Subjects without Selves

Harvard Studies in Comparative Literature
Founded by William Henry Schofield
43

GABRIELE SCHWAB

Subjects without Selves

Transitional Texts in Modern Fiction

HARVARD UNIVERSITY PRESS

Cambridge, Massachusetts
London, England
1994

Adapted from Gabriele Schwab, *Entgrenzungen und Entgrenzungsmythen*
(Stuttgart: Franz Steiner, 1987).

This book is printed on acid-free paper, and its binding materials
have been chosen for strength and durability.

Library of Congress Cataloging-in-Publication Data

Schwab, Gabriele.
  Subjects without selves : transitional texts in modern fiction / Gabriele Schwab.
    p. cm.—(Harvard studies in comparative literature; 43)
  Includes bibliographical references and index.
  ISBN 0-674-85381-4 (alk. paper)
  1. English fiction—20th century—History and criticism. 2. American fiction—History and
criticism. 3. Modernism (Literature) I. Title. II. Series.
PR888.M63S39 1994
823'.91209—dc20
                                                                    93-11692
                                                                        CIP

Contents

Preface

If translating in general can be understood as an experience of moving and negotiating between two cultures and two languages, then the task of translating a book whose first version was my own German *Habilitationsschrift* is an unusual one. I emigrated to the United States in 1983; thus, when *Entgrenzungen und Entgrenzungsmythen* was published in Germany in 1987 (Stuttgart: Franz Steiner), I had already been teaching for four years at different American universities. Translating the work allowed me to travel back and forth through the cultural space between two continents as well as through the different "time zones" of the German and English versions of *Subjects without Selves*. No longer completely at home in the German academic world, but still a foreigner (or, as it says so nicely on my Green Card, an "alien resident") in my new academic home at the University of California, I often found myself an ethnographer in two foreign cultures. Some of the stages of this travel are reflected in the folds and fissures created by the contact between two very different cultures and historical moments.

It seems curiously apt, then, that *Subjects without Selves* is concerned with boundaries, transitions, and transitional spaces; and almost a joke or "a revenge of the God of semantics"—to use Vladimir Nabokov's mocking phrase—that my German title, *Entgrenzungen und Entgrenzungsmythen,* turned out to be virtually untranslatable. *Entgrenzung* is a word whose connotations run from the action of the lifting of boundaries—their transgression, transformation, or expansion—to the syncretistic experience in which details and structures are grasped holistically. Moreover, *Entgrenzung* also recalls the fragmentations and dissolutions of form and structure prominent in modernism and post-modernism. It is a word that calls up such different realms of discourse as geography and geopolitics, morphology, psychoanalysis, and aesthetics. To my knowledge, no English word combines all of these connotations and resonances. I have therefore chosen to replace this term with the notion of "transitional texts." This invokes one of the key concepts in my theoretical framework: I hold that literature is a transitional space of speech whose function consists in continually reshaping the boundaries of language and subjectivity.

This book draws mainly from psychoanalysis and reader response theory to explore the relationship between language and subjectivity in modernist fiction. I use both theories to illuminate the cultural politics and psychological functions of aesthetic practices and literary forms. I am concerned with the development of artistic forms and their impact on the changing forms of subjectivity in our culture. Literature, I argue, creates a cultural space whose primary function consists in a continual shaping and reshaping of the boundaries of language and subjectivity on both an individual and a collective level. Modern and postmodern experimental texts, in particular, fulfill this function with their multifarious exploration of the boundaries of poetic language and their opening up of language toward the unconscious. They mark important transitions in the development of new literary forms and practices as well as new modes of literary reception in an increasingly global and hybrid culture.

The German version of this book was written at a time when many theorists and critics proclaimed the "death of the subject" both in literature and in theory. My intervention was aimed at the reductive way in which this notion pervaded the critical debates of the time. It was out of fashion to deal with literary subjectivity, but I deliberately chose this unfashionable topic because of my conviction that modernism and postmodernism have not outgrown the notion of the subject, but on the contrary have created completely new and unexplored notions of subjectivity. Those who speak of the "death of the subject" propagate a philosophical and epistemological refutation of the relatively stable and well-bounded subject commonly attributed to the tradition of Cartesianism. *This* subject may well be dead, yet the highly experimental texts of the twentieth century have created forms of literary subjectivity that are as far removed from the Cartesian subject as one can possibly imagine. These texts have produced vital forms of a new literary subjectivity with culturally relevant philosophical and epistemological implications. Different from a philosophical, Cartesian concept of the subject, this new literary subjectivity must be analyzed on its own terms and according to the modes of production and reception that generate it.

But literary subjectivity differs not only from philosophical notions of subjectivity; it also differs from the manifold manifestations of what philosophers call the "empirical subject"—that is, the subjectivity of human beings who live in material worlds. Literary subjectivity relates to empirical subjectivity, philosophical conceptions of subjectivity, and in fact all other cultural productions of subjectivity; but it is generated and disseminated according to its own laws and conditions and therefore constitutes a field of its own that cannot be understood in merely referential terms. Moreover, since language is the material that produces literary subjectivity, its analysis cannot be separated from a theory of poetic language.

Subjects without Selves is thus concerned with the relationship between language and literary subjectivity or, from a slightly different perspective, the capacity of poetic language to generate literary subjectivity. In a larger sense, I am investigating the cultural function of aesthetic production and the politics of changing literary forms. Problems of literary reception play a crucial role in this investigation, because the experimental texts I consider in this volume all aim at changing familiar habits and modes of reading. I hold that literary texts and cultural objects in general form a kind of ecological relationship to their different environments—the specific culture by and within which they are produced, the communities of recipients they address, cultural concerns and social issues they voice, aesthetic practices they share or aim to change, and other cultural objects with which they establish an intertextual relationship. In order to keep this relationship vital, continual negotiations with these different environments are necessary, and a decision in relation to one environment affects all the others. For example, if literary texts become highly experimental, challenging linear and monolingual narratives and generating a variety of new forms of poetic language and aesthetic practices, their changing literary forms affect everything from the cultural production of subjectivity and familiar practices of reading to the politics of aesthetic forms and theories of language.

In this context, it is no coincidence that literary texts have become increasingly sensitive to their different environments. Less concerned with a mere representation of referential worlds, they have become more and more interventionist, reflecting social concerns, philosophical and epistemological premises of their time, other discursive and aesthetic practices, the dramatic impact of technology and the media on our way of life, and the increasing globalization of our culture.

While involved in my translation, I have also been working on other projects, in particular a new book, *The Mirror and the Killer-Queen: Aesthetic Experience of Otherness*. Both projects emphasize the fact that reading not only forms part of our cultural production of subjectivity, but also constitutes a specific experience of otherness. While *Subjects without Selves* focuses on the relationship between language and subjectivity, my new projects focus on intersubjectivity and in particular on those forms of intersubjectivity that create cultural or imaginary others/Others. I hold that patterns of reading are formed on the basis of the much more general patterns through which a culture mediates its relations to otherness; but I also hold that one of the main functions of literature (and other cultural objects or aesthetic practices in general) may be to change these patterns of relating to otherness. After all, we read literatures from many and very different cultures and historical periods, and we also read texts whose use of language differs so radically from what is familiar to us that we must expose ourselves to, deal with, and relate to their formal otherness. This is precisely what I have tried to do in *Subjects without Selves:* to expose myself to the otherness generated by the unfamiliar experimental forms of modern and postmodern texts and to translate this experience into an analysis that takes this otherness to be a challenge to our own cultural assumptions and practices, our ways of living in a language, our habits of reading, and our cultural formations of subjectivity.

My translation plays out the differences between two cultures. The main reason for translating the work myself was to be able to produce a freer, more liberal translation of the German edition. I did, however, resist the insistent temptation to totally rewrite the book; therefore, I have not turned to texts that appeared after the publication of my German volume, nor have I referred to new turns in the theoretical debates. My intention is to present my original argument in order to expose it to the challenge of a reception in a completely new context. In a certain sense, this reception will take the form of a mediation between the two different academic cultures. I have taken certain steps in order to facilitate this mediation. Even though the German version of *Subjects without Selves* is informed by the debates in literary criticism and theory in West Germany, France, and the United States, the problem of a very different audience and cultural context in each country must be taken into account, since those differences dictate the terms of the debate. The reception of psychoanalysis, poststructuralism, deconstruction, and especially feminist theory is radically different in Germany than it is in the United States. This has mostly affected Chapter 1: I cut parts of the German version and expanded others according to the new implicit audience of my translation. But I have changed neither my arguments nor the overall organization of the book, nor have I attempted to explain or apologize for certain cultural and temporal gaps. On the contrary, I was delighted to see that in some respects there are more varied and diverse contexts for the reception of my work than when I wrote the original German version.

Nonetheless, I could not refrain from asking myself what would have changed had I been able to rewrite the book instead of simply translating it. I certainly would have emphasized gender more, especially in the theoretical chapters. Many of the issues I address are directly pertinent to feminist theories or, more generally, to a gender-specific theoretical perspective. This is particularly relevant to the issue of boundaries in the acquisition of language and the symbolic order and the related formation of subjectivity. Many American as well as French feminist theorists (among them Chodorow, Gilligan, Benjamin, Dinnerstein, Kristeva, Irigaray, Cixous, and Clément) have argued that in patriarchal cultures women acquire a different, more flexible, fluid, and provisional sense of boundaries than men. Many French feminists in particular have used modernist experimental texts as paradigms for an *écriture féminine*. Julia Kristeva's distinction between the symbolic and the semiotic, which figures in both my theoretical framework and my readings, opens up another road for further developing a gendered perspective, since Kristeva herself has identified the semiotic with the cultural space of the maternal. My readings show that the theoretical framework I have developed inevitably leads to considerations of gender once it is confronted with specific literary texts and historical perspectives. In particular, the chapters on Melville, Woolf, Joyce, and Pynchon draw out problems of gender implicit in my theory.

Another cultural difference between the German and American context for critical theory concerns the construction of theory as such. In Germany more weight is placed on building theoretical models than in the United States, where literary critics during the last decades have focused primarily on either applying or criticizing existing theoretical models. Many American critics tend to adopt theories that have become mainstream at a given historical time—such as, for example, deconstruction, Lacanian psychoanalysis, the new historicism, and American or French feminism. These theories then provide the tools for professional affiliation by creating specific critical and interpretive communities with their own modes of reception and circulation based on relatively stable premises and concepts. In Germany, perhaps due to the strong impact of philosophical and dialectical thought on literary scholarship, theories are rather treated as open heuristic concepts in need of continual change and further development. Rather than the mere transmission of a given theory or the perpetuation of a theoretical school, the emphasis is on the further development or reconstruction of theories. The critical reception and integration of different theoretical models or the building of a new theory in the spirit of creative eclecticism plays a crucial role in this process. Without wanting to suggest too rigid a dichotomy between U.S. and German theorizing, I want to emphasize that building a theory is very different from applying a specific theory and from criticizing existing theories.

I am therefore more interested in the strength of theories and in their undeveloped potential than in their weaknesses. Accordingly, I place various theories in new contexts and confront them with literary texts and other theories in order to develop new theoretical perspectives on problems concerning the cultural function of poetic language, the relationship between language and subjectivity, and the functions of different literary forms, aesthetic practices, and politics of reading.

The construction of theories is for me an endeavor that entails an ongoing process of reshaping the boundaries of theoretical concerns, often by exposing the questions I have asked from the start of my career to foreign contexts that offer new perspectives and challenges. Inspired by different cultural and theoretical environments, I have seen my own theory continually grow and change as, for example, in the direction of my new project on the otherness of poetic language. But even the trajectory of the present volume does not follow the logic of a linear teleology. I began this book as a reader response critic with a psychoanalytic orientation, but I expanded my theoretical boundaries after becoming increasingly interested in the cultural formation of subjectivity through textual and aesthetic practices as well as in the notion of textual ecologies.

The last chapter therefore is not truly an "end" to the book. Instead, that chapter opens up the theory of this work to other theories that bear a certain family likeness to my project. Accordingly, the interdisciplinary reflections in Chapter 9 should be read less as a conclusion than as a confrontation of the aesthetic practices I have described with similar developments and trends in other fields. The psychoanalytically oriented theory of poetic language I developed at the beginning as a framework for my readings is there confronted with a larger cultural environment of other theories ranging from philosophy, systems theory, and cybernetics to the new physics and anthropological theories concerned with an ecology of mind. This chapter tries to spell out perhaps the most basic assumption underlying this book, namely that the textual and aesthetic practices of a specific culture continually and dynamically interact with all its other facets. In other words, literary texts create a textual ecology of their own that not only reflects the cultural ecology at large but also intervenes in it and, in the best case, tries to maintain its flexibility and work toward important historical changes in our signifying practices and cultural formations.

Acknowledgments

My indebtedness to people and institutions that have supported this project extends over ten years. I want to reiterate my thanks to all those who helped me shape my German book—especially former colleagues, students, and friends from the University of Constance and the Constance School. My warmest thanks go to Wolfgang Iser, my *Doktorvater* and friend, to whom I dedicated the German version and whose intellectual vitality, generosity, and continued enthusiastic interest in my work has provided the most crucial and invaluable support anyone could possibly wish for.

I wish to extend special thanks to Murray Krieger and Ed Schell, who were crucial in bringing me to the University of California at Irvine, and the many friends and colleagues who have read and supported my work: Mike Clark, Alex Gelley, Renée and Judd Hubert, Ruth Klueger, Jim McMichael, Jane Newman, Margot Norris, John Rowe, John Smith, Martin Schwab, and Brook Thomas.

Many others provided invaluable assistance. Lindsay Waters was the driving force behind this translation. His energetic support far exceeded the tasks of an editor, and his critical comments are among the most insightful intellectual responses I have received. Thanks also to Donna Bouvier, my copyeditor, for many suggestions that greatly improved this book. I was also most fortunate to gain Judith Pike and Gregg Lambert as my research assistants. Their dedication to this project was as invaluable as their sense of humor and the meticulousness with which they assisted me during the final stages of the translation. I am indebted to the Organized Research Unit on Women and the Image at the University of California—Irvine and the Center for

German and European Studies at the University of California—Berkeley for providing this research assistance.

My gratitude extends also to the readers of *Subjects without Selves,* who gave me encouragement, valuable criticism, and suggestions for improvement. Lore Iser provided me with informed, imaginative and challenging criticism and insightful suggestions. Jochen Schulte-Sasse has for a long time been a loyal supporter of my work and was an excellent reader of both the German and the English versions. I also benefited greatly from Nancy Armstrong's astute comments and suggestions for the translation.

I owe a special debt of gratitude to the John Simon Guggenheim Memorial Foundation, which has supported this translation in an indirect way and greatly facilitated its completion. I worked on the translation during a leave on a Guggenheim Fellowship I received for my new project on the otherness of poetic language. This fellowship was supplemented with a research fellowship from the University of California—Irvine and a stipend from the School of Humanities. My thanks go to both institutions.

Last, but not least, my warmest thanks go to the three men who support my life and my work on a daily basis: my companion, Paul Harris, who is also one of my most inspired readers; my son, Manuel Schwab, who came with me to this country when he was five years old and has now become an American poet from whom I learn what it means to "live in a language"; and finally Leon, the "little man," who keeps me in touch with the imaginary worlds of a three-year-old.

Subjects without Selves

1

The Insistence of the Subject

Then perhaps the subject returns, not as illusion, but as fiction.
—*Roland Barthes*

"Where is the subject? It is necessary to find the subject as a lost object. More precisely this lost object is the support of the subject and in many cases is a more abject thing than you may care to consider . . ."[1] The manner in which Jacques Lacan here puts the subject in question as an accessible psychological entity is paradigmatic of a much larger epistemological suspicion concerning subjectivity that has governed debates in philosophy, critical theory, and literary criticism for over three decades. The subject, in fact, must be rediscovered as a lost object not only in its psychological but also in its theoretical constitution—and, as Lacan's own theory illustrates, it may easily turn into an abject theoretical thing as well, "a fading thing that runs under the chain of signifiers."[2]

For Lacan, as for many other critics, the subject is indivisible from the language it speaks; yet this language may only constitute it as a lack, a void to be filled with phantasms. Respectively, language is filled with an as yet unknown power and agency, but it nonetheless becomes as ubiquitous and problematic as the subject itself. Language may well "speak the subject" instead of being spoken by a subject, but simultaneously communication appears often as reduced to what Lacan terms "empty speech." Consequently, literature has played its own distinct role in this cultural reconfiguration of language and the subject. Since the beginning of the twentieth century, highly experimental literary texts have gloried in exploding (and imploding) the bounda-

1

ries of poetic language, while philosophers and literary critics have celebrated the undecidability of meaning in these texts. The literary subject seems to be all but lost in their unbounded celebration of pure language games.

In this twilight of the age of poststructuralist and postmodern sensibility it might seem anachronistic to engage in a *recherche* of the lost subject. My motive for doing so—regardless of the suspicious intellectual mood of the time—is my conviction that those who prematurely announced the death of the subject have ignored the challenge presented by twentieth-century literary experiments with language and subjectivity. Rather than merely replacing the novel's historical emphasis on subjectivity with other concerns—foremost, the concern with the intricacies and power of language—these experiments have presented radically new figurations of subjectivity. They have opened up larger perspectives on how the subject is intertwined with other things, such as language, culture, and the politics and aesthetics of representation. What is at issue is the intricate and ambivalent connection between language and subjectivity as well as the question of how to define and where to locate agency and power—in language or the subject. The problem of the subject, in other words, has become politicized and exists as much in a cultural as in a psychological framework.

Literary critics should recognize that the singular and determinate philosophical subject of the Cartesian tradition that provoked the epistemological suspicion in our time is not all there is to the subject. In fact, the critique of the subject might not be related to the abundant new forms of literary subjectivity that have already sprung up in the wake of the critique of the subject that has continued since the nineteenth century. Moreover, literary critics are faced with a wholesale reconsideration of the function of aesthetics in light of these changing cultural and epistemological configurations. It is no coincidence that some of the most provocative theories of language and subjectivity—especially those that are loosely called "French thought"—have been inspired by and continue to draw upon literary models of high modernism and postmodernism. The highly experimental literature of these periods explores ever new connections between language and subjectivity and attempts to transgress or expand the boundaries of each. Given the wide range of these literary experiments, as well as their impact on philosophy and critical theory, it is astounding that terms such as the "death of the subject" or the "end of representation and communication" continue to mark theories of both modernism and postmodernism.[3]

In *The Order of Things,* Michel Foucault traces the roots of the modernist experiments with poetic language back to the "demotion of language to the mere status of an object" at the beginning of the nineteenth century. Foucault sees what he calls the "appearance of literature" as one of the compensations for this cultural demotion of language: "Finally, the last of the compensations for the demotion of language, the most important and also the most unexpected, is the appearance of literature, of literature as such—for there has of course existed in the Western world, since Dante, since Homer, a form of language that we now call 'literature.' But the word is of recent date, as is also, in our culture, the isolation of a particular language whose peculiar mode of being is 'literary.'"[4]

According to Foucault, the development of a particular literary language is accompanied by a decrease in referentiality and representational functions and an increase in self-referentiality, which turns language into an object that reflects on itself. Instead of representing, for example, a fictional subjectivity of literary characters, poetic language increasingly "addresses itself to itself as a writing subjectivity."[5] Foucault links this process with an episteme marked by the end of representation. Within this epistemological configuration, literature takes on a paradoxical function. It can no longer represent the ruling regime of knowledge, or episteme, in which it is generated since, if it were to merely represent the end of representation, it would still remain caught within the old paradigm of representative literature. Thus, according to Foucault, in the twentieth century literature posits itself as "experience of the unthought," joining psychoanalysis in its paradoxical "task of making the discourse of the unconscious speak through consciousness."[6] For Foucault the "end of representation" also implies that, instead of simply mirroring a current epistemological configuration, the new literary forms actively take part in shaping a new episteme.

Curiously, this constructive dimension of the disruptive and fragmented forms of poetic language has found only a very limited resonance in contemporary criticism. Often the emergence of a language that speaks itself has mistakenly been identified with the disappearance of the subject. This perspective fails to account for the curious yet highly significant fact that in direct proportion to the seeming disappearance of the subject, poetic language develops a subjectivity of its own. The following investigation is stimulated by this question: How can we relate the new forms of poetic language—including what Foucault calls the "writing subjectivity"—with the emergence of new forms and notions of subjectivity?

Among literary critics, the narrative of the end of the subject reflects a persistent tendency to interpret the shifting boundaries of language and subjectivity in negative, even apocalyptic, terms, as a sign of decay, a crisis of representation, meaning, and communication; or as a dismissal of the subject from the scene of writing. The very categories of the subject, of representation, or of meaning all too often appear to be nothing but outdated values of an obsolete humanist tradition. Notions of the loss of the self or the death of the subject have dominated discussions for over thirty years, both in literary criticism and in philosophy. Wylie Sypher's *Loss of the Self in Modern Literature and Art* (1964)[7] exemplifies a type of literary criticism that analyzes the experimental forms of poetic language in modern literature as indications of a vanishing of the subject. The Cartesian model of centered subjectivity becomes the standard against which the new forms of literary subjectivity are measured and found to be deviations. Historically and conceptually, however, the category of a centered subjectivity had at the time already been fundamentally challenged by a number of theoretical perspectives.

Psychoanalysis, with its profound impact on the intellectual currents of the twentieth century, and in conjunction with philosophical traditions such as phenomenology, hermeneutics, structuralism, poststructuralism, and deconstruction, provides different theoretical models for viewing experimental literary subjectivity in a new and more positive light. Modern and postmodern experimental texts alike deploy formal and linguistic ruptures, artistic experiments, and violations of aesthetic norms that reach far beyond mere negative representations of the subject in crisis. One of the most challenging new modes of representation consists in the aesthetic use of structures that draw upon what psychoanalysis calls the primary processes. It is these very structures that open poetic language to the effects of the unconscious.

In the theoretical field, structuralism, poststructuralism, and deconstruction set major new trends in exploring literary modernism. The otherwise radically different theoretical models of Barthes, Lévi-Strauss, Foucault, Lacan, Derrida, Lyotard, Deleuze and Guattari, and Kristeva all display traces of their encounter with psychoanalytic thought. Instead of mourning the loss of the self, poststructuralism and deconstruction privilege experimental fragmentations and (dis)figurations of language as open and dynamic processes of textualization. The dominant tenor of their discourses about the subject is, however, still one that celebrates its end. Foucault, Derrida, Baudrillard, Lyotard, and Deleuze and Guattari all in some way convey the sense that we are beyond the subject. Especially in the United States, the death of the subject has enjoyed such astounding popularity that related theoretical categories—such as identity, author, origin, history, or literary work—have largely been abandoned as mere relics of the dark age of humanism. Nevertheless, the narrative of this historical revaluation remains a tale thought to have a decisive ending, or at least to feature a radical break with the whole tradition of Western philosophy. In the introduction to a recent volume entitled *Poststructuralist Joyce*, for example, we read about the "subject" of *Finnegans Wake:* "The aim is not to produce a *reading* of this intractable text . . . but to look at the mechanisms of its infinite productivity; . . . to record the perpetual flight of the subject and its ultimate disappearance."[8] Once the "ultimate disappearance" of the subject is taken for granted, the "infinite productivity" of *Finnegans Wake*, however, seems to dissipate in the void of an entropic linguistic universe.

My own readings develop a very different narrative. Instead of an ending or a radical discontinuity, I tell the story of dynamic change within an ongoing process. Such a story is less interested in endings than in beginnings; it emphasizes the emergence of new forms over the disappearance of old ones. In order to understand the significance of these new forms, one must ask why literary games with the boundaries of language and subjectivity have exerted such a strong fascination. What is their psychological appeal for the reader? And how do these new forms of literary subjectivity relate to the dissolution of subjectivity brought about by schizophrenia, paranoia, or the so-called new narcissism?[9]

The rhetoric of the end of the subject is, of course, directed against conventional notions of a subject defined as a bounded unity with a specific structure that bestows identity—a subject, in other words, that we have come to identify historically with the Cartesian subject.

Strictly speaking we cannot conceive of language without presupposing a subject. As Kristeva has argued throughout her work, every theory of language relies on a conception of the subject, which implies that "a theory of meaning . . . must necessarily be a theory of the speaking subject."[10]

From this perspective, invoking the death of the subject reveals little more than a negative fixation on the old norm of a centered subject. By contrast, the new forms of poetic language call for a new conception of literary subjectivity that meets the challenge posed by the great variety of experimental forms developed in modern and postmodern texts. Because literary subjectivity is not a mimetic representation of other cultural forms of subjectivity, poetic language and aesthetic experience develop their own implied concepts of subjectivity. From this perspective, literary subjectivity appears as an effect of poetic language rather than of the fictional subjectivity of literary characters. And often it gains its cultural relevance less through its affinities with than through its differences from other cultural manifestations of subjectivity.

The indeterminacy of experimental literary forms and the polyphony of voices structure an aesthetic experience that can no longer rely on familiar forms of literary communication. Often the texts require readings that exceed the semantic dimension, producing the well-known symptoms of what Samuel Beckett once called "the withdrawal of semantic crutches." More than in conventional narratives, the aesthetic experience of experimental texts is stimulated by asemantic qualities of speech, by sounds, echoes, and rhythmic undulations—in short, by what Kristeva termed the "semiotic" as opposed to the symbolic functions of language. The semiotic functions have, of course, always been emphasized in poetic language. But while conventionally the asemantic qualities of poetic language support semantic signification, modernist "semiotizations" tend to subvert it. By inverting the use of asemantic qualities, literary language often reactivates and privileges the so-called presymbolic functions of language—that is, the primary processes.

Numerous theories have emphasized the effects of the unconscious in language and accordingly acknowledged the role of the primary processes in experimental poetic language. Lacan's concept of the "sliding signifier," for instance, is based on a shift from the semantic to the syntactic functions of language. Lacan's decentered subject is engendered by a play of signifiers and imaginary identifications, where "a signifier represents the subject for another signifier." In this play of signifiers the subject moves between the hollowness of "empty speech" and the sporadic emergence of its "truth" in a "full speech" that subverts the confines of coded signification. In his seminar on Poe's "The Purloined Letter," Lacan chooses poetic language as his model for this transgressive quality of speech.[11] Just as the purloined letter remains undetected because it is exposed to everybody's view, poetic language hides the truth of the subject at its very material surface. This observation contains the seeds for a positive conception of a poetic language that creatively uses the inscriptions of the unconscious. Reading poetic language against the grain of semantic signification lays bare what the signifier hides visibly at the surface. But, as in his theory of the mirror phase, Lacan is more interested in the falsifications and misrecognitions provided by the imaginary than in its constructive functions and thus refrains from developing an elaborate concept of poetic language.

In contrast to Lacan, Derrida weaves a much closer tie between the subject and textuality. Characterizing subjectivity and textuality in the same way, Derrida conceives of the subject/text in terms of a dynamic flow that may assume temporary identities around focal points, but only in order to dissolve them again into new forms. Like Lacan, Derrida develops his notion of the subject in opposition to a codified language. However much their theories differ in detail, style, and direction, both Lacan and Derrida are interested in those areas where language functions beyond a stable semantic signification. The signifier's reach into the unconscious or its working against the prescriptions of a code redefines the subject's position in relation to the constraints of social and symbolic orders. In both theories poetic language is but one example of such a possible expansion of the boundaries of language.

Neither Lacan nor Derrida are, of course, primarily interested in a theory of poetic language. While Lacan still attributes a distinct status to specialized forms of speech such as therapeutic discourse or poetic language, Derrida deliberately forgoes such conceptual differentiations. Julia Kristeva, on the other hand, links the transgressions of poetic language directly to the emergence of new forms of subjectivity. Like Derrida and Lacan, Kristeva is interested in linguistic features that function beyond signification, since meaning and signification do not exhaust the function of poetic language.[12] Analyzing the poetic use of the presymbolic sensoric and rhythmic functions of language, she develops a theory of poetic language based on the distinction between the symbolic and the semiotic or between what she calls the "genotext" and the "phenotext." According to Kristeva, poetic language creatively uses rhythms, intonations, glossolalia, and sound-plays, which are so important in the experience of language in early childhood. Though pervasive in language, this sphere of the semiotic—which Kristeva identifies with the maternal space in our culture—remains largely unconscious unless it is deliberately activated in order to protect the subject from being completely absorbed by the symbolic. Even though the semiotic is inseparable from the signifying function, it constitutes itself beyond thetic consciousness and beyond the functions of the ego. Kristeva's subject is, accordingly, a "subject-in-process," which retains the potential of the semiotic even after acquiring the capacity to function within the symbolic order. Poetic language becomes Kristeva's privileged model for the semiotic, which is, of course, closely linked to the primary processes. According to Kristeva, poetic language mediates between the symbolic and the semiotic or between primary and secondary processes. Poetic language, she argues, is neither an imaginary discourse of the I, nor a discourse of transcendental knowledge, but an intermediate discourse that continuously oscillates between the two, balancing the sign and the rhythm of consciousness and drive.[13]

For Kristeva, poetic language and literary subjectivity are located within an intermediate space between the speech and the subjectivity of empirical subjects on the one hand and the discourse and transcendental subject of philosophy on the other. Inspired by the literary modernism of Lautréamont, Mallarmé, Baudelaire, Rimbaud, Artaud, Joyce, and Sollers, Kristeva's literary "subject-in-process" is an anarchistic, subversive subject of desire, more oriented toward the pleasure principle than toward the reality principle. The unbounded forms of literary modernism serve as paradigmatic examples of an emergent episteme, which, though shaped by modernism, has often been associated with postmodernism.

Other theorists have linked the open and fragmented forms of experimental literature with the increasing fragmentation of subjectivity in our culture and accordingly evaluated them in much more critical terms. Fredric Jameson, for example, understands the rhetoric of the end of the subject within the larger cultural context of late capitalism.[14] In *The Political Unconscious*, Jameson places the notion of the end of the subject at the center of his critique of postmodernism. However, in a countermove to the more positive poststructuralist view of postmodernism, Jameson criticizes what he sees as its inherent cultural pathologies. In Jameson's view, the modern alienation of the subject culminates in its postmodern fragmentation. Inverting Deleuze and Guattari's theory of the postmodern "schizo," Jameson diagnoses "cultural schizophrenia" as the pathology of late capitalism, emphasizing, in place of the subversive potential of the Signifier in language, the colonization of the unconscious through signifying practices. In doing so, he inverts a common tenet of postmodernism. While poststructuralism and deconstruction trace the subversive potential of the inscription of the unconscious upon the symbolic order, Jameson instead diagnoses the pervasive invasion of the unconscious by the symbolic order.

Adopting the Lacanian understanding of schizophrenia as a breakdown of the function of the signifier as a "suggestive aesthetic model," Jameson sees the postmodern subject reduced to an experience of pure material signifiers. Cut off from the orienting function of a transparent symbolic order, the postmodern subject shares a schizophrenic's loss of reality, temporality, and history and his or her spectacular sensation of intensity. In relation to this loss of orientation, literature and other cultural objects may, according to Jameson, assume the function of a "cognitive mapping": "The political form of postmodernism, if there ever is any, will have as its vocation the invention and projection of a global cognitive mapping, on a social as well as spatial scale."[15]

By limiting the function of literature and cultural objects in general to a merely cognitive orientation, Jameson curiously enough adapts a conventional notion of *Bildung* to postmodern conditions. Lost in a global culture and dispersed into pure intensities, the fragmented postmodern subject suddenly finds himself or herself once again on the surface of a cognitive map. And yet the new fragmented forms displayed by postmodern cultural objects call for an "equivalent mutation in the subject," according to Jameson: "The new architecture therefore . . . stands as something like an imperative to grow new organs, to expand our sensorium and our body to some new, as yet unimaginable, perhaps ultimately impossible, dimensions."[16]

Similar claims that cultural objects change perceptual habits and, by extension, the very structure of subjectivity had been made much earlier by the modernists themselves and were reinforced by the early critics of postmodernism—most insistently by Ihab Hassan, who understands the postmodern "will to unmaking" in the context of a broadly mapped "historical mutation," a "transhumanization" of our "global culture" that transforms the very organization of the subject. For Hassan, the postmodern subject is a gnostic, self-constituting subject whose fluid boundaries appear under the double perspective of continuity and discontinuity.[17]

Current debates tend to eclipse any notion of such a radical impact of cultural objects on their recipients in much the same way as they underplay the continuity between the experimental forms of modernism and postmodernism. My own readings focus on the new ties woven between language and the subject in order to elucidate the new notions of literary subjectivity implied in the experimental language games in modernism and postmodernism. Emphasizing relative continuity rather than a complete rupture between these two periods, I look at a series of texts, ranging from Herman Melville's *Moby-Dick* to Thomas Pynchon's *Gravity's Rainbow,* in order to investigate the dynamic relationship they entertain with the cultural system from which they emerge and to which they react in a transformative way.

The next chapter sets up a theoretical framework for these readings, and combines aesthetic, psychological, and cultural perspectives. I draw upon psychoanalytic theories that are concerned with the boundaries of subjectivity. D. W. Winnicott's theory of play and object relations serves as a starting point. Winnicott's analysis of the positive role of the imaginary in the genesis of the subject prepares the ground for a psychoanalytic theory of cultural objects. I supplement Winnicott's model with specific notions from Anton Ehrenzweig's theory of creativity in order to formulate my own theory of poetic language, aesthetic production, and reception. My revision of Winnicott and Ehrenzweig will provide a theoretical model that is more attuned to the modern and postmodern texts under consideration. Moreover, I submit their theories to some major revisions motivated by current theoretical discussions in literary criticism, philosophy of language, and psychoanalysis.

Winnicott locates literature and cultural objects in a transitional space[18] of experience, the roots of which go back to the function of play in early childhood and to the formation of the first symbolic objects. According to Winnicott, this transitional space generates a continual process of differentiation, dedifferentiation, and redifferentiation of the subject's boundaries, whose processual and partly autopoietic[19] formation requires mediations between conscious and unconscious experiences and between primary and secondary processes. From this perspective, temporary dedifferentiations of subjectivity are not necessarily indications of a fragmentation of the subject, but may on the contrary be a precondition for the flexibility and the processual development of its boundaries.

For Ehrenzweig, aesthetic dedifferentiations may activate unconscious modes of experience that are crucial for creative processes in general. Ehrenzweig's theory of art inverts our culture's privileging of the secondary processes over the primary processes. The equation of these processes with order and chaos is, for Ehrenzweig, a stifling and widespread epistemological error. He contends that primary processes follow their own system of order and provide the method for a holistic and syncretistic "unconscious scanning" that is more encompassing, inclusive and—as Ehrenzweig asserts—superior, in some respects, to the scanning capacities of the secondary processes. For Ehrenzweig a process of unconscious scanning followed by a dynamic interaction between primary and secondary processes forms the very basis for aesthetic production and reception.

The central role that Ehrenzweig attributes to the primary process and unconscious scanning in creative processes makes his theory directly relevant for theoretical discussions concerned with the boundaries of language and subjectivity. Jean-François Lyotard, for one, perceives the dedifferentiation of stable forms in postmodern culture as a new way of dealing with dimensions of experience that resist representation and conceptualization.[20] He argues that without awareness of the incommensurability of reality (experience) and concept—the basis of Kant's philosophy of the sublime—a crucial dimension of postmodernism, namely what has been termed the "postmodern sublime," escapes critical evaluation. Postmodernism, according to Lyotard, aims at the paradoxical task of representing the unrepresentable through the invention of new forms that reach beyond the grammatical, lexical, syntactic, or semantic codification of language. For Lyotard, Joyce is exemplary for having developed experimental forms of language that resist the harmonization of the unrepresentable in favor of the ineffability of the postmodern sublime.

It seems no coincidence that Lyotard would find interest in Ehrenzweig's theory of art and introduce his work to a French audience. But it is also clear that he would refute its epistemology, which, for Lyotard's postmodern sensibility, seemed to resonate too much with a more traditional aesthetic of harmony *(Harmonieästhetik)*. In his introduction to the French translation of *The Hidden Order of Art,* entitled "Beyond Representation,"[21] Lyotard criticizes Ehrenzweig for grounding the creative function of the unconscious within a model of literary communication.[22] Lyotard links the postmodern turn against representation to a refutation of the communicative structure of aesthetic experience. Like the unconscious, postmodern texts for Lyotard efface the distinction between inside and outside without which there can be no communication.

This is where Ehrenzweig's model differs radically from Lyotard's. Ehrenzweig sees the conscious and the unconscious as synthetic functions in the creative process. Thus, both unfocused attention and unconscious scanning have a culturally relevant communicative function. I consider Ehrenzweig's insistence on the communicative function of the unconscious and the primary processes as a strength, because it allows one to account for, among other things, the undeniable appeal of literary texts that use primary processes and linguistic forms derived from them for aesthetic purposes. We would eclipse one of the most powerful effects of these texts if we were to deny the existence of unconscious communication, which, after all, also forms one of the most crucial assumptions in Freud's own work.

Lyotard further equates Ehrenzweig's use of the terms "unity" and "wholeness" with the rhetoric of a conventional organicist theory or aesthetic of harmony. If we understand, however, that for Ehrenzweig the term "unity" has very different and far more complex connotations, we may grasp the much more radical implications of his theory. Instead of referring to an organicist concept, Ehrenzweig's notion of wholeness refers to an open system based on continual synchronic and diachronic processes of change. Far from replicating the hierarchical order of a conventional aesthetic of harmony, this dynamic wholeness pertains rather to a holistic model that reveals significant epistemological affinities to holistic models developed in postmodern theories—

such as systems theory, cybernetics, ecological theories, and cognitive and dynamic theories of mind. Instead of constructing false unities or totalizing conceptualizations, these theories presuppose an opening toward precisely those domains of experience that appear as unrepresentable from a conventional perspective.

A holistic model allows one to see the syncretistic forms of experimental literary subjectivity in connection with the emergence of a new episteme. To grasp those experimental forms of language and subjectivity, consciously or unconsciously, requires a mediation between modes of experience that have already been conceptualized and modes that seem to resist conceptualization. I reconsider the function of experimental poetic language, literary subjectivity, and the unconscious in modernism and postmodernism in light of these holistic theories. Ultimately, such a reconsideration might even affect our notion of the "postmodern sublime" by overcoming the traditional dichotomy between the representable and the unrepresentable, because the evocation of the unrepresentable within representation can be read in two directions: either as defying conceptualization altogether, or as calling for conceptualization on a higher level of abstraction and complexity.

Both Winnicott and Ehrenzweig develop holistic models, presupposing a continual process of mediation between primary and secondary processes as indispensable for an "ecology of the subject." Like poststructuralism and deconstruction—albeit in different ways—they, too, value those forces in language that either resist or try to reach beyond the bounds of a codifiable signification. Ehrenzweig's privileging of the primary processes as a mode of unconscious scanning, however, has to be seen as a reaction to the widely established cultural privileging of the secondary processes that provide the foundation for the symbolic order. Far from globally rejecting the secondary processes or antagonistically polarizing the two modes of experience, both Winnicott and Ehrenzweig assert the need continually to balance primary and secondary processes. They insist on the importance of the primary processes in their work against the restrictive power of the symbolic order; yet, instead of attributing an alienating quality to the very existence of a symbolic order as such, they regard the degree of restrictiveness and alienation as contingent upon and related to concrete cultural and political practices.

Ehrenzweig's notion of a dynamic interaction between primary and secondary processes shows certain systemic affinities with Derrida's notion of continual dissemination. The latter generates a process of continuous dispersion, a self-reflexive recoiling from stasis or the development of a pattern. According to Ehrenzweig, the oscillation of the boundaries between primary and secondary processes is supposed to prevent stasis by keeping the two different modes of production and reception in constant flux. The two theories, however, differ in their assessment of the creative process. While Derrida attributes the central agency to language and textuality and makes the text speak beyond the control of the speaking subject, Ehrenzweig retains the agency of the subject while also requiring that it temporarily relinquish the controlling functions of consciousness. In other words, for Ehrenzweig, too, the text speaks beyond the control of the speaking subject—but only because the subject's unconscious temporarily takes over the creative functions. The main difference between the two positions can be described in terms of the constitution of meaning and the receptive process. While Derrida postulates an irreducible undecidability of meaning, thus turning the receptive process into an endless semiosis, Ehrenzweig contends that the differentiated aesthetic structures of a work contain an undifferentiated matrix that is perceived and scanned unconsciously. Meaning may thus be undecidable, but only relative to our conscious perception. For Ehrenzweig aesthetic response therefore requires a reception that oscillates between focused and unfocused modes of attention.

In *Deconstruction Reframed*, Floyd Merrell has compared two different models of relativity, one developed by Derrida, and the other by David Bohm.[23] Merrell criticizes Derrida's notion of undecidability by using Bohm's critique of absolute relativism. Bohm, a quantum physicist, refutes models of absolute relativity, which are centered exclusively upon conscious perception and reception.[24] Even if an object of perception cannot be objectively described or conceptualized, this does not, according to Bohm, mean that we must dissolve the conceptual difference between subject and object or between a subject/object and its other. Like Ehrenzweig, Bohm assumes an implicit alternative order within the realm of concrete manifestations or representations. For Bohm, this "enfolded order" is holistic; it defies our categories of space and time and can therefore only be experienced "unconsciously."[25]

Ehrenzweig's relativity of orders is grounded in the assumption that all notions of order depend upon the perspective of the observer. Moreover, conscious perception relies on different structures of order than unconscious perception. According to Ehrenzweig, any perceivable order is based on a matrix that, from the perspective of this order, appears as disorder. What appears as ordered to conscious perception participates in an undifferentiated matrix that can only be perceived through unconscious scanning. Most likely, this alternate order of the unconscious is first experienced as dissolution or chaos. Ehrenzweig concludes that temporary dedifferentiations and emergent chaotic shapes do not result exclusively from a dissolution of order, but may be a necessary precondition for the emergence of new forms of order. This does not mean that Ehrenzweig rejects the idea of chaos, contingency, or noise altogether. But he distinguishes between two forms of chaos, namely one that is contingent and one that is based on the hidden order of the unconscious. The instrument used to distinguish between the two is what Ehrenzweig calls "unconscious scanning"— that is, a capacity for unconscious reception crucial for aesthetic experience.

What is perceived as order changes over time because the unconscious is, according to Ehrenzweig, not an innate structure but the product of a historical formation. Ehrenzweig argues that the history of aesthetic reception reveals a culturally variable and changing order of the unconscious, which in turn affects what recipients perceive as order or chaos. For example, to his contemporaries Mozart's music sounded painful to the ear and was perceived as musical chaos, whereas over time and due to the historically shifting boundaries between consciousness and the unconscious we have learned to perceive its harmonious aspects. This assumption accounts for the fact that the boundaries of consciousness and the cognitive order are relative in the sense that they shift according to historical changes in the modes of perception. Moreover, we may assume with Ehrenzweig that literary texts contain an undifferentiated matrix as "the Other" within textuality. From this perspective, literary texts that unsettle the boundaries between differentiated order and undifferentiated matrix may then aim at changing or expanding the boundaries of consciousness and communication.

What interests me in Ehrenzweig is his revision of the psychoanalytic notion of the primary processes from the perspective of their role in the creative process. This revision allows one to develop a model of aesthetic reception that comprises conscious and unconscious responses as well as their interplay. Such a model seems especially fruitful in light of the fact that modern and postmodern experimental texts use primary-process structures in so many creative ways. If it is true that these texts speak beyond the control of their authors or resist the confines of unambiguous meaning, then perhaps we need to develop new receptive attitudes, and some of them may well be unconscious. As Ehrenzweig shows us, the unconscious in literary texts need not necessarily only be the product of repression; it may also emerge as a "structural unconscious" that forms the source of our most creative energies.

One of the most crucial features shared by modern and postmodern experimental texts is their use of structures that resemble the primary processes. But this aesthetic use of primary-process structures is not merely a rendition of dreamlike qualities in literature, nor is it a mere dedifferentiation of rhetorical conventions and linguistic codes. My readings of modernist and postmodern experiments with language open up a larger theoretical and cultural context and draw out not only the aesthetic dimension of these experiments but also their epistemological, conceptual, cultural, and political implications. This may best be understood from the perspective of an "ecology of the text"[26] in which all discrete features of a text bear upon its overall function within various and expandable contexts, past, present, and future. Changing literary form is not merely an aesthetic game played by writers concerned with innovation and originality or haunted by anxiety of influence. Rather, it is primarily a response to pressures or challenges arising from different "environments"—such as other literary or discursive forms, cultural formations, psychological needs, social changes, or political concerns. Such an "ecological" perspective grasps the different spheres that bear upon literary production and reception in connection with, rather than in isolation from, each other.[27]

Accordingly, the experimental forms of modernism and postmodernism can no longer be described exclusively in negative categories, such as the rejection or disruption of former textual or aesthetic practices. The necessity of a conceptual model capable of emphasizing what these forms achieve instead of what they leave behind becomes obvious. In this larger context, the theoretical move from such notions as the "death of the subject" and the "end of literature" to such notions as the "proliferation of multiple subjectivities" and the "cele-bration of language" can no longer be reduced to a rhetorical gesture or an inversion of aesthetic values. Above all, such a move is a cultural intervention, a manifestation of a politics of reading inspired by the new aesthetic practices and interested in their impact on shaping new modes of speech, perception, and communication as well as new literary emotions and moods.

From this perspective, modernism appears no longer as a unified aesthetic and aestheticizing movement of esoteric (if not reactionary) writers, but as a diverse and heterogeneous cultural practice that not only reflects the larger trends of its own time but also resists them and works toward shaping new ones. My choice of texts for close readings is inspired by authors who have shaped our aesthetic and cultural practices in singular ways. But it is also motivated by their different uses of primary-process structures. Woolf, Joyce, Beckett, and Pynchon share what Foucault once called an "opening of language toward the unconscious." Such an opening constitutes much more than a mere psychological device. It testifies to a cultural politics that uses the capacity of language to draw from unconscious energies and creative skills in order to resist the unifying and codifying powers of language and thus to expand the boundaries not only of language but, mediated through it, of perception, communication, and emotion.

This is why the subjectivity of these texts may well be seen as paradigmatic for much more encompassing changes in the cultural formations of subjectivity. Boundaries in these texts function less as fixed demarcations of territorial or rhetorical politics than as provisional differentiations and temporary shaping devices within a continual process of change. Perhaps the transgression of boundaries is one of the most cherished literary practices in these texts; but I see this transgression less in its merely reactive impetus or its (imperial) drive toward the appropriation of new territories than in its challenge of existing cultural formations and its use or release of interior unconscious or repressed resources.

The preceding discussion of various theoretical perspectives on the open and fragmented forms of modernism and postmodernism has highlighted the role of the unconscious in aesthetic production and reception. The following chapter outlines the basic features of Win-

nicott's and Ehrenzweig's theories in order to unfold their implications for a theory of poetic language.[28] The first part of the chapter
traces the functions of the imaginary for the genesis of the subject. I
begin by evaluating the different epistemologies of Lacan's and Winnicott's theories of the mirror phase. Both Lacan and Winnicott stress
the role of the imaginary in the formation of the subject, which
requires ongoing mediations between primary and secondary processes. As Winnicott has shown, cultural objects provide a transitional
space for experimenting with such mediations in a protected cultural
space. My reflections on the psychogenesis of the subject become the
basis of a psychogenetic theory of poetic language. With Winnicott,
Ehrenzweig, and (from a different perspective) Kristeva, I assume that
poetic language forms a kind of intermediate or transitional speech
that affects the boundaries of subjects, who make creative use of this
speech in literary production or reception.

The theoretical part of my investigation is followed by five chapters
of close readings that reflect upon the assumptions and categories
developed by my theoretical model. Herman Melville's *Moby-Dick* is
a landmark in the historical development of fictional subjects and
literary subjectivity. In certain respects, Melville presents an early version of the modernist concern with the dissolution of the subject
and/or its dispersal into a multiplicity of voices. *Moby-Dick*'s grandiose
myth of the transcendence of subjectivity shapes Melville's cultural
opposition to Enlightenment values and the bonds of Cartesian subjectivity, while its proliferant intertextuality experiments with a multiplicity of voices and the ambiguities of narrative authority.

My choice of texts from the twentieth century is motivated by an
attempt to gain a variety of very different perspectives on new forms
of poetic language and literary subjectivity. All these texts experiment
in very different ways with the boundaries of language and subjectivity
and mark the transition to a new paradigm, or episteme. I have
decided to call them "transitional texts."[29] At its most general level,
this term recalls Winnicott's assumption that cultural objects are the
descendants of the so-called "transitional objects" formed during the
psychogenesis of the subject. In this respect, of course, all literary texts
are, in a sense, transitional. However, I use the term here more
specifically in relation to the crucial role that transgressions of boundaries and transitions to new orders play in these texts. These twentieth-century novels not only transgress familiar boundaries of poetic

language and literary subjectivity, but also mark a much more general transition toward new epistemological configurations, notions of order, and forms of aesthetic production and reception.

Virginia Woolf's *The Waves* is one of the first texts to develop formal consequences for the literary presentation of unbounded subjectivity. It abandons the narrative structure of the novel in favor of an interior dialogue, a dialogue based on a new form of abstract and recurrent poetic images that does not unfold within characters but between them as a form of unconscious dialogical interaction. Highly structured aesthetic devices present experimental characters who possess the formal qualities that have come to make up modernist experimentalism. Woolf's text marks a crucial transition toward the emerging new configurations of poetic language and literary subjectivity.

Experiments with a transitional literary language culminate in *Finnegans Wake*. Here, driven to its utmost extreme, a dedifferentiated language modeled after the primary processes is no longer unequivocally connected to literary characters, but can be read as engendering a specific subjectivity of language. Joyce's linguistic experiments explore not only a completely new mode of literary production, but also a utopia of reading that engages the eye and the ear in a holistic perception of language. *Finnegans Wake* may be said to become the training ground for a new kind of reader who must develop his or her skills in syncretistic perception and unconscious scanning. On a different level, this text also provides a testing ground for contemporary theories of language and their implied epistemologies. It is based on the idea of an "Ur-writing" at the time of its technological reproduction, a hologram that contains, as Joyce has claimed, the meaning of the whole text in each of its parts. Playfully exposing the multiculturalism and polycentrism of a global culture, this text also reflects the historical dynamic of (linguistic) colonization that underlies this colossal condensation of different languages and cultures. On a more general level, *Finnegans Wake* explores a new way of exceeding what cultural codes define as the boundaries of language.

Through quite different means, Samuel Beckett's *The Unnamable* pushes the boundaries of subjectivity to their extreme with the implosion of a first person narrator's discourse. The literary subject of this text transgresses its own boundaries in a highly reflexive self-exploration. This creates the fictional paradox of a first person narrator who invents himself as the fiction of an Other, who, himself a fiction, can only come into existence by inventing other fictions or voices, one of whom is *The Unnamable*. Combining the features of literary characters, empirical subject, and the transcendental subject of philosophy, the unnamable becomes a transitional character who challenges our most basic assumptions about subjectivity.

Gravity's Rainbow explores a new type of fictional presentation of history. Pynchon's apocalyptic metafiction exposes the function of myths of transcendence through the destructive realities of war. Supported by a dense intertextual network, Pynchon creates a carnivalesque "simultaneous fiction," which mixes different historical periods and blends World War II with the 1960s—the time during which Pynchon wrote the novel. The characters are often cast as replicas of film stars or other historical figures, "flat characters" copied from the two-dimensional surface of a filmstrip. This macrostructural frame turns *Gravity's Rainbow* into a simulated film narrative from the sixties about World War II. Pynchon's intriguing theoretical intertextuality, moreover, links his historical fiction to contemporary epistemological configurations of knowledge—especially the so-called postmodern theories in the sciences, systems theory, and cybernetics.

I have deliberately chosen novels that have created new forms of poetic language and literary subjectivity. These new forms are systematized in Chapter 8, which outlines the basic features of a cultural theory of transitional texts. Among these features in the texts under consideration are their activation of primary processes, their rejection of Cartesian subjectivity, their resistance to a horizontal division of subjectivity, and their insistence on new forms of aesthetic experience.

Chapter 9 links the new forms of literary subjectivity to paradigmatic changes in current theories. In this speculative outlook, I have deliberately chosen an interdisciplinary perspective derived mainly from cybernetics, systems theory, cultural ecology, and the so-called postmodern sciences. Remarkably, not only literary texts (such as *Gravity's Rainbow)* but also new theories of language (such as, for example, Julia Kristeva's theory of poetic language) use metaphors and models from the new sciences. Heisenberg's theory of quantum physics, for example, has become a most influential paradigm in the humanities.

Entropy, as both a metaphor and a conceptual model, figures prominently in postmodern literature and theories of postmodernism. Entropy is a key metaphor not only in *Gravity's Rainbow,* but also in numerous theoretical models—for example, those of Derrida,

Blumenberg, and Bateson. With its negative connotations, however, the entropy metaphor invites readings that equate transitional texts with manifestations of literary entropy. In order to avoid this focus on dissolution, decay, chaos, and apocalypse and to grasp the fundamental ambivalence of transitional texts, I contrast the model of entropy with the more productive model of the hologram. The holographic paradigm has inspired holonomic theories of mind, such as the theories of David Bohm and Karl Pribram. These holistic theories confirm from a very different perspective Ehrenzweig's assumption that undifferentiated forms may release syncretistic and holistic experiences that complement cognitive experiences. The affinities between notions of subjectivity implicit in transitional texts on the one hand and in holonomic theories of the mind on the other allow one to perceive transitional texts as part of a larger cultural and theoretical development that demands a new understanding of subjectivity.

This speculation will complement, but never replace, one's fascination with the fundamental otherness of transitional texts, the sense that they anticipate the future of a subjectivity that has not yet been formulated discursively and perhaps even resists discursive formulation, but that, precisely because of this resistance, presents such a profound challenge to our available models of poetic language and literary subjectivity.

2

The Transitional Space of Literature

To understand poetry one must be able to put on the soul of a
child, like a magic cloak, and to prefer the child's wisdom to that
of the adult.   —*Johan Huizinga*

The Psychogenesis of the Decentered Subject

In his theory of carnivalesque literature Bakhtin writes that "the word
is not a thing, but the ever-moving, ever-changing medium of dialogical intercourse."[1] Bakhtin's theory can also be read as a socioge-
netic theory of poetic language: "A single consciousness, a single
voice, is never sufficient. The life of the word consists in passing from
mouth to mouth, from context to context, from collective to collective, from generation to generation . . . Every member of a speech
collective . . . receives the word from an alien voice, is filled up with
this alien voice. The word comes into a context from another context,
saturated with alien meanings. His own thought finds the word already
occupied."[2]

Operating in the unconscious, these dialogical relations are rooted
in language prior to any dialogue and exist beyond the meanings that
emerge from the relationship between signifier and signified. According to Bakhtin, dialogical relations lie beyond the bounds of metalin-
guistics; and when he speaks of the occupancy of the word by an alien
voice, he indirectly invokes the psychogenesis of the word. Only one
further step leads to a metapsychology in which the subject's occupancy by an alien voice is already built into the structure of the
unconscious—which is, as Lacan argues, "the discourse of the Other."[3]

In a similar vein, the anthropologist Plessner writes, "I am, but do not possess myself,"[4] thus casting the subject as an ex-centric being that is partly concealed from what motivates its actions. If we supplement Plessner's dictum with the answer given by Bloch—"I am, but do not possess myself. That is why we must become"[5]—we have already pointed to the earliest anthropological function of the imaginary, namely the formation of the boundaries of subjectivity.

Once the infant has learned to distinguish between self and other, or inside and outside, it also develops a sense of play. Most cultures create a special cultural space with its own rules and conventions for imaginary activities such as, for example, play, ritual, and aesthetic experience. Both the individual and the collective formations of subjectivity in a specific culture use the creative potential of this space— often in the form of institutions such as collective ritual practices, the arts, and, more recently, the proliferating forms of leisure culture. A basic function of all the diverse cultural objects is thus the shaping of the boundaries of subjectivity through ritualistic or aesthetic experience.

In this chapter, I use Lacan's conception of the mirror phase and Winnicott's theory of play in order to elaborate a psychogenetic conception of the imaginary and of poetic language. Both theories assign the imaginary a fundamental role in the psychogenesis of the subject and the creation of otherness. While Lacan emphasizes the deeply ambivalent role of the imaginary in the constitution of the subject, Winnicott focuses on its creative role in the continual reshaping of the boundaries of the subject.

Psychoanalytic theories posit the earliest phase in the subject's development as one of relative undifferentiation, where there is as yet no mental separation between self and other. During the subject's development the primary processes—as an early mode of experience— are increasingly thrust into the background, while the secondary processes become the basis of what is commonly experienced as a relative continuity of the subject. According to Freud's *Civilization and its Discontents*, the subject's integration into the symbolic order requires the subordination of the pleasure principle to the reality principle, and this process in turn leads to differentiation and the formation of boundaries. The secondary processes thus evolve as functions of the symbolic order and presuppose the ability not only to postpone immediate satisfaction, but also, and more significantly, to include logical thinking and its requisite law of contradiction, as well as the capacity for negation and discrimination. Moreover, the secondary processes form the mental operations necessary for the mastering of syntax and semantics and the correlative production of systems, hierarchies, and polarities. Finally, they also provide the ground for what Freud calls "reality-testing"—that is, the ability to differentiate between a wish or a claim and its fulfillment.

Once these capacities have been developed, all the features of primary-process experience that prove irreconcilable with the new order become more and more subliminal. Simultaneity of experience and the conflation of temporal hierarchies is abandoned in favor of a spatiotemporal order. The interchangeability of part and whole, the fusion of objects and thoughts, their freely floating cathexis, and their imaginary investment give way to more stable and bounded representations of objects (Freud's *Objektrepräsentanz*). And, finally, the immediate visual experience, the production of alogical connections without hierarchy or polarity, the coexistence of opposites, and the system of overdetermination give way to an elaborate system of categorization. The basic achievement of this phase is the differentiation between I and Not-I—that is, the constitution of the subject's boundaries.

Primary processes, however, are not simply substituted by secondary processes, but survive as a form of unconscious experience that complements, counteracts, and shapes conscious experience in decisive ways. The gradual transition from one mode of being to the other during the infant's acculturation and socialization is the outcome of its confrontation with a cultural environment—a process that Freud perceives as deeply agonistic. Instead of following a linear development, the process unfolds in extremely heterogeneous patterns as an ongoing struggle with varying success and exceedingly ambivalent results. Feeding on the energies of the pleasure principle, the primary processes, after having been pushed underground, continue to exert a subversive effect upon the symbolic order. While they find their dominance restricted to the unconscious, manifesting themselves in special areas of experience, such as dreams, fantasies, and other alternative states of consciousness, they nevertheless operate simultaneously within the symbolic order and pervade the secondary processes.

Winnicott's narrative of the subject's psychogenesis is less agonistic than Freud's. Instead of emphasizing the struggle between primary and secondary processes, he highlights their complementarity. He does acknowledge that the symbolic order imposes restrictions, but he weighs them against the enabling functions and the pleasure derived from differentiation and the creative use of the symbolic order. From this perspective, the continued operation of the primary processes within the secondary processes is not only agonistic, but may also be invigorating since it guarantees the permeability between conscious and unconscious experience and opens up a channel between conscious and unconscious energies. In a similar vein, Ehrenzweig emphasizes the creative force of the primary processes as a tool for unconscious scanning. This productive force of the primary processes becomes crucial for an analysis of their use in poetic language. I see the agonistic and the productive aspects of the primary processes not as exclusive or incompatible, but as the result of their fundamental ambivalence in relation to the symbolic order. My model of poetic language therefore stresses not only the tensions between the two modes of production and reception but also their productive interaction.

This fundamental ambivalence determines the manifold operations of the imaginary and of poetic language. In dreams and phantasms, for example, the primary mode of being may acquire the status of a lost paradise or a threatening abyss. And while the capacity to differentiate between self and other is bought at the price of a cleavage within the subject, the very imaginary functions that enabled the differentiation may later be used to temporarily suture this cleavage. Psychoanalysis has traced this fundamental ambivalence back to the earliest stages of development, particularly to the so-called mirror phase and the role of the gaze for the constitution of boundaries and otherness.

The look and its other, the gaze, also play a fundamental role in the constitution of the imaginary functions. In the phase of relative undifferentiation, where self-experience is bound up with experience through others, the mother's look and touch[6] are internalized by the subject as a mirroring structure, and occasion the first affective cathexes of the body, which in turn engender a kind of "bodily ego" (*Körperich*).[7] We can see here the psychogenetic foundations of a whole philosophical and epistemological tradition of the *esse est percipi*.

This mode of mirroring determines how the first sensory experiences of the body are affectively invested and becomes crucial for the later differentiation of an image of the body from an image of the self. To experience its own body as an organized gestalt with perceptual qualities, the infant must be able to see it from without—that is, from a distance. This experience is facilitated in the so-called mirror phase, which plays a central role in Lacan's theory. The discovery of one's mirror image as an image of oneself—in which one's own look becomes the medium of the experience—proves to be as fundamental for the cognitive cathexis of the "bodily ego" as the mother's look for the affective cathexis. According to Lacan, the discovery of the mirror image as an image of oneself is decisive because it identifies the body as a bounded and organized unity at a time when undeveloped motor control makes the infant feel uncoordinated, helplessly dependent, and fused with its environment.

Although this bounded and organized gestalt in the mirror is an illusion, it nevertheless provokes the wish and capacity to overcome the lack of motor coordination and achieve independence through differentiation and the formation of boundaries. In contradiction to the infant's own experience of bodily incoordination, the mirror image fulfills the dual function of anticipation and achievement, and thus instills a primary capacity for representation—not yet conceptually organized, to be sure, but a pictorial capacity that enables the infant to relate to an "outside." The reality effect of this outside is, according to Lacan, always "duplicated, whether it consists of his own body or of the persons, or even objects, around him."[8]

Lacan argues that the structure of this mirror experience becomes the matrix for all further self-experience: the difference between image and reality will remain constitutive for self-consciousness in general. Keeping self-experience and self-image in harmony henceforth requires the exclusion of discrepant experience. Hereafter, however, the excluded or repressed experiences also make use of the imaginary in their striving for recognition. The repressed returns in phantasms of the fragmented body: in images of detached, independent body parts, of organs equipped with a life of their own, of particular body parts in a state of fusion with natural objects, and the like. These phantasms not only incorporate wishes for liberation from the bounds of the body or the ego and a return to the experience of unbounded fusion with the environment; they also incorporate complementary anxieties about disintegration, fragmentation, and dissolution. Like the mirror image itself, the phantasms of the fragmented body are exceedingly ambivalent with regard to self-experience and self-representation. In the mirror phase, the imaginary not only circumscribes a bodily gestalt for the subject, but also, through the phantasms of the fragmented body, represents what has been excluded from this circumscription. In other words, the imaginary functions not only to stabilize but also to destabilize boundaries. This ambivalent status of the imaginary becomes more obvious during the subject's later development.

The relation to oneself acquired in the mirror phase meanwhile furnishes no more than an initial frame or, as Lacan calls it, a "matrix." In general, this frame becomes part of the processes of delimitation and differentiation and the organization of social relations. The gradual differentiation between self and other, or I and Not-I, provides a release from the original symbiotic fusion, and the symbiotic dependence gradually turns into the need for recognition, in which the original dependence is internalized. This recognition, in turn, is embedded in a complex set of interactions. The Other, created within the matrix of the mirror experience, forms a complicated duality: an internalized Other shapes all our perceptions of the concrete other encountered in social and symbolic interactions. Yet the boundaries between the two always remain fluid. The subject's sense of recognition is not only derived from the actions and demands of concrete others, but is also structured by internalized demands of the Other.

Because of the need for recognition, social norms and the imperatives of the symbolic order associated with the Other begin to operate in the subject. As an effect of the internalized Other, the subject recognizes, above all, qualities that satisfy those norms. Hence the subject's recognition by the Other is rarely based on what the subject is, but is from a very early stage linked with demands for what it must become. The internalized Other codetermines the subject's anticipatory strategies and exclusionary practices.

Anticipation plays an important role not only in the mirror stage but also in the phase of social self-constitution. To be recognized, the subject must posit itself as something it is not, or not yet. And while everything that does not comply with the Other's norms is threatened with exclusion, it is only by way of exclusions that the subject can become what it is supposed to be. At the same time, these very exclusions cause a rift in the subject between what may be acknowledged and what must be repressed. An element of self-estrangement is thus necessarily built into whatever the subject eventually posits as an "I." Therefore, the very constitution of a subject, its capacity to say "I" or to picture itself as bounded and relatively coherent, is unthinkable without the role of the imaginary.

This capacity to feel or to say "I" increases in proportion to the renunciation of symbiosis, socially instilled in favor of differentiation. The cleavage within the subject is reflected by the two modes of being and their continual negotiations between undifferentiation and differentiation, pleasure principle and reality principle, symbiosis and individuation. Ultimately, any successful renunciation of symbiosis and the differentiation of the subject must be culturally mediated. This mediation takes place through the creative function of the imaginary and through cultural objects such as security blankets, teddybears, soothing sounds, books, and the like. In fact, the ways in which a culture produces a "facilitating environment" (Winnicott) for the processes of differentiation generate a whole style, if not aesthetics, that guides the subject's development. Autopoiesis is here the driving force that determines the unfolding and the aesthetics of this development.

The Transitional Space

While the earliest threat to symbiosis is generated by the mother's absence, the infant learns to create supportive structures in order to be able to endure her temporary absences. The exemplary game of *fort-da*, in which, according to Freud, a little boy gains imaginary control over his mother by making her disappear and come back in the form of a reel and string, is a classic example.[9] Gradually a transitional space is formed between the child and the mother, a space that, according to Winnicott, has its own aesthetic and, in a way, even its own epistemology. The boundaries of this transitional space are fluid, since the infant—and later the adult—keeps drawing them anew in response to internal or external demands.

According to Winnicott, this transitional space is created by the earliest use of the imaginary. From a psychogenetic viewpoint, we might regard the transitional space as a space for the imagination's testing and mastering of the demands and tasks posed by the gradual development of intersubjectivity. This space, which at first takes shape within the original symbiosis, prepares the ground for the gradual differentiation of the boundaries between self and other.

At this point the infant creates specific objects equipped with imaginary cathexes. These so-called transitional objects are objects whose primary function consists in helping to create otherness by establishing the first boundaries between self and other. Subsequently, the infant's creation of transitional objects evolves into the creation of a transitional space between self and other, a space reserved for play and other imaginary activities. Even though, in one sense, this space furthers differentiation and creates otherness, in another sense it also reduces the pressures that result from differentiation and otherness. The infant experiences transitional objects as Not-I but, paradoxically, not yet as separate objects. Winnicott regards this paradox as constitutive of the transitional space in general. Security blankets or stuffed animals are most often used as transitional objects, but almost everything else, including living beings or even movements and sounds, may serve the same function. According to Winnicott, transitional objects that develop the infant's capacity for symbolization are precursors to cultural objects. Even later, after the capacity to distinguish between self and other and to form object relations is acquired, the subject still uses the transitional space to play with its own boundaries by constantly undoing and reshaping them. Free from the pressures of the reality principle and unchallenged by reality testing, the subject can produce illusions of sameness and difference in a protected space, a no-man's-land between I and Not-I.

Seen from the outside, the child's experiences in the transitional space may seem to be illusory. Yet the transitional objects or phenomena antedate the formation of reality testing. Even later, the distinction between being and seeming will always be suspended in the transitional space. The creative production of temporary illusions in the transitional space relieves the subject from the pressures of distinguishing between inner and outer reality.[10] These experiences are, however, no longer identical with those in the phase of undifferentiation. Elements of both primary and secondary processes form these experiences; and, more important at this stage, both processes are compatible with each other, since the boundaries between them are temporarily suspended.

According to Winnicott, this transitional space retains its significance in later life: along with the creative use of cultural objects, it becomes the place for the subject's continual reshaping of its own boundaries. These transitional experiences are, in fact, precursors of aesthetic experience. The temporary suspension of the boundaries between outer and inner reality does not mean, however, that the primary processes automatically regain their dominance. On the contrary, the transitional space gradually develops into a space where there can be interaction and mediation between the two modes. The experimental forms assumed by the subject are simultaneously the product of these mediations and the vehicle for potential change in the relationship between these two modes. Like the mirror phase, the transitional space establishes a linkage between the boundaries of the subject and the imaginary. Moreover, the function of the transitional space in shaping the boundaries of the subject becomes exceedingly more complex and ambivalent. While initially it functions as a protected space for the constitution of boundaries, this space later is used to keep boundaries flexible, to expand or reshape them, and possibly to reintegrate what had been repressed during their formation.

Both the mirror phase and the transitional space provide the ground for the subject's very ambivalent development within the symbolic order. During the mirror phase as well as during the early uses of the transitional space the infant posits itself as something it is not, or has not yet become, and thereby moves toward or is pushed into dramatic change. In each instance the infant acquires mental or affective differentiations that are crucial for functioning within the symbolic order: the capacity to experience oneself as bounded is acquired by internalizing an image of one's body, while the capacity to distinguish between I and Not-I is acquired through transitional objects.

After the infant has both literally and metaphorically moved away from the mother during the mirror phase, it begins to use the transitional space as a protected area, populated with imaginary objects that are, as Winnicott formulates it, seen as part of the self, but paradoxically also as the first Not-I possessions. From a psychogenetic viewpoint, these objects facilitate differentiation on both cognitive and affective levels. Differentiation is to a large extent achieved by fostering the capacity for representation and symbol formation. As stated earlier, though initially the transitional space helps to form and stabilize boundaries, the subject increasingly uses this same space to keep boundaries flexible—to relax, undo, and reshape them. The stronger a culture imposes its pressures for differentiation on the basis of a suppression of primary processes, the more it becomes a function of the imagination to retain primary-process experiences and to facilitate temporary dedifferentiations. The transitional space provides a culturally sanctioned sphere where the subject may use the imagination to reconnect with what has been excluded or repressed during its development. This implies that, once the basic differentiations and boundaries are formed, the transitional space develops into a very heterogeneous conglomeration of disparate and discontinuous cultural spheres whose boundaries remain fluid and whose functions vary greatly. One of the most prominent characteristics of the transitional space is its ambivalence toward the cultural environment in which it is created. While it is the most important space for the differentiation of cultural life, it is also an agency of transformation and, under specific conditions, subversion. This ambivalence can be attributed to the continual negotiation of boundaries in the transitional space.

The dynamic of a continual differentiation and dedifferentiation of boundaries gradually forms the main activity in the transitional space. The very constitution of decentered subjectivity demands the continual drawing and redrawing of boundaries, and this process in turn depends upon the generation of certain areas or functions where the unconscious can retain access to operation and meaning. Due to the polarization of two modes of being within decentered subjectivity, temporary dedifferentiations of boundaries become as necessary as the drawing of new ones. The transitional space can, in fact, be seen as a space where the subject seeks to come to terms with and make creative use of its decentered position. Fashioned according to an aesthetic of its own, this space ultimately turns the predicament of the cleavage between the conscious and the unconscious or between self and Other into an incentive for creative production.

Language and Symbol

The acquisition of language, the engine and bearer of the secondary processes, is generally considered a fundamental achievement in the subject's development. But, as Lacan has not ceased to remind us, we are already molded by language before we even learn to speak, since the symbolic order pervades and structures every cultural negotiation, including the earliest phases of psycho- and sociogenesis. Accordingly, even the unconscious is structured like a language and forms, in Lacan's words, a "discourse of the Other."[11] On the basis of its capacity for symbolization, language becomes the privileged medium for the secondary processes and the vehicle of the symbolic order. Yet the ambivalent function of the imaginary and cultural objects created in the transitional space also permeates the whole domain of language and symbols. Pervaded by the unconscious, language speaks more than its subject intends to say and thus may assume a certain agency of its own. It may at the same time be more removed and closer to the speaking subject than this subject is consciously able to perceive. Under special conditions, language may stage a performance of the unconscious and thus open up an ambivalent communicative space for what is otherwise excluded from communication.

Hence the fundamental split within the subject, expressed as a polarization of two modes of being, is also reflected within language. In order to express the unconscious, or the Other, language functions paradoxically, at the same time revealing and concealing the unconscious—a quality that has been described by Freud as a structure of double meaning. Our symbolic order tends to organize these two levels of meaning hierarchically. The so-called manifest meaning, consciously constituted along the lines of semantic information, dominates a latent meaning, operative at an unconscious level. The latter uses the ambiguities of linguistic structures and the formal qualities of language as a means of speaking against the codified signification. In other words, a tacit negotiation goes on within language between what is admitted and what is excluded from the symbolic order. In our quotidian discourses the unconscious forces its way into consciousness only exceptionally—for example, in certain derailments of speech or in the classic example of the so-called Freudian slip.

When the dynamic relation of primary and secondary processes is expressed—as in these simple cases—as a dynamic between manifest and latent meaning, the tension between them is somewhat pacified, since the unconscious does not visibly disrupt the process of signification. This dynamic changes as soon as primary processes take part in shaping the manifest expression and thus become explicit communicative signals. In addition to dreams and other states of alternative consciousness where primary processes are used spontaneously, cultural objects in the transitional space often deliberately employ in culturally significant ways figurations and structures borrowed from the primary processes. Because the transitional space is only initially a developmental phase and then becomes a general sphere of cultural and artistic production, its use of primary processes is part of an ongoing cultural negotiation concerning the two alternative modes of mental and creative production and experience. In particular, the use of poetic language in the transitional space remains part of a continual reshaping of the cultural boundaries of subjectivity.

The fact that initially the transitional space develops as an experimental space protected from the pressures of the reality principle does not mean that it will remain free from cultural determination. To the extent to which a child has contact with cultural objects—in the form of toys, books, and media, but also in the form of culture-specific ways of playing—the transitional space assumes a specific cultural shape, however much this shape can be molded in turn by the child's familial environment with its own style of care. Both the formational and the transformational qualities of cultural objects and in particular (due to their specific use of language) literary texts are therefore inherently ambivalent in relation to the culture that produces them.

Regarding poetic language, one must emphasize that its formative qualities exceed its representational functions. The transitional objects are neither merely representing elements (signifiers) nor represented elements (signifieds), but function as ambiguous and complex molders of subjectivity. Accordingly, if we see poetic language less as a representational than as a formational object, we emphasize the cultural function of literary form. This becomes especially relevant when one tries, for example, to assess the status of primary-process structures in literary texts. Even if a literary text performs primary-process operations, we may never simply read it as a mere primary-process production. Translated into a consciously shaped aesthetic production, primary processes do not merely represent the unconscious, but play a formational role by shifting the boundaries between conscious and unconscious modes of production and reception. Primary-process operations in literary texts may thus shape unconscious material, but as textual figurations they pertain completely to neither the primary nor the secondary processes.

Seen from this perspective, cultural objects facilitate negotiations between inner and outer reality and between primary- and secondary-process experiences. Their specific achievement, then, does not lie primarily in what Freud emphasized—namely in their referring to a latent meaning and thus revealing the operations of the unconscious—but lies rather in their creating specific figurations of language able to provide an aesthetic experience formative for subjectivity. Unlike the relatively private objects the child creates in the transitional space, cultural objects must adjust to the requirements of intersubjective communication. But if, with Winnicott, we wish to locate cultural objects in general in the transitional space, they constitute what Winnicott calls a third-order level—that is, a level where primary and secondary processes are no longer experienced as exclusive of each other, but where they are mediated in a significant way.

Poetic language then generates a transitional space of speech—that is, it becomes the medium of a third-order speech. Its intermediacy reaches beyond the Freudian structure of double meaning in that it dehierarchizes the two modes of signification and causes them to interact in a more complex way. From this perspective, it is above all the move beyond the level of representation toward the level of formation that makes this third order of speech culturally relevant. A theory that locates poetic language in a transitional space of speech thus revises and complements the basic assumptions of such hermeneutic theories as those developed by Freud and Ricoeur with their models of a poetic structure of double meaning.[12]

Poetic Language as a Transitional Space of Speech

To place poetic language in a transitional space means to loosen the exclusive affiliation with the secondary processes and the symbolic order. Such a premise has considerable epistemological implications, since it asserts a difference between poetic and other forms of speech—a conceptual move in the direction of theories that define poetic language by its difference from so-called ordinary language.[13] But while most theories attempt to locate the difference in the phenomenology or structure of poetic language, a theory of the transitional space describes poetic language functionally, from a psychogenetic perspective, thus emphasizing its formative qualities.

But how far can we follow Winnicott in concluding that cultural objects in general retain the functions of such a transitional space? At first glance, this perspective seems to conflate genesis with function and structure, especially since poetic language already presupposes all the differentiations of the secondary processes. In other words, what is the difference between an infant creating its first objects in the transitional space at a time when it as yet has no command of spoken language, and an adult operating with the highly differentiated symbolic system of poetic language? Even if we accept that poetic language operates within a transitional space of culture, we must still make distinctions of genre or periodization and differentiate between specific forms of poetic production according to the extent of deviation from other forms of speech.

Historical and generic differences I take to be distinctions internal to poetic language itself, as the distinction between its function and mode of operation within a transitional space—not as constraints that affect the conceptual scope of the theory. In other words, I share Winnicott's view that cultural objects in general operate within a transitional space of culture, with its own modes of operation. This generalized conceptual framework, however, allows for a wide range of historical specifications. Different cultural environments produce considerable variation in the forms and uses of cultural objects, which in turn can be described from historically specific perspectives. For example, authors of early forms of the novel, which rely on various models of integrated subjectivity for their literary constitution of a bourgeois subject, mold their poetic language according to the conventions of literary realism—notwithstanding that these texts, too, are generally ambivalent toward the models that inspire their aesthetic framework and its epistemological implications. By contrast, once literary texts emphasize the split within the decentered subject, they increasingly abandon the forms of realism for the fragmented, open, and mobile forms of the primary process. These open forms, in turn, relate in ambivalent ways to the formation of decentered subjectivity. Thus poetic language can, in varying degrees, approach or move away from the function of the (psychogenetically) earliest cultural objects that helped form the boundaries of subjectivity. It can emphasize the shaping of boundaries or their dissolution, depending on historical or artistic considerations. But its inherent tendency is always to do both at once.

Just as we find changing historical forms of subjectivity, so too do we find historical changes in the transitional space. The development of the transitional space depends not only upon its cultural environment but also upon its own historical dynamic. Poetic language has two distinct historical fields of reference, one working in a more diachronic field of reference and the other in a synchronic one. Poetic language relates primarily to the history of literature and its rhetorical and aesthetic conventions, but it is also mediated through other current discursive practices. The internal field of reference constitutes what we commonly call intertextuality, a phenomenon that is itself constituted by a transgression of boundaries from text to text or even from text to other media.

In other words, concrete forms of poetic speech within a specific cultural environment, form a dialogical relation not only to other forms of speech used within this environment but also to the traditions of poetic language to which it is intertextually affiliated. And just as, psychogenetically, the objects created in the transitional space assume changing functions, so do the different forms within the transitional space of poetic speech.

Generally, the transitional space is a space for protected cultural negotiations. The notion of protection here has psychological and political implications that are clearly distinct from conventional notions of art as a sphere of compensation and free play. While conventional notions of art consider the space of literature and the arts a relatively closed system whose "autonomy" also means a certain isolation from social and political processes, Winnicott's notion of a "protected transitional space" emphasizes that this space is to some extent exempted from the rules and restrictions that operate outside. At the same time, however, the boundaries of the transitional space remain fluid; and this flexibility accounts for the fact that experiences in the transitional space may have a tremendous impact on the sociocultural environment at large. Protection, then, means mainly a certain release from the common operations of internal and external censorship. Winnicott therefore insists on a ground rule in the transitional space, namely that its activities and inventions must not be challenged. The dictum "Do not challenge" is a productive and receptive disposition that bears certain affinities with what literary critics know as a willing suspension of disbelief.

But this receptive attitude is itself not free from the ambivalence that marks cultural productions in general. Under certain conditions, the verdict on challenge makes the transitional space vulnerable to co-optation—as we may witness, for example, through the cultural invasion of mass cultural products that channel and shape the imaginary activities of historical subjects. We may well evaluate a culture according to the extent to which it tries to gain access to and mold or control the transitional space—especially given our increasingly invasive media culture. The transitional space is, in short, not only the space where desire is mediated, worked through, transformed, and sublimated, but also a space where new forms of desire may be created.

Poetic language as a transitional space of speech can mediate desire most particularly through what Lacan calls "the discourse of the Other" within speech. In defining poetic language as a transitional space of speech, one can assume that it becomes a privileged medium to mediate this discourse of the Other—that is, to make it readable. Locating literary texts within the transitional space allows one to highlight those qualities derived from the psychogenetic function of cultural objects: the shaping of the unconscious, the excluded, or the "unrepresentable"; and the respective shaping of the boundaries of subjectivity and language.

While transitional objects facilitate the early formation of the subject's boundaries, poetic language, in mediating the discourse of the Other, takes part in shaping the various forms of subjectivity generated by a specific culture. Poetic language operates on the cultural boundaries of subjectivity, just as it operates on the boundaries of subjects who produce or read it. It thereby confers a certain reality on imaginary productions. By way of shaping the undifferentiated or the unrepresentable it takes part in the continual production of subjectivity. During this process, established conventional boundaries of language have to be suspended, along with the boundaries of what critical judgment would admit as real or realistic.

The effect that poetic language has on the boundaries of subjectivity can be described in terms of differentiation—even in those cases where the most immediate result is dedifferentiation. The presence of the excluded or the voice of the Other in poetic language activates the unconscious and exposes it to change. Seen in this way, one of the functions of poetic language is to serve as a mediator for the unconscious. This, of course, presupposes that the unconscious in general is subject to historical change. Poetic language, especially when it makes use of primary processes, may become the vehicle of such a change.

Psychoanalytic theories of literature have not fully explored this creative potential of poetic language. Freud is mainly concerned with unconscious modes of production and the possibilities of detecting unconscious motives behind literary narratives. Lacan emphasizes the imaginary mainly as a sphere of the subject's misrecognition. Winnicott's theory of play and creativity mentions only in passing the implications of his model for a more encompassing theory of culture. One of the most challenging aspects in developing these implications for a theory of literature lies in the fact that Winnicott refuses to treat cultural objects reductively as mere affirmations of psychoanalytic assumptions and instead highlights their own dynamic contribution to cultural processes.

Conceptually, Winnicott allows us to analyze poetic language in accordance with the more general operations within the transitional space of cultural objects. This perspective allows one to highlight a dual function of poetic language in the formation of subjectivity: on the one hand, poetic language loosens the boundaries of subjectivity by admitting the unconscious or the voice of the Other into its signifying processes; on the other hand, poetic language shapes the unconscious and thus redraws the boundaries of subjectivity in more complex ways. In a manner characteristic of the transitional space, poetic language is thus both stabilizing and subversive at once—in regard to not only the boundaries of subjectivity but also those of language. Poetic language is able to subvert the order of language, which is developed in connection with and based on secondary processes, by integrating the form and material of primary processes into the domain of communication. Ultimately, this very process has a stabilizing effect because it allows for new differentiations within language and thus for an expansion of language and communication.

Often poetic language develops its aesthetic effects and cultural functions precisely through its difference from the codes and rules of the symbolic order. The most creative use poetic language makes of the transitional space extends the boundaries of language in two directions. Poetic language either produces extreme stylizations and formalizations and thus creates a relatively strong bounding and structuring of linguistic material, or breaks up syntax and semantics, fragments and subverts meaning, and opens itself to the free-floating connections of the primary processes—that is, toward destructuring and dedifferentiation. Experimental texts in particular have used this potential of poetic language.

It is clear that the transgression of boundaries between I and Not-I or self and Other is already part of the process of literary production. An author such as Virginia Woolf, for example, uses her own speech to give voice to imaginary characters or utterances, thus derealizing herself in an "alien speech" that is nevertheless her own. Like transitional objects, poetic language belongs to the I and the Not-I at the same time. The possibility of language to transgress the boundaries of its speaker is pushed to its limits in the modern and postmodern texts I call "transitional texts," where it is even difficult to attribute the multiple voices to specific characters or character-effects. In exploring the most refined ways in which language can dissolve its unequivocal attachment to a speaking subject, poetic language migrates into a space between the boundaries of I and Not-I. It uses that special potential for which the transitional space lays the psychogenetic foundation, namely to speak the voice of the Other in one's own voice.

In order to reshape what has been repressed by the symbolic order, poetic language must use the structure of double meaning in a way that, paradoxically, undoes this structure while using it. As a tacit dimension, the excluded, or the voice of the Other, always has a potential space within our speech. But it becomes overtly significant only under the special condition of slippages, breaks, or dedifferentiations of language. Poetic language develops its own forms and conventions for satisfying such conditions, most often by making strategic use of rhetorical figures and tropes that produce indeterminacy and multiple meanings. It is not a question of a manifest text concealing a latent meaning in need of translation—as Freud constructed the interpretation of dreams—but of a text offering the endless productivity of multiple meanings. When it comes to hearing or deciphering the voice of the Other, the libidinal cathexis of poetic language is crucial. As one of the major mediums for effecting change in the structure and content of the unconscious, poetic language appeals to the unconscious in multiple ways. One can even assume that the effects of unconscious aesthetic experience are more lasting than those of conscious experience because they are structural rather than formal or thematic. And because they are so hard to grasp and describe, the unconscious effects of literature are hardly ever conceptualized in aesthetic theory or, indeed, in reader response theories.

The Creative Process of Literary Production and Reception

> The primary process is a precision instrument for creative scanning that is far superior to discursive reason and logic.
> —*Anton Ehrenzweig*

Just as the author of poetic language derealizes him or herself in order to speak voices that are neither wholly I nor Not-I, so the reader, too, has to temporarily suspend his or her own boundaries during the reception process in order to slip into an imaginary world made of alien thoughts, voices, and characters. Confronted with imaginary voices that resonate with or create dissonance to their own interior polyphony, readers may establish complex relations to these voices and, in extreme cases, even experience states of aesthetic fusion with them. Reader and text are, in this sense, never in a simple subject-object relation, for reading temporarily effaces the divison of subject and object. Furthermore, playing across subject-object divisions is a fundamental operation in the transitional space, and this very operation also shapes the process of literary reception. Moreover, the willing suspension of disbelief, the basic receptive attitude in the transitional space, supports the malleability of the reader's boundaries and furthers unfocused attention, unconscious scanning, and the processing of undifferentiated structures.

This disposition facilitates the shaping of the unconscious or the unrepresentable. The plasticity of the recipient's boundaries during unfocused attention heightens the sensitivity for unconscious material and modes of connection and increases the chances for their admittance as part of aesthetic experience. It must be stressed once again that the aim is not to make conscious what has hitherto remained unconscious but rather to reach beyond what Ehrenzweig calls the "surface-sensibilities"[14] in order to create a "negative capability" for the reception of unconscious structures and their often more complex order. Over time, transitional experiences may extend receptive boundaries. Due to the cultural polarization of primary and secondary modes of experience, literary texts have to deploy complex strategies in order to get these two modes to interact. In other words, not only do textual strategies have to take into account the resistance or the censorship of the recipient, but they must also actively deploy poetic devices that facilitate unconscious reception and the recognition of primary-process structures. Instead of keeping conscious and unconscious experience at two separate levels, poetic language brings the two forms into a delicate yet productive interaction with each other. The inherent receptive ambivalence toward the primary processes holds true for aesthetic experience as well. The fascination with primary experiences always contains a potential threat, which is felt all the more intensely when texts dissolve narrative or semantic structures and deploy formal fragmentation and dedifferentiation to such an extent that they undermine a reception based exclusively on focused attention.

Because poetic language operates at an intersubjective level, it must integrate primary-process material and structures in a culturally significant manner and furthermore take into account what is required to circumvent censorship. In this sense, poetic language provides a cultural form of balancing the increasing exclusion of primary processes from the symbolic order. Just as transitional objects were initially used to cope creatively with cultural constraints and challenges, poetic language creatively copes with the requirements of the symbolic order while simultaneously challenging potentially restrictive cultural norms and practices.

This perspective has important implications for a theory of literary reception. The act of reading is neither a merely individual process nor a merely cultural or collective one. Individual forms of reception are inextricably fused with cultural ones. Transformations of the boundaries of poetic language and literary subjectivity, for example, also affect the reader's language and subjectivity. Unfamiliar forms of poetic language challenge the reader's receptive disposition and habits—an effect that of course does not remain restricted to experiences within the transitional space. The special communicative situation in the transitional space may thus help to differentiate not only aesthetic experience but also, mediated by aesthetic experience, perceptual habits and patterns of reading or communication in general. However, given the ambivalence that marks the cultural use of the transitional space, the opposite may also be true. Cultural objects may, for example, induce regressive desublimation, sensationalization of affect, or a numbing of our perceptual or rhetorical sensorium.

The special conditions of the transitional space thus account for its ambivalent, if not paradoxical, relationship to the symbolic order. As a protected experimental space, it affects the boundaries of the symbolic order, despite—or perhaps even precisely because of—its being generated within this order. The creative potential of the transitional space is always relative in respect to the symbolic order. The vicissitudes of postmodern media culture, for example, whose technologically refined seductions and multiple forms of colonizing the unconscious enable it to intrude more efficiently than any other culture into the transitional space, considerably reduce the chances of the creative use of transitional space. But in opposition to theories that presuppose a total control and co-optation of literature and hence of the subject, a theory of the transitional space emphasizes the basic ambivalence of all cultural objects as well as the fact that recipients may use them in very different ways. While retaining the assumption that the transitional space is shaped by cultural forces, this allows one to account for both strategies of adaptation or co-optation and strategies of resistance.

The readings of texts in the following chapters are grounded in a theory of aesthetic experience and reader response developed under the assumptions of the transitional space. Only an analysis of the specific communicative situation in the transitional space and the strategies with which cultural objects appeal to their recipients can help us understand the status of these objects within the symbolic order. The communicative strategies of transitional texts reveal a paradoxical structure typical of the transitional space. These texts often communicate in a mode of seeming noncommunication. The literary integration of the unconscious as the Other of subjectivity or culture appears alien, if not unrepresentable, to our consciousness. In addition, poetic language must guard itself against the absorption of its subversive or transgressive strategies. Withdrawing the semantic bridges of narrative, or even of obvious signification in general, may serve this purpose and simultaneously sharpen sensitivity for the perception of unconscious resonances. Aesthetic events have, of course, always happened at the boundaries of poetic and rhetorical conventions. What appears specific to transitional texts, however, is that while these texts preclude immediate access to meaning, they mobilize unconscious forms of reception in order to bring conscious and unconscious aesthetic experience to a new form of interaction.

As we have seen, Anton Ehrenzweig argues that unconscious scanning is indispensable for creative processes in general. Focused and unfocused attention are two modes of reception that reflect the decentered position of the subject. To our focused attention, primary processes appear undifferentiated and chaotic; but unconscious scanning may reveal a hitherto unseen order. The notion of primary undifferentiation is thus to be understood as relative to the forms, structures, and norms of conscious perception/reception.

The assumption that primary undifferentiation is not the same as chaos or lack of organization requires a revision of psychoanalytic notions of the primary process. Ehrenzweig develops such a revision in close connection with an analysis of creative processes. According to Ehrenzweig, creative processes mediate between primary and secondary processes and between the undifferentiatedness of the unconscious and the differentiated organization of consciousness. The hidden order of the unconscious reveals itself to unconscious scanning. The transgression of boundaries between primary and secondary processes is, according to Ehrenzweig, the most vigorous source for creative energies: "Unconscious scanning makes use of undifferentiated modes of vision that to normal awareness would seem chaotic. Hence comes the impression that the primary process merely produces chaotic phantasy material that has to be ordered and shaped by the ego's secondary processes. On the contrary, the primary process is a precision instrument for creative scanning that is far superior to discursive reason and logic."[15]

Undifferentiated or syncretistic perception[16] is especially apt for grasping multidimensional structures, because it suspends the scheme of figure and ground. Conscious perception, steered by secondary processes, focuses on salient features to which it attributes the status of "figures," while respectively turning their environment into "ground." Unfocused attention, on the other hand, attributes equal weight to every detail and renounces the hierarchies of figure and ground in favor of unprejudiced undifferentiation. The loss of accuracy in delineating salient features is compensated for by the grasping of holistic orders that escape conscious perception. Unconscious scanning reverses the priorities of analytic consciousness by temporarily dissolving the dominant features of a textual or perceptual surface. The distinction between these two modes of attention proves especially fruitful for analyzing the dedifferentiated or fragmented forms of poetic language in transitional texts.

If aesthetic experience combines conscious and unconscious reception, we must differentiate textual qualities according to the ways in which they appeal to conscious or unconscious receptive dispositions. Hermeneutic theories of a double meaning structure of language work with the assumption of a surface and depth structure of language. Ehrenzweig assumes as much when he talks about our conscious "surface-sensibilites." We can make the same distinction within the surface structure of language if we insist that language has only a surface. We then assume that different forms of order are effective within one and the same surface level of language. In order for us to experience an aesthetic event the conventional relationship between these two forms of order must be disrupted. Once the differentiation of a new structure has been established long enough as a literary convention, it has to be "perturbed" in order to keep the boundaries between the two orders flexible. Each new order at first appears as chaos, but the aesthetic experience of changing modes and sensibilities of perception is a fundamental process pertaining to the historical development of the transitional space of cultural objects.[17] Whether we perceive a text as ordered or undifferentiated changes over time because the experience of order depends on the historical development of perceptive capacities and conventions. In this respect, Ehrenzweig shares the assumptions of an aesthetics of reception that works with the notion of a horizon of expectation—as developed, for example, by Hans Robert Jauss.[18] Ehrenzweig describes a dynamic in the aesthetics of reception according to which our conscious experience tries increasingly to integrate what is experienced as chaos or undifferentiation. This process becomes the basis for changes in our notions of order, our epistemologies, and the cultural forms of language and subjectivity.

With their linguistic breaks and semantic breakdowns, their overdeterminations, and their multiplicity of voices, transitional texts open up multiple forms of aesthetic experience that transcend consciousness. Their unbounded creativity expands the boundaries of poetic language toward the unconscious by dedifferentiating its conventional order and by integrating primary processes. Thus poetic language becomes the material basis for subtle play with the boundaries of subjectivity.

The Hidden Core of Subjectivity and the Tacit Knowledge of Literature

that time you went back to look was the ruin still there where
you hid as a child . . . on the stone where none ever came . . .
and they all out on the roads looking for you.
                                            —*Samuel Beckett*

The montage created from Samuel Beckett's *That Time* combines two fantasies that together expose the subject's ambivalence toward its own boundaries: the fantasy of hiding and the fantasy of being found.

Together these fantasies stand for the paradoxical wish to protect a core of oneself from communication but simultaneously to be discovered and acknowledged in this core. Winnicott describes this ambivalence in terms of a core self that is protected through inner boundaries.[19] This core self is known and experienced through a tacit form of knowledge that must be excluded from any form of discursive explication. It is formed during the constitution of the subject as an inner area of protection against total usurpation by others or by its absorption in the symbolic order. The subject harbors a paradoxical desire of wanting social recognition for its entire being, while the disclosure of its inner core simultaneously inspires fears of being devoured. Winnicott writes, "It is a sophisticated game of hide-and-seek in which it is a joy to be hidden but a disaster not to be found."[20]

The personal core forms the most vulnerable but also the most resistant part of the subject. On the one hand, this core largely withstands the norms and constraints imposed by the symbolic order; on the other hand, it must gain social recognition to avoid an alienating split between the social and the private. Freud wrote to Binswanger, "I have thought for a long time that not only the repressed is unconscious but also the most dominant part of our being, the true part of our self—unconscious, but knowable."[21]

This means that the subject establishes double boundaries: outer boundaries beyond which it expels what it does not want to admit into the self; and inner boundaries, which enclose what it wants to keep protected from intrusion by others. The inner core forms a space of tacit self-knowledge that is not exposed in direct communication but nevertheless shapes every interaction with others. In a significant tacit communication the subject operates on the basis of an unthought, shared knowledge that is never allowed to become explicit. Winnicott relates this tacit communication to the experience of cultural objects, maintaining that every aesthetic experience involves a tacit contact with the subject's inner core. Poetic language affects this inner core by enabling a protected form of inexplicit communication about it. Thus it also takes part in shaping the inner boundaries of the subject. In the protected transitional space those boundaries can be traversed without threat. Experiences that relate to the inner core can be translated into aesthetic experiences because they do not violate the taboo of communicating explicitly about the inner core of an individual person. Aesthetic experience provides the protection of an anonymity in which the subject can be found in its inner core without this being a threat or an intrusion.

Tacit literary communication is by no means restricted to an individual aesthetic experience; it also unfolds at a cultural level. Literature allows for a cultural communication of "tacit knowledge," which can be seen as equivalent to its communication about the personal core.[22] A culture may harbor at its core forms of tacit knowledge that, if communicated openly, would violate a cultural boundary or taboo. Just as certain areas of subjectivity may be excluded from conscious experience and communication, similar exclusions occur on a cultural level. Part of what is excluded may then be converted into a collective tacit knowledge. Certain forms of symbolization, then, take over the function of mediating this knowledge without making it explicit. Ritualized actions can become the mediators of this tacit experience, within small groups such as a family or a dyad as well as within larger cultural communities.

It is important to see that even though explicit communication of this knowledge is a cultural taboo, the members of the culture in question nevertheless indirectly refer to this knowledge in their actions and judgments. Michel Leiris has pointed out that the cults of the *zâr* in Ethiopia function on the basis of such a collectively shared tacit knowledge.[23] During the ritualistic performances of a *zâr* (a spirit), the possessed person—in most cases a woman—can act out wishes and desires that are otherwise culturally taboo. The official interpretation of the community is that she acts under the spell of a *zâr* and is thus not responsible for her acts. Tacitly, however, she is held responsible as soon as she violates the boundaries of what is admissible within the ritualistic performance. She can, for example, publicly punish her abusive husband (in the name of the *zâr*) but is not allowed to kill him.

These ritualistic performances are an excellent example of a collective use of the transitional space. Leiris reads ritual as a theater that conceals its own theatrical character. The very distinction between theater and reality is eclipsed. The obsession is a first person experience that is officially defined as an alien or Not-I experience. The collective tacit knowledge thus allows for a collectively lived experience of a dimension of subjectivity that is excluded from the official cultural code.

In our contemporary cultures, the most prominent cultural carriers of tacit knowledge are cultural objects that, due to the specific conditions in the transitional space, provide a protected form of communication free from the threat of personal intrusion. Evidence of such a collective tacit knowledge, its cultural availability, and its effective use can be found in the same ways as evidence of the effect of the unconscious—that is, mainly through the traces that are left when subjects act on the basis of tacit knowledge.

One can thus assume that not only individuals but also cultural groups form a tacit core of subjectivity, known by everybody but excluded from explicit communication. Even though this core is formed as a protected space against the total reduction or absorption of subjectivity by the social, it is at the same time shaped by sociocultural conventions—especially by the ways in which a culture facilitates or tries to control the experience of cultural objects. One can assume that the unconscious premises of a culture, including its epistemological errors, form part of such a tacit core.

The intersubjective negotiations concerning tacit knowledge take place on the boundary between communication and silence. Something is brought to experience that is nevertheless excluded from public discursive knowledge and explicit interaction. This tacit knowledge resists direct representation and interpretation, but it does not resist the translation into something else, namely into indirect forms of symbolization, which evoke rather than spell out what is known but not thought. In order to read the unthought known, one must follow the symptomatic traces of tacit knowledge that are left within language along with the traces of the unconscious. Just as we can detect the effect of tacit knowledge in certain forms of interaction, we can also detect it in certain forms of discourse.

We may assume that, under certain conditions, aesthetic experience may entail an unconscious experience of the tacit core of subjectivity. This experience would allow for a form of indirect, unconscious communication about this core, while it would at the same time retain the silence in relation to the symbolic. From a different perspective we could define the transitional space as a space that expands the boundaries of the symbolic order from within, allowing one to experience what remains, otherwise, tacit knowledge or inaccessible silence. Thus the transitional space functions continually to reshape not only the outer but also the inner boundaries of subjectivity—even where such shapings remain unconscious.

The relationship to the unconscious, however, changes when boundary transgressions become one of the most obvious and crucial forms of—if not a condition for—aesthetic experience. In the transitional texts at hand they determine the whole structure of literary effects and the strategies guiding reader response. These shifting boundaries seem to signal a general change in the cultural functions of the imaginary and of literary subjectivity. The reception of primary processes, which has over a long period remained unconscious, increasingly moves into the focus of aesthetic experience. This shift engenders new cultural forms of subjectivity, which in turn affect the symbolic order itself. If the dynamic between structuration and destructuration is a basic condition for creative production in general, what is the cultural specificity and function of transitional texts in relation to this dynamic? And how do these texts affect the boundaries of their recipients on both an individual and a collective level and thus contribute to the emergence of a new episteme? These questions will provide the theoretical horizon for the following readings of literary texts.

3

Aesthetics of Blankness in *Moby-Dick*

But as in landlessness alone resides the highest truth, shoreless,
infinite as God—so better is it to perish in that howling infinite
than be ingloriously dashed upon the lee, even if it were safety.
                              —*Herman Melville*, Moby-Dick

The Frame of Narration

Herman Melville's *Moby-Dick* enacts a familiar romantic myth of the
sublime: according to the narrator Ishmael, the whiteness of the whale
"shadows forth the heartless voids and immensities of the universe,
and thus stabs us from behind with the thought of annihilation."[1]
The romantic discontents of civilization release an ambivalent yearning
for the magnitude and terror of unrestricted nature. Combined with
an imperial drive to explore and appropriate foreign spaces, this romantic desire shapes Melville's monumental myth of the white whale
shared by Melville's main characters—Captain Ahab, the protagonist
of the drama; and Ishmael, the narrator.[2] Each in his own way seeks
the challenge of oceanic unboundedness in order to explore the immense spaces of subjectivity buried beneath the surfaces of cultural
formations.

Melville's myth of the white whale constitutes one of American
literature's most prototypical manifestations of imperial male subjectivity and its philosophical groundings. One symptom of this subjectivity is the troubling relation between a spiritual quest for transcendence—which gave rise to the movement of Transcendentalism—
and the mercenary American dream of an imperialist expansion of
boundaries through the appropriation, subjugation, or extermination

of everything that figured as nature or wilderness. *Moby-Dick*'s exploration of the boundaries of subjectivity, moreover, reveals on a different level how this imperial drive toward the unlimited expansion of boundaries is culturally enforced by a formation of male subjectivity that uses myths and even reenactments of ancient rituals in order to conjure, as a defense against the thought of annihilation, the phantasm of absolute male power and invulnerability.

While *Moby-Dick* casts Captain Ahab as the carrier of this myth, its narrator, Ishmael, figures as a kind of involved mythographer—one who, after participating in this drama of mythical proportions, remains the sole surviving witness able to relate the shattering of the myth and the perishing of its hero. The narration thus breaks and explores the myth through the narrator's oscillation between inside and outside perspectives. Ishmael is cast as an impassioned intellectual narrator who, as a transcendentalist philosopher of sorts who has "gone native" in the perusal of his romantic spleen, retrospectively assumes various positions of distance toward both the myth of the white whale and his own function as narrator and perpetrator of this myth. He achieves this distance partly by breaking up his narration or dramatic staging of the events with interspersed reflections upon their historical, philosophical, or metaphysical implications, and partly by exposing the weaknesses and failures of his narration with a good dose of self-irony.

Being "landless," "shoreless," and as "infinite as God" are the narrator's metaphors for a mystical experience of transcendence. From the very beginning, when Ishmael declares meditative transcendence of the self to be the aim of whaling, his narration explicitly raises issues of subjectivity. Ishmael links the magical attraction of the wide ocean not only to the romantic spleen but also to the myth of Narcissus: "Surely all this is not without meaning. And still deeper is the meaning of that story of Narcissus, who because he could not grasp the tormenting, mild image he saw in the fountain, plunged into it and drowned" (p. 95). Melville links this spleen of an intellectual addicted to melancholic brooding and exotic nostalgia of distant oceans with what Harold Beaver describes in his introduction to *Moby-Dick* as the American dream of imperialist expansionism:

> By mid-century the United States was dizzily entering an era of expanding wealth and power. The ever-shifting frontier expressed the untold opportunities of the vast power-house of American life. Emer-

son, Thoreau, Whitman—the writers of the eastern seaboard—all felt this as keenly as the pioneers . . . Between land and sea spread the boundless prospects for that free American spirit transcending both. "Transcendentalism" itself was the expression of this free play of mind, rapturously caught up in an infinite spiritual quest.[3]

Undoubtedly, the romantic notion of subjectivity in *Moby-Dick* finds a fertile philosophical ground in the transcendentalist aesthetic philosophy of Carlyle, Emerson, and Thoreau. The narrator, however, also evokes Cartesianism by deploring his Cartesian ego as a burdening intellectual inheritance of the times. And yet we will see that Ishmael's own narration never completely escapes the confining boundaries of this cultural tradition. As Harold Beaver put it:

Even the antics of his intellectual pride—shoring these fragments, statistics, quotations against his ruins—is capable of no justification except the now meaningless Cartesian proof: "Cogito ergo sum." Over such "Cartesian vortices" Ishmael hovers. This Cartesian nightmare is the sole heritage: the capacity of human consciousness to reflect upon itself and to entertain its own end.[4]

Melville's choice of a narrator who is entangled in Cartesian consciousness colors the literary presentation of the romantic myth of the white whale with a certain scepticism. Cartesianism and Romanticism become competing philosophical positions both in the text and within the narrator. Ishmael presents us with a discourse full of complex tensions that reveal how his attraction to the romantic myth and his involvement in Ahab's drama are tinged with Cartesian rationality. These tensions are reflected through a variety of narrative and aesthetic devices sometimes complementing, at other times relativizing or even undermining each other. The myth itself unfolds within the narration of Ahab's chase after Moby Dick, and forms the center of the textual presentation; yet Ishmael's narrative mirrors and contrasts the myth from the retrospective of an involved but critical protagonist.

Ishmael's narrative forms a decisive break with the literary precursors of *Moby-Dick* as well as with other romantic narratives of transcendence. With its multifaceted narration, its different styles and forms of presentation, and its varying perspectives, the text displays a self-reflective consciousness and critique of the multiple and conflictive cultural influences that underlie the myth of the white whale. Even though Melville has created one of the great transcendentalist myths of subjectivity, the narrative establishes a decisive tension toward this myth and draws some of its most productive cultural energies from this tension.

Ahab's White Whale

The textual enactment of Ahab's drama draws on mythologies and archetypes of various historical periods and cultures. Due to its rich intertextual network, its overdetermined narrative, and its complex textual organization, *Moby-Dick* opens itself to a whole spectrum of different approaches.

After three attacks by a white whale, which leave him traumatized and mutilated, Ahab turns the whale into a godlike incorporation of evil and embarks upon his fatal chase. His whole being becomes absorbed by this chase, to a point where he blinds himself not only to the world around him but also to the "white monster" itself. The narrator describes Ahab's world as one where the "mystical cosmetic" (p. 296) of colors, which light casts onto earthly substances, disappears, leaving a Manichaean world of black-and-white polarities. Ahab's mutilated body is transformed into the metallized container of an "iron self": "His whole high, broad form, seemed made of solid bronze, and shaped in an unalterable mould, like Cellini's cast Perseus" (p. 218).[5] The whiteness of the whale, which for Ishmael symbolizes the transcendent ground of subjectivity, turns for Ahab into a white screen onto which he projects his demonic self. As Harold Beaver has pointed out, the myth of Narcissus is crucial for Ahab's myth of the white whale: "A blank is hunting a blank, in his madness, pursuing a mirror image of his own mad self—both dumb and vacated things. Narcissus is drawn through an enchanted labyrinth of reflections."[6] Unable to perceive the boundaries between self and world as boundaries between self and other, Ahab's "grandiose self"[7] sees all earthly greatness as a mirror of himself: "The firm tower, that is Ahab; the volcano, that is Ahab; the courageous, the undaunted, and victorious fowl, that too is Ahab; all are Ahab; and this round gold is but the image of the rounder globe, which like a magician's glass, to each and every man in turn but mirrors back his own mysterious self" (p. 541).

Harold Beaver argues that during his chase, Ahab, as in a Nietzschean proteanism, assumes the features of the whale. Narcissistic mirror images and phantasmic projections reveal that he needs absolute control over his environment in order to stabilize his fragile self-boundaries. His confrontation with Moby Dick, the god of destruction, allows him to erect a grandiose, gargantuan self that stylizes him as a god of salvation—that is, an inverse mirror image of the whale. As Ahab's demonic Other, the white whale thus fulfills the omen of the sign of the cross that has been inscribed in Ahab's body. In order to prepare for the fight with Moby Dick, Ahab stages a "symphony"[8] of a god chasing another god.

Ahab shares with his nemesis an aura of impenetrability and elusiveness, which endows him with a charismatic authority over his crew. He forges them into a collective body through phallic rituals and magic ceremonies and refers to them as parts of his own person: "Ye are not other men, but my arms and my legs, and so obey me" (p. 679). The myth of the white whale becomes for Ahab a means of securing control over his *corps social*. Before the threatening confrontation with Moby Dick, Ahab's men become increasingly obsessed with collectively shared images of fragmented bodies. Fantasies of being devoured by the gigantic maternal body of the whale, as well as fantasies of a violent mutilation of this body, reveal the crew's regression to the level of a collective self embodied by Ahab. Its organization is based entirely on the archaic phantasms of penetration, ejection, and devouring, and their passive correlates, being penetrated, ejected, and devoured.

Ahab's chase also enacts the old myth of the birth of the hero. Born as the son of fire, Ahab accuses his father of forcefully depriving him of his mother: "But thou are but my fiery father; my sweet mother I know not. Oh cruel! what hast thou done with her? There lies my puzzle" (p. 617). This male fantasy, which entails a phantasm of incomplete birth, pervades the myth of the white whale. Harold Beaver recalls Mircea Eliade's description of a cosmogonic myth: "To enter into the belly of the monster is equivalent to a regression into the primal indistinctness, into the Cosmic Night—and to come out of the monster is equivalent to a cosmogony: it is to pass from Chaos to Creation . . . Every initiatory adventure of this type ends in the creation of something, in the founding of a new world or a new mode of being."[9]

Ahab, however, is not granted the good fortune of Jonas, who, after a belated symbiosis in the belly of the whale, is reborn as a hero.

In constrast to the legendary whale in Jonas's tale who initiates Jonas into a mythic formation of self-boundaries, Moby Dick causes Ahab to restage the drama of a loss of self-boundaries. Ahab's attempt to heal his fragmentation and become reborn through the destruction of the white whale fails. Like Ahab's artificial leg made from the bone of a whale, the artificial boundaries that Ahab erects during the chase can only function as prostheses.

In a certain sense Ahab fails because he refuses to recognize himself in the white whale. By turning Moby Dick into the absolute Other, Ahab projects onto him those qualities he rejects in himself. In order to orchestrate Ahab's use of others as extensions of himself, the text introduces two characters who serve as prosthetic selves: Pippin, the black cabin boy; and Fedallah, the Parsee. Together the two incorporate and mediate Ahab's split subjectivity.

When Pippin falls into madness he turns into Ahab's dialectic figure. The dissolution of Pippin's self after his exposure in the wide ocean has the same structure as Ahab's mania. Both Pippin and Ahab suffer from what Ishmael calls the "concentration of the self" in the face of infinite emptiness.

While Pippin cannot bear this concentration of the self and succumbs to madness—which can be seen as a flight from his own boundaries—Ahab uses his absolute focus on the whale to maintain the concentration. In contrast to Pippin, who with the loss of his boundaries gains prophetic clarity, Ahab is blinded by his rigid self-containment. Ahab's "strength" and Pippin's "weakness" are thus dialectically mediated and collapse into each other. Ahab ends up hiding Pippin in his cabin, the space that symbolizes the core of his self: "Ahab's cabin shall be Pip's home henceforth, while Ahab lives. Thou touchest my inmost centre, boy; thou art tied to me by cords woven by my heart strings" (p. 631).

Pippin's closeness, however, also threatens Ahab with its healing force. Ahab needs to cut himself off from his personal core, since only such a split can maintain the energies needed for his monomaniacal chase. "There is that in thee, poor lad, which I feel too curing to my malady. Like cures like; and for this hunt, my malady becomes my most desired health" (p. 641). Pippin, on the other hand, pictures himself as a bodily supplement able to compensate for Ahab's fragmented body: "Ye have not a whole body, sir; I ask no more, so I remain a part of ye!" (pp. 641–642).

Ahab's addiction to his malady explains why he must abandon Pippin as soon as he is about to confront the whale. He needs a supplementary self, not for his cure, but for his mania. Fedallah, the second supplementary self, embodies Ahab's "evil shadow": "In the Parsee Ahab saw his forethrown shadow, in Ahab the Parsee his abandoned substance" (p. 645). While Pippin symbolizes Ahab's core self, Fedallah incorporates the dark side, which Ahab rejects in himself. Fedallah is thus turned into a curious double not only of Ahab, but also of the whale—which makes him all the more an ideal opponent. Without Ahab's awareness, he comes to represent what Ahab and the whale have in common. During the chase Ahab amalgamates the demonic nature of the Parsee as an opponent of the whale. A mystic pact is supposed symbolically to unite the two opposite poles. Ahab finds in Fedallah what he could not find in Pippin, and what he rejects in the whale: a dark mirror of himself.

It is as if the text reveals something about the security of unconscious choices by having Ahab, without being fully aware, choose Pippin as his rejected core and the Parsee as a shadow. Without Ahab's knowledge, Fedallah incorporates precisely those aspects that Ahab persecutes in Moby Dick as the unacknowledged Other of his own subjectivity. The Parsee therefore can only intensify Ahab's tragedy, since his very role reveals that the chase must end in self-destruction. Even if Moby Dick had not destroyed him, Ahab, in killing Moby Dick, would only have destroyed himself, for the whale as his imaginary Other *is* himself.

Aesthetics and psychology are synthesized perfectly in the mirror effects produced by Ahab's relationships to Moby Dick, Pippin, and the Parsee. Both aesthetically and psychologically, Pippin and the Parsee dialectically mirror what cannot become manifest.[10] The topos of a representation of the unrepresentable is supported by a wide variety of archaic myths evoked in the text. All these myths symbolize the paradoxical desire for both wholeness and dissolution of the self. Since the imaginary subjectivity that Ahab attributes to Moby Dick is the Other of his own subjectivity, the myth of the white whale performs an imaginary domestication of this Other. But, at the same time, the persecution of this Other is a self-persecution. The demonization of an Other who is really a dark mirror of the self turns the mythic chase into a ritual of self-destruction. Moreover, the archaic mythologies that Ahab invokes symbolize the whale as an androgynous god who incorporates the rejected or inaccessible potential for rebirth and wholeness.

This unrealized aspect of the myth is evoked again and again throughout the novel. It contains the seeds of Ahab's tragedy, and yet it remains hidden from Ahab during his own reenactment of the myth. Lévi-Strauss once said that myths think themselves in men without their knowledge.[11] Ahab's drama reveals this very dynamic of an unconscious power of myths. Unable to achieve mythic wholeness, Ahab tries to stage a grandiose cosmic transcendence. But just as he had dismissed Pippin when he threatened to cure him of his malady, he also represses those parts of the old mythologies of the whale that would counteract his mania. By repressing the myth's potential for symbiosis and rebirth—that is, its feminine aspect—Ahab turns an androgynous myth into a myth of imperial male domination and independence.

Calling upon mythical fire-worshippers, Ahab, the son of fire, subjects himself to the very element that forges his "iron soul": "Oh, thou dear spirit, of thy fire thou hast made me, and like a true child of fire, I breathe back to thee" (p. 616). This submission to paternal power is marked by the scar on Ahab's forehead, which identifies him as a reincarnation of an Egyptian fire-worshipper branded by a god. At the same time it also evokes the Christian god of salvation as a later version of the same myth. This lineage sheds new light on Ahab's fierce obsession with the white whale. His god of fire is a god of destruction who steers his destiny as an "unseen agency." By choosing Moby Dick, an equally destructive god of water, as his opponent, he engages in a fight with the most powerful rival of the god of fire.

As a god of water, the white whale is also a divine incorporation of transcendence. In contrast to Ishmael, who respects and fears this mythic quality as an ineffable reality of the whale, the same vision of inscrutability releases in Ahab a raging desire for violent intrusion: "How can the prisoner reach outside except by thrusting through the wall, shoved near to me. Sometimes I think there's naught beyond. But 'tis enough. He tasks me; he heaps me; I see in him outrageous strength, with an inscrutable malice sinewing it. That inscrutable thing is chiefly what I hate; and be the white whale agent, or be the white whale principal, I will wreak that hate upon him" (p. 287).

Ahab's phallic rage expresses itself in his blind obsession "to pierce the profundity." Behind his battle against the terror of inscrutable transcendence lurks the *horror vacui* of an empty self. The white whale becomes the white space on the map of cosmic subjectivity, a space Ahab tries to colonize with the hybrid gesture of imperial usurpation. Melville's text thus continually frames the myth of the white whale from a double perspective. The myth that Ahab enacts in his confrontation with the whale reveals his male hubris and will to power. However, Ishmael repeatedly evokes the myth's other side: its androgynous potential. The narrative perspective thus explicitly exposes what is repressed in Ahab's myth. Ahab's failure, in fact, appears increasingly to be the result of a powerful cultural repression. Potentially, the whale symbolizes the desire for both wholeness and transcendence. The text reveals, however, that Ahab's reenactment of the myth is doomed to fail because he represses the desire for wholeness. Instead of using the myth's potential for integration, Ahab attempts to annihilate in the whale the demonic Other; yet, unaware of the complete absorption of his own subjectivity in this Other, he thus works toward his own destruction.

The Literary Composition of the Myth

The intertextual and intercultural network that mirrors the myth of Moby Dick reaches back to the earliest whale mythologies in the history of mankind. Ishmael evokes the Egyptian myth of Isis and Osiris as the myth of origin: "Whaling may be regarded as that Egyptian mother, who bore offspring themselves pregnant from her womb" (p. 205).[12] The Egyptian Nut, whose daughter Isis was impregnated by her twin brother Osiris in their mother's womb, was also the mother of Typhoon who caused the bitter fate of his divine brother Osiris and, through him, all mankind. Melville's text establishes multiple connections between the myth of Osiris-Typhoon and the myth of Ahab and the white whale. Like Osiris, Ahab sails around the world assuming simultaneously the functions of priest, king, and god. Like the water monster Typhoon, Moby Dick incorporates both oceanic transcendence and destructive evil. And like Osiris, Ahab suffers three consecutive mutilations while chasing the whale. Ahab ends his withdrawal into the total isolation of his "cure" with phallic rituals of fire-worship, based upon the ritualistic gathering together of Osiris's fragmented body as a restoration of the earth's fertility. The three basic symbols of the myth of Osiris are to be found in Melville's text:

the falcon is nailed as an emblem to the mast of the sinking Pequod; Queequeg's coffin, in which Ishmael survives, recalls Osiris's coffin; and Osiris's phallus is retained in the phallic cathexis of Ahab's lost leg.

The myth of Osiris's fragmented and reassembled body symbolizes the dissolution of subjectivity into a primordial undifferentiation, which in turn prepares for a new individuation. The biblical story of Jonas and the whale enacts the same archaic dynamic through the mechanisms of devouring and ejecting. The narrative of *Moby-Dick* abounds with fantasies of fragmented bodies, as well as those of devouring or being devoured: "Judge then to what pitches of inflamed, distracted fury the minds of his more desperate hunters were impelled, when amid the chips of chewed boats, and sinking limbs of torn comrades, they swam out to the white curds of the whale's direful wrath into the serene, exasperating sunlight, that smiled on, as if at a birth or a bridal" (p. 282).

Ishmael's imagery contains visions of fragmented bodies within a basic structure of destruction and rebirth. His narrative thus evokes the ideal form of a cosmogonic myth. As a gigantic, individual gestalt emerging out of oceanic undifferentiation, the white whale symbolizes unity and boundedness. By contrast, his immortality and omnipresence symbolize absolute unboundedness: "These were his prominent features; the tokens whereby, even in the limitless, uncharted seas, he revealed his identity, at a long distance, to those who knew him" (p. 281).

Melville's intertextual play with the myth of Isis and Osiris also draws on variants of the same myth from other cultures, as, for example, from the primordial myth of the gnosis, the Hebrew version of Leviathan as Satan, and the Greek myth of Typhoon. Ahab's myth is thus mirrored in the different shapes of a collective myth shared by a variety of cultures. In this kaleidoscope of shifting mythological affiliations Ahab appears as a Gnostic demiurge under the power of his mother, Sophia, the holder of wisdom. She incorporates the archetype of the devouring Great Mother, the threatening female aspect of the myth. The mythological relationship with the biblical King Ahab, a worshipper of Baal, the sun god and water dragon, again evokes Moby Dick as a mirror of Ahab because it asserts a deeper connection between those contrary principles whose violent division leads to Ahab's destruction.

These ancient whale mythologies are all based on myths of individuation whose function is to define the cultural boundaries of subjectivity. The whale, as an androgynous symbol, presents an archaic challenge for decentered subjectivity because it contains the polarization of the subject within a primordial undifferentiation. The mythological structure of a transition from chaos to creation that underlies this formation of subjectivity is shared by all of the diverse myths cited in *Moby-Dick*. In the Hindu myth, for example, Vishnu is reincarnated as Matse Avatar through Brahma's periodic dissolution and recreation of the world. "When Brahma, or the God of Gods, saith the Shaster, resolved to recreate the world after one of its periodical dissolutions, he gave birth to Vishnoo, to preside over the work" (p. 472).

Melville's recourse to mythology as an intercultural framework for his casting of Ahab's subjectivity emphasizes collective procedures of individuation. But at the same time he also emphasizes historical specificity, mediated through Ishmael's reflections upon contemporary philosophical issues, such as romantic or transcendentalist ideas, or his abundant scholastic parodies in the chapters on cetology. These reflections complement the mythological material and situate Ahab's myth within the specific historical context of European Romanticism and its American variant, Transcendentalism. The challenge of Ahab's myth to contemporary cultural notions of subjectivity arises out of this historical revaluation of ancient mythologies within the romantic and transcendentalist traditions. The narrator's multiple voices play the crucial role in this historical mediation. From the outset, Ishmael is cast as a prototype of European Romanticism—the melancholic pursuing his spleen—while, by contrast, Ahab is cast as the maniac—the American counterfigure of the melancholic. The way in which Ishmael's role as a melancholic mythographer is contrasted with Ahab's mania reflects the ways in which the figure of melancholy in European Romanticism has been transfigured in American Transcendentalism into that of mania. Thus the difference between myth as story and narration as mythography implicitly reflects the European heritage of Romanticism and its transformation within a different cultural climate in America.

Ishmael's Ambivalent Discourse

Ishmael not only evokes a whole network of mythic allusions that testifies to the anthropological force of the myth of Moby Dick; he also repeatedly interrupts his narrative with a series of highly academic reflections on the problem of whaling. Aesthetically, these quasi-scientific chapters are problematic, and it comes as no surprise that they have elicited conflicting reactions.

Ishmael's academic reflections are ambiguous and full of irony. With the passion of a pedant, he first constructs an encyclopedic masterwork containing all available historical and scientific data about the whale. But as soon as all of this knowledge is meticulously displayed for the reader, Ishmael discredits it with the most condescending intellectual tone. His biting derision mocks his contemporaries, the naturalists, who think that their knowledge is objective truth. In addition, the passages on whaling are full of parodies of myths, comic submyths, and ironic allusions to whalers' susceptibility to myths.

Moreover, Melville parodies the methods of comparative mythology, a discipline that was fashionable among his contemporaries. H. Bruce Franklin has emphasized Melville's critique of both nineteenth-century comparative mythology and competing historical and psychological interpretations of myths. In the chapter entitled "Moby Dick," Ishmael, according to Franklin, indirectly critiques the methods of the historical school of comparative mythology by revealing how their historical knowledge is already pervaded by anthropomorphic projections. Franklin further interprets Ishmael's dramatizing of the psychological relevance of Ahab's drama for the whole crew as support for psychological theories of myth, whose tradition reaches from Bayle and Hume to Jung.

Ishmael's critique of historical representations of myths is further spiced with snide remarks against the pictorial representations of myths in Hinduism, Judaism, and Christianity. "It is time to set the world right in this matter, by proving such pictures of the whale all wrong" (p. 367) asserts Ishmael, in a laconic conclusion to his wholesale deconstruction of all those mythologies that he himself had evoked earlier in order to frame the dramatic encounter between Ahab and Moby Dick. And yet, rather than undermining the effects of the old whale mythologies, Ishmael's narrative creates a challenging opposition between the lived myth and its academic reconstruction. Similar to the ways in which comic subplots disrupt Shakespearean tragedies, Ishmael disrupts the mythic drama between Ahab and Moby Dick with comic submyths, only to intensify its effects.

Ishmael's double role as a protagonist in the drama and as a distanced narrator introduces a significant ambiguity into the text.[13] The effects of doubling and mirroring in the coupling of Ishmael and Ahab as literary characters is one of Melville's masterpieces of composition. As protagonist, Ishmael had himself succumbed to the myth; as narrator, he reenacts the myth in his narration, but only to undermine it in a double way: first he distances himself from the myth by interspersing his narrative with philosophical reflections and quasi-scientific observations, but then he, in turn, undercuts his own metadiscourse with his black humor. The complexity of Ishmael's retrospective is in strong contrast to the limited perspective of unconditional submission he had as a protagonist of the drama. According to his own report, he had at the time succumbed to Ahab's myth as much as the rest of the crew.

But in his role as narrator, Ishmael nearly effaces his role as protagonist. As a consequence, Ishmael's subjectivity is not fictionalized under the conditions of immediate action, but under those of retrospective reflection. And yet, even from his historical distance to the events, Ishmael still struggles with the challenge of the whale's impenetrability and transcendence. This ties Ishmael's intellectual pursuit to Ahab's passion of penetrating the white whale and its secrets. However, this pursuit is as futile as Ahab's monomaniacal chase. Whenever he lets his intellectual pride take over, Ishmael ends up dispersing the whale's mystery in the dry and pedantic intellectualizations of his retrospective narration. His rhetoric of penetration reveals how much Ishmael speaks under a compulsion to repeat Ahab's chase within his narrative. This compulsion leads to a grotesque spectacle when Ishmael defies the decorum of a sacred space and enters the skeleton of the holy Whale of the Arsacides in order to measure its insides. An uncanny desire for autopsy reveals itself as the dark side of Ishmael's mythography: "Sutting the green measuring-rod, I once more dived within the sceleton. From their arrow-slit in the scull, the priests perceived me taking the altitude of the final rib. 'How now!' they shouted: 'Dar'st thou measure this our god! That's for us.' 'Aye, priests—well, how long do ye make him, then?'" (p. 562).

By transposing Ahab's monomaniacal chase onto an intellectual level, Ishmael's narration not only domesticates his earlier avowed spleen but also turns him into an involuntarily comic narrator. Ishmael's own drama unfolds symptomatically within his fetishism for detail and the maniacal learnedness of the chapters on whaling. Even the sublimation of Ishmael's passions within the strategies of his narration is a reversed image of Ahab's regressive desublimation. If the text shows how Ahab suffers from a negative fixation on the demonic Other as incorporated by the white whale, it also shows how Ishmael suffers from a related negative fixation on precisely those intellectual positions that he shuns rhetorically with sarcastic condescension. Ishmael can present the unrepresentable only in a mode of negation. Thus, he exhibits his meticulous knowledge of all that the whale is not. His parody of the naturalist's positivist research on the whale, however, collapses under the ballast of negative knowledge that Ishmael unfolds in his narration. The narrative turns inadvertently into a critical exposure of the psychology of the narrator. Ishmael's double negative fixation on both Ahab's myth and a rejected Cartesian rationalism culminates in his maniacal attempt to chase down the whale on paper.

And yet Melville has endowed Ishmael with an astute awareness of his own limitations. Ishmael presents his own fixation on the myth of the white whale as an obstacle to his attempts to grasp the ineffable. Trapped in his Cartesian nightmare, Ishmael fails in both his actions and his narration and is unable to realize his dream of transcendence and the unboundedness he yearns for in his melancholy spleen. He comes to recognize his submission to Ahab's myth and his fixation on the Cartesian mind as two complementary forms of failure that mark his narrative.

On a different level of abstraction, this double failure itself becomes an important theme in the text. Ishmael confronts us with the epistemological dilemma of a narrator who, knowing the limitations of self-reflexivity for the presentation of transcendence, remains nonetheless entangled in his rationalist mind and therefore chooses self-consciously to expose his own failure. According to Ishmael, no representation can ever grasp the transcendent ground of subjectivity—especially not a myth of transcendence, which transforms illimitable unboundedness into a closed form. By evoking the power of myth and its discontents, as well as the respective dilemma of representation, Ishmael's narration escapes being caught in a mere romantic desire for remystification.

Ishmael problematizes both the myth of the white whale and his own modes of narration as two different ways of dealing with the challenge of transcendence, namely romantic mythologizing and Cartesian rationalization. Melville's answer to this challenge becomes paradigmatic for the cultural consciousness of the time and the break-through to modernism. To be sure, romantic myths of transcendence express a cultural will to escape the confines of Cartesian subjectivity. On the other hand, however, Ishmael inadvertently reactivates his Cartesian heritage to challenge the myths of Romanticism. Melville thus carefully chooses a highly ambivalent narrator, who, against his own will, is torn between a Romanticism, which he deems unlivable, and Cartesianism, which he wants to discard as a burdening heritage. This tension ultimately creates the energy of a text that works against its own boundaries in order to reveal the limitations of the two cultural traditions in which it is grounded. The Cartesian dream of stable boundedness and the romantic dream of transcendence and unbound-edness thus appear as two polar forms of a continuous cultural for-mation.

By combining the opposite qualities of bounded concentration and infinite blankness, the white whale is an ideal focus for the Cartesian as well as the romantic dream. Ishmael's negative fixation to both is presented as symptomatic of the cultural sensibility of his epoch, a cultural sensibility torn between a romantic desire for the ineffable and a Cartesian desire for certainty and control. Ishmael's discourse reflects this tension. Even though a shared desire for unboundedness provides the energy for the dramatic events as well as the narration, Ishmael continually subjugates this desire to a domesticating intellec-tual control. His repeated assertion that it is impossible aesthetically to grasp the transcendent aspect of the whale—which constitutes the always deferred ideal object of the text—sounds like an incantation used to work against the limitations of the text's own narrative situ-ation and its forms of discourse.

The Borrowed Speech of Ahab's Drama

Ishmael's narrative, however, is not the only textual perspective. Sev-eral chapters deploy a dense intertextuality drawn from the most diverse cultural periods. *Moby-Dick* had various literary models in the first half of the nineteenth century, the most important of which are J. N. Reynolds's *Mocha Dick: Or the White Whale of the Pacific: A Leaf from a Manuscript Journal,* Owen Chase's *The Wreck of the Whaleship Essex,* and Jules Leconte's *Le Cachalot Blanc.*[14]

While these stories of whaling do not provide more than an idea of plot, other literary foils are much more tightly woven into the network of Melville's text. During Ahab's encounter with the whale, the narrator disappears behind the curtain of a drama staged with elements and props of other texts. Just as Ahab's performance draws on borrowed myths, the textual performance borrows "alien voices" (Bakhtin) from other texts. This intercultural and intertextual network produces the effect of a removal from the narrow confines of one specific historical time. The various myths support the idea of a trans-historical validity of Ahab's myth; and the dramatic language borrowed from Shakespeare's tragedies evokes a drama whose meaning is already loaded with the meaning of those earlier texts, whose voices still resonate in our time. Melville's text plays with the simultaneity of all times that we find in every great myth. His monumental textual universe is populated by such diverse intertexts as Shakespeare's dramatic language, the metaphysical prose of the seventeenth century, lyrical allusions to Milton's *Paradise Lost,* and the density of detail from Dickens's realism. These literary forms are supplemented by the discursive forms of sermons, philosophical reflections, and scientific treatises. The composition of the myth of Moby Dick borrowed from parts of other whale myths finds its aesthetic equivalent in the composition of *Moby-Dick* borrowed from parts of other literary texts.

The chapters that present Ahab's drama most forcefully play with the borrowed speech of Shakespeare's tragedies.[15] Modeled after Shakespearean characters, their protagonists speak in the dialectic images of Elizabethan drama, while the crew surrounds Ahab like a choir. Ahab and Pippin, for example, invoke the roles of Lear and his Fool: "Now, then, Pip, we'll talk this over; I do suck most wondrous philosophies from thee!" (p. 637). The chapters before the encounter with the whale are full of allusions and rhetorical invocations of *Hamlet, Macbeth,* and *King Lear*—as may be seen in the chapter about Queequeg's coffin, "The Deck," which resonates with the scene of the grave diggers in *Hamlet:* "The grave-digger in the play sings, spade in hand. Dost thou never?" (p. 636).[16] Intertextual density culminates in the chapter called "The Candles," in which dark rituals prepare the destruction of the Pequod. The fight with the storm Typhoon, the God who mirrors Moby Dick, is announced by an allusion to the Typhoon in Milton's *Paradise Lost.*[17] Ahab's ritual conjuration of Lucifer answers the divine *menetekel* of the three corposants. The following ritual of blood bondage, a symbol of the subjugation of Fedallah, the dark shadow, recalls both Ahab's fire worship during his earlier Persian incarnation and, on a literary level, Carlyle's *Sartor Resartus*. Retrospectively, these condensed mythological and literary echoes appear to be an anticipation of Joycean condensations—especially when Ahab's monologue pours forth like an Elizabethan torrent of speech in which Ahab is mirrored in the most diverse literary figures.

The borrowed speech provides a means to dramatize Ahab's myth that Ishmael's narrative lacks. Melville's intertextuality repeats formally the same dialectic of bounding and unbounding we have already observed in his characters. Alien voices open the boundaries of Ishmael's narrative and simulate a mythic coexistence of multiple epochs, cultures, and languages. Like the multiple breaks in textual perspective, they anticipate the increasing self-reflexivity and experimentalism of twentieth-century literature. From the perspective of this later development, *Moby-Dick* might appear to be a text that works against its own boundaries from within. The choice of Ishmael, a narrator split between Cartesian and romantic desire, creates a historically significant tension. This tension signals a change in the cultural formation of subjectivity and its forms of literary presentation. The transcendence of the subject in *Moby-Dick* is based on a romantic myth of transcendence enacted—if not acted out—by a "hero" who perishes by it, and told by a narrator who remains captivated by the myth even though he breaks its force in a self-critical narration. This textual performance of a wrecked passion and an unrealized desire for transcendence, with all its tension and ambivalence, accounts for the continuous fascination of *Moby-Dick*.

Blankness as an Aesthetic Principle

Aside from those more obvious considerations touching Moby Dick, which could not but occasionally awaken in any man's soul some alarm, there was another thought, or rather vague, nameless horror concerning him, which at times by its intensity completely overpowered all the rest; and yet so mystical and well nigh ineffable was it, that I almost despair of putting it in a comprehensible form. It was the whiteness of the whale that above all things appalled me.   —*Ishmael*

Moby-Dick contains the seeds for a new aesthetic that is only partially realized in the text itself, but that anticipates later forms of literary presentation. This implied aesthetic focuses upon the representation of the unrepresentable, the ineffable ground of subjectivity, and the experience of the sublime or of transcendence. All these ideal objects, which the text invokes, call for new aesthetic forms and devices. *Moby-Dick* explores the aesthetic paradox of a literary or mythical bounding of unboundedness as a mode to make the experience of transcendence imaginable. This aesthetic paradox underlies the structural tensions in the composition of the text. When he first sets out for his adventure, Ishmael yearns for an experience of transcendence that he hopes will free him from his Cartesian nightmare. His retrospective aesthetic dramatization of the myth of Moby Dick, however, exposes the failure of this experience. Moreover, his narrative reflects the epistemological ground of this failure by doubling and, in a certain sense, repeating it as a problem of representation.

For Ishmael, the whiteness of the whale incorporates nothingness in a bounded and well-defined shape. This bounded nothingness inspires both absolute peace and silence as well as utmost terror, the ecstacy of oceanic fusion with the cosmos as well as the *horror vacui* in the face of its total emptiness. The explosive fusion of polar opposites in the experience of the sublime can easily lead into the abyss of regressive desublimation. For Ishmael the white whale is a figure in which these poles are already mediated: the whiteness symbolizes transcendence and infinity; the bounded form and the definite shape function as a counterbalance able to contain it. In a similar way, the bounded shape of a myth is supposed to mediate a paradoxical experience of the unrepresentable. Once again, it seems as if the sublime experience of European Romanticism invoked by Ishmael, the melancholic, is radicalized in Ahab's imperialist mania of transcendence.

With its lure of transcendence and its lurking terror, the whiteness of the whale represents for Ishmael the ineffable, which he seeks to experience in the pursuit of his romantic spleen.[18] In the midst of the utmost extreme of self-experience Ishmael finds the threat of total self-annihilation. Ishmael's metaphysical *horror vacui* is the inverse of his ecstacy of mystical transcendence and reveals his fear of a complete annihilation of his subjectivity:

> Is it that by its indefiniteness it shadows forth the heartless voids and immensities of the universe, and thus stabs us from behind with the thought of annihilation, when beholding the white depths of the

milky way? . . . is it for these reasons that there is a dumb blankness, full of meaning, in a wide landscape of snows—a colorless, all-color of atheism from which we shrink? (p. 295)

When the tragedy reaches its culmination, Ishmael remarks that, like Moby Dick, Ahab also comes to incorporate those metaphysical qualities: "Therefore, the tormented spirit that glared out of bodily eyes, when what seemed Ahab rushed from his room, was for the time but a vacated thing, a formless somnambulistic being, a ray of living light, to be sure, but without an object to color, and therefore a blankness in itself" (p. 303).

The old topos of a mystic or meditative transcendence of the self, the "blankness, full of meaning"—like the Shakespearean "signifying nothing," which Ishmael evokes as a supplementary trope (p. 142)— refers to an experience by which one can ward off the underlying threats of a metaphysical *horror vacui*. The horror is sublimated by the shape of the myth, which fills the void with meaning. Even though whiteness symbolizes a metaphysical absence of meaning, its incorporation into the defined shape of the white whale generates a secondary meaning. It is a form of retaining, but also a mastering of, the horror of the unformable and ineffable whiteness by making it accessible to a paradoxical representation and experience.

From this perspective, the myth of the white whale appears as the convergence of a subjectivity that confines the experience of transcendence to a myth. The myth fulfills the paradoxical task of integrating an experience of sublime terror. It provides narrative boundaries for the unbearable lack of definition inherent in transcendence. Just as Ishmael sees white as simultaneously a visible absence of color and the condensation of all colors, the whiteness of the whale symbolizes for him both the metaphysical absence of meaning and the absolute concentration of meaning in a symbol of transcendence.

The whiteness of the whale thus bestows focus and shape on a subjectivity whose ultimate ground remains transcendent. Ishmael's epistemological and aesthetic reflections upon these problems give *Moby-Dick* the status of a text on the boundary between metaphysics and anthropology.[19] The myth of Moby Dick raises the metaphysical question of transcendence, if not of the existence of a god; but this question is raised under the conditions of a self-confrontation of the subject. Transcendence is no longer primarily an object of metaphysics but, according to post-Kantian epistemology, an object of anthropology. From the perspective of a theory of subjectivity, transcendence is a specific experience of decentered subjectivity. The fact that, on a cosmic scale, a subject can no longer occupy the middle of the universe is supplemented by the experience that this subject also no longer has access to the ground of its own subjectivity or, as Freud puts it, that it is no longer master in its own house. Both displacements from the center evoke the desire for myths able to shape the ineffable and thus make it available or controllable on a mediated level. Such "concord-fictions" (Kermode) allow one to create an imaginary control over both the cosmological and the subjective displacement from the center.

This shaping of the mythological material from the perspective of a "radical anthropology"[20] motivates both the myth of Moby Dick and Ishmael's relativizing deconstructions of this myth. Ultimately, he asserts over and over again, the ineffable cannot be confined within an aesthetic form or a theoretical system. This is the insight formulated in Ishmael's speculations about blankness. These speculations gain programmatic validity not only as a metaphor for the ineffability of subjectivity but also as an aesthetic category. Ishmael's reflections in the chapter "The Whiteness of the Whale," in fact, point beyond the aesthetic devices realized in *Moby-Dick* itself. They establish a textual self-reflexivity that can be read retrospectively as an anticipation of the major aesthetic principles of modernism. In such a retrospective reading, "The Whiteness of the Whale" gains specific importance because its self-reflexivity affects the status of the novel's various forms of aesthetic presentation.

Melville's self-reflexive challenging of his own modes of representing subjectivity can be seen as a decisive step toward the transition from late Romanticism to modernism. The actual devices used in the text are systematically polarized and divided into Ahab's reenactment of a great myth of transcendence and Ishmael's parodistic demonstration of what fails to grasp the transcendent reality of the whale. The implicit aesthetic of blankness developed in "The Whiteness of the Whale" and "The Spouter Inn" remains a utopian construct. In both chapters Ishmael calls for a presentation of transcendence in a mode of negativity. In such a presentation, transcendence could be evoked without becoming merely a projective screen for something else. Because transcendence pertains to the ineffable, the object of the text is a "No-Thing,"[21] and thus its aesthetic presentation requires devices that reflect the irreducible surplus of the ineffable in any representation. By imagining blankness as a fundamental aesthetic category for the presentation of transcendence or the ineffable, Ishmael indirectly challenges the very forms of his own narration.

Ishmael discovers the aesthetic potential of blankness spontaneously when he contemplates a pictorial representation of whaling:

> On one side hung a very large oil-painting so thoroughly besmoked, and every way defaced, that in the unequal crosslights by which you viewed it, it was only by diligent study and a series of systematic visits to it, and careful inquiry of the neighbours, that you could any way arrive at an understanding of its purpose. Such unaccountable masses of shades and shadows, that at first you almost thought some ambitious young artist, in the time of the New England hags, had endeavoured to delineate chaos bewitched . . . But what most puzzled and confounded you was a long, limber, portentous, black mass of something hovering in the centre of the picture . . . Yet was there a sort of indefinite, half-attained, unimaginable sublimity about it that fairly froze you to it, till you involuntarily took an oath with yourself to find out what that marvellous painting meant. (p. 103)

"Defaced," the painting gains a supplementary aesthetic quality that it did not have in its original form. Only the blurring of its contours evokes the most basic feature of the whale, which Ishmael mentions throughout the text: that the whale "has no face." Although in this painting indeterminacy is not an intentionally deployed aesthetic category but is rather the result of extrinsic forces, for Ishmael it is precisely the indeterminacy that turns the experience of the painting into an aesthetic event.[22] The accidental defacement adds to the oil painting that very dimension of the whale that its original version as well as all the "erroneous pictures" lacked.

Ishmael's aesthetic experience of the defaced oil painting is paradigmatic for his antinaturalist aesthetic conception. The painting in the Spouter Inn affects him deeply because it evokes the idea of chaos. In this chapter, as well as later in the chapter about whaling, the whale is equated with the idea of chaos and lack of structure. Accordingly, Ishmael depicts the paradox of structuring what cannot be confined to any structure as the basic aesthetic problem. Only a text that is structured as a "blankness full of meaning" can communicate the experience of the ineffable. Ironically, Ishmael professes this aesthetic principle especially at those moments when he practices its opposite by indulging in the positivistic collection of data about the whale. To be sure, Ishmael has abandoned the illusion of the naturalists, who believe that one can obtain a mimetic replica of one's object. Ishmael's negative demonstrations of the failures of representation, as well as his endless enumerations of what the whale is not, ensure that the order of the text appears as the order of his own narration and not as the order of things or events. The abundant use of the most diverse rhetorical and literary conventions and styles, as well as of the whole tradition of mythological and mystic representations of transcendence, the ineffable, and the sublime, reveals the extent to which Melville's text explores the historically available means of representation.

A true aesthetic of blankness as envisioned in "The Spouter Inn" would, however, reach beyond a kaleidoscopic syncretism of available forms and styles. In Melville's novel it remains but an implicit utopia. And yet there is a productive tension between the multiple alien voices from mythological, literary, and theoretical intertexts and the blankness of an aesthetics of negativity. It is because of this tension that *Moby-Dick* assumes a transitional position between Romanticism and modernism. Intertextuality and self-reflexivity in combination with indeterminacy and blankness have become the foremost experimental devices in high modernism. Melville's implicit aesthetics of blankness thus anticipates conceptually what later becomes a dominant aesthetic device. His combination and intermixture of genres and literary devices prepares the ground for a presentation of decentered subjectivity that resists mythological centering. With its interfacing of voices, genres, and rhetorical devices, *Moby-Dick* is one of the first novels that implode the genre from within. The oscillating mixture of mythic, epic, novelistic, dramatic, lyrical, and discursive elements and the constant shifts in perspective, style, and rhetoric establish an early form of those floating literary discourses that have become the trademark of modernist experimentalism.

The history of reception of *Moby-Dick* shows furthermore that the text gained its status as a classic only during the twentieth century, a generation after Melville's death. Contemporary success was most likely undermined by Melville's refusal to satisfy the expectations derived from the well-established and successful genre of whaling lore. Melville's earlier texts, *Typee* and *Omoo* better fit this genre. Certainly, the reception of *Moby-Dick* was further complicated by the fact that this novel also frustrated the expectations of a literary taste trained by the romantics and pre-romantics. Despite its deep affinities with the romantic imagination, its mystic notions of transcendence, its fascination with evil, demonic, or magical forces, and its visions of self-transcendence, Melville's text breaks away from the conventional romantic forms of presenting these topics. The use of montage and intertextual mirrorings, as well as the condensation of whole traditions of cultural material, create a density and overdetermination of the literary discourse that reaches beyond Romanticism and becomes formative for both the style and rhetoric of modernism.

Melville's vision of saying the unsayable without the comforts of mythological closure stretches his text beyond its own boundaries. No wonder his anticipated aesthetics of blankness inspired experimental modernists to mold their desire for unbounded subjectivities into literary forms that resist the closure of mythologies.

> Drain off the prop ocean and leave the white whale stranded.   *William Burroughs*

4

Eyeless Silence: Interior Dialogue in *The Waves*

But how to describe the world seen without a self?
            —*Virginia Woolf*, The Waves

Fictions of the Unconscious

In 1956 Nathalie Sarraute wrote, "The word 'psychology' is one that no present-day writer can hear spoken with regard to himself without casting his eyes to the ground and blushing."[1] Only a quarter of a century earlier, however, in 1931, when Virginia Woolf published *The Waves,* attitudes were different. Literary circles in England, foremost among them the famous Bloomsbury group, which counted among its members not only Virginia Woolf but also Freud's translator, James Strachey, eagerly circulated and discussed Freud's texts. In France, the movements of symbolism and surrealism developed highly experimental forms of voicing the unconscious in literature and the arts. This was a time when the most urgent task for a novelist was the invention of new literary devices capable of creating characters with interiority and an unconscious. Psychoanalysis as a new theoretical orientation determined the intellectual climate when Virginia Woolf wrote *The Waves.* One would think that this aesthetic interest in psychoanalysis would have reinforced the primacy of the so-called psychological novel. Yet the most prominent literary attempts of the time to create fictions of the unconscious abandon psychological realism in favor of experimental techniques of stream of consciousness or interior monologue. Among Woolf's diverse explorations of such techniques, *The Waves* is surely the most unconventional. Considering Nathalie Sar-

raute's verdict on psychology, it is ironic that this "playpoem" anticipates techniques of the *nouveau roman* and other experimental forms
of fiction that, after the turn from psychology toward *écriture,* came
to be cherished as purely linguistic and formal innovations. But the
high level of abstraction and the distancing artificiality of Virginia
Woolf's poetic speech, as well as her dismissal of a linear narrative and
of realistic characters, are all linked with her aesthetic interest in the
unconscious.

In her diary, Virginia Woolf imagines *The Moths,* later renamed *The
Waves,* as "an abstract mystical eyeless book: a playpoem" involving
an insubstantial world free from reality.[2] One of the most esoteric texts
of its time, *The Waves* cannot easily be ascribed to any particular genre.
Neither purely a novel, drama, or poem, it is an unusual amalgam of
all three, and defies the boundaries of genre. Its language, now replete
with poetic images, then suddenly highly abstract, always keeps one
at a certain distance. Six characters are involved in a dialogical exchange of sorts; yet it is neither a real dialogue nor a direct speech
addressed to an identifiable other. Although the individual speeches
resonate with each other, they do not directly address or answer any
one in particular. The poetic sequences remind one of interior monologues—but are also clearly distinct from them.

Initially, the esoteric aura of poetic speech leaves even the status of
the characters in the dark. Are they purely roles? Disembodied speakers? Or just internal voices? Their highly stylized speech is as remote
from familiar forms of everyday speech as it is from conventional
novelistic discourse, poetic monologue, or dramatic dialogue.

> "I see a ring," said Bernard, "hanging above me. It quivers and hangs
> in a loop of light."
> "I see a slab of pale yellow," said Susan, "spreading away until it
> meets a purple stripe."
> "I hear a sound," said Rhoda, "cheep, chirp; cheep, chirp; going
> up and down."
> "I see a globe," said Neville, "hanging down in a drop against the
> enormous flanks of some hill."
> "I see a crimson tassel," said Jinny, "twisted with gold threads."
> "I hear something stamping," said Louis. "A great beast's foot is
> chained. It stamps, and stamps, and stamps." (p. 6)[3]

Only toward the end of the first chapter do we learn that this poetic
language game is being played by little children. Voiced by five-year-

olds, the stylized phrases seem even more esoteric.[4] At the same time, we learn that we are not faced with disembodied and timeless poetic voices, but with three male and three female characters, each endowed with an individual biography. A series of gatherings at different stages of their lives frames their poetic exchanges spatially and temporally. Biographical details of their social lives provide the vestiges of a narrative; yet they are only evoked as catalysts for a complex intrapsychic drama, which takes the place of a traditional plot. Every concrete event is enfolded in a discourse of emotions that transforms both action and emotion into poetic abstraction. Whether the characters are telling stories or voicing their memories and perceptions, their environment is never more than a stage for poetic performance of inner speech. Penetrating everything from the most trivial activities of daily life to the most exotic or archaic fantasies and moods, their speech always externalizes subjective acts of processing the world.

The most provoking aesthetic challenge, however, consists in how Woolf uses her much acclaimed stream-of-consciousness technique in order to have her characters voice a shared knowledge of the most painfully intimate and often indecorous fantasies or experiences. While commonly such tacit knowledge is excluded from explicit communication or social interaction, Woolf's characters voice it explicitly in their dialogical exchange of poetic images. Their little pathologies and inhibitions, their fantasies, fears, and failures are turned into poetic images and musical rhythms. Their oedipal or homoerotic desires, their voracious sexual urges, their fantasies of returning to the womb, their delusions of grandeur, and their paranoid fears and self-lacerations are all endowed with an aura of naturalness and ease. We find these expressions of unconscious or tacit spheres of experience in the characters' poetic dialogues juxtaposed to sublime experiences of nature or mystic moments of ecstacy and communion. If the characters would use a rhetoric of transgression to voice these experiences, their discourse would be in accordance with a long tradition of transgressive poetic practices. Woolf, however, incorporates them seamlessly into the poetic articulation of other spheres of daily experience as well as of states of ecstatic elation. Instead of privileging certain experiences as poetic ones, *The Waves* uses poetic speech in order to elevate all experiences to the same level—just as the unconscious uses the dream to dehierarchize the dream-thoughts.

In general, poetic speech in *The Waves* is open to the unconscious, which seems to flow freely between the characters without the boundaries imposed by censorship. This formal opening toward the unconscious resonates thematically with the characters' desire to escape from their narrow, bourgeois social life into the exuberance of their inner worlds. *The Waves* thus mediates the split between a social self and a "private self" (a term used in *Mrs. Dalloway*) through a poetic speech that formally ignores this split. Yet Woolf's characters remain prisoners of their bourgeois culture—divided subjects, suffering from their ambivalent desire for unboundedness and its antagonism with their social lives.

Nonreferential Images

The characters' desires, fears, and fantasies are woven into poetic images that recur in ever new modulations throughout the various stages of their lives. Because each character owns a specific set of poetic images, these images function as paradoxical "identity themes" in a speech that constantly runs against the confines of identity.[5] The most dominant images are those that evoke fears of fragmentation or a loss of self along with a complementary desire for fusion with others or with the surrounding world. Louis, for example, pictures himself as a flower stem whose roots reach into the utmost depths of the world. The weight of the earth presses on his ribs; his eyes are blind, green leaves.[6] Rhoda's images resemble psychotic dissolutions of the body: "Month by month things are losing their hardness; even my body now lets the light through; my spine is soft like wax near the flame of the candle. I dream; I dream" (p. 38). And Bernard, who expresses his desire to fuse with others through what he contemptuously terms his "phrases," says in his final monologue: "I am not one person; I am many people; I do not altogether know who I am—Jinny, Susan, Neville, Rhoda or Louis; or how to distinguish my life from theirs" (p. 237).

All these fantasies—of being freed from the boundaries of a material body, of fusing with others or melting into the environment, of returning to the womb, and of remaining in a perpetual flow between multiple selves—draw upon recollections of primary undifferentiation. The dreamlike effacement of the contours of the outer world and the dissolution of its hard materialities seems to hold all the promise of Freud's "oceanic oneness." Yet Freud was also the one to insist that these primordial states are more ambivalent than later visions of a lost paradise, whose dark side Lacan explored in the phantasms of the fragmented body and the dissolution of the subject. These threatening fantasies haunt Rhoda, whose "transparent body" is breaking apart into fragments. Her phantasms of the fragmented body, such as her vision of melting into other bodies or of softening like malleable clay, all signify states of disembodiment or dissolution of the self.

Poetic speech in *The Waves* thus moves between the extreme poles of a relentless desire for unboundedness and fusion and an even more relentless fear of dissolution and fragmentation. The inadequacy of self-boundaries from which all of Woolf's characters suffer forms the core theme of the text. Fears of and desires for unboundedness become all the more haunting when the characters depict them as a response to their all too bounded, conventional, and rigid social lives. The oscillating and fluid poetic self-images are evoked as potential inner states. These states, however, are never realized in their outer world, except perhaps for a few moments of mystical fusion experienced during their gatherings. Thus, the poetic appears to be that surplus of the subject that exceeds the social. But, at the same time the very form of the characters' speech allows this excess to insinuate itself into the social and public domain.

In other words, *The Waves* conveys the theme of a split subjectivity by using a poetic discourse that symbolically heals the split on a formal level. This tension between the psychological disposition of literary characters and their mode of expression removes us from the conventions of psychological realism as well as from familiar stream-of-consciousness techniques. One can hardly overemphasize the innovative character of Woolf's highly artificial poetic speech: it presents a completely singular form of decentered subjectivity while, at the same time, embedding it in a critique of social codes.

In this context it is interesting to see that Rhoda, who suffers the most from her inability to adapt to social norms, is the only character who cannot establish a boundary between inner and outer realities. Her inability to define herself through boundaries eventually drives her to commit suicide. Characteristically, Rhoda has also given up the least of what the other characters define as a "true self." Already as a child, Rhoda expresses a terror of being excluded from the symbolic order. Letters for her are nothing but empty configurations of lines. She attempts to replace the system of conventional meaning and the codes of the symbolic order with an architecture of private symbols. Unable to experience herself as a temporal and historical subject, she remains outside of space and time: "The world is entire, and I am outside of it, crying, 'Oh, save me from being blown for ever outside the loop of time'" (p. 17). Rhoda is at home only in the timelessness of her unconscious, never in the external world or in interactions with others, not even in her own body. Only when daylight fades and the rough edges of the material world dissolve can she drift into a stream of private symbols, for then she "is relieved of hard contacts and collisions" (p. 22).

Rhoda never learns to perceive herself as being bounded by a body or individualized by a face. "I have no face" is the formula she repeats over and over again in order to visualize her exclusion from the symbolic order (pp. 27, 35, 191). Even when she looks at her face in the mirror she cannot transform this into a real mirror experience:

> "That is my face," said Rhoda, "in the looking glass behind Susan's shoulder—that is my face. But I will duck behind her to hide it, for I am not here. I have no face. Other people have faces; Susan and Jinny have faces; they are here. Their world is the real world. The things they lift are heavy. They say Yes, they say No; whereas I shift and change and am seen through in a second." (pp. 35–36)

Here Rhoda evokes the absence of precisely those two basic functions that, from a psychogenetic perspective, mark the entry into the symbolic order: the capacity of identifying with one's own mirror image and the capacity of negation.[7] Both achievements not only form the basis of self-boundaries, they are also prerequisites for the function of representation, communication, and interaction. Rhoda can never relinquish her timeless world of undifferentiation; instead she continues to drift as a disembodied entity, fusing with her dreamlike environment whose objects are visual, fluid, inclusive, and nonhierarchical. In order to feign assimilation into the symbolic order, she copies the gestures of her friends. Choosing a strategy of mimickry, she endows her gestures of imitating others with animistic power: "I will seek out a face, a composed, a monumental face, and will endow it with omniscience, and wear it under my dress like a talisman" (p. 27). Nonetheless, she remains emotionally imprisoned in herself. Under the onslaught of archaic emotions that she cannot share with others, Rhoda takes refuge in an autistic rocking, like a child who is threatened by self-dissolution even in her own fantasy world.[8] Her "ill fitting body" is bound to the "here and now" as to a monster, but outside the body lurks the *horror vacui* of a spaceless and timeless world: "Alone, I often fall down into nothingness. I must push my foot stealthily lest I should fall off the edge of the world into nothingness. I have to bang my hand against some hard door to call myself back to the body" (pp. 36–37).

Thrown back and forth between two worlds without ever being able really to inhabit either one of them, Rhoda becomes increasingly fragmented. Her attempts to force herself back into her body fail, since this body does not give her a protective form. During adolescence, in place of a gendered image of her female body, she creates more phantasms of a fragmented body. Yet later during the course of her life, she tries willfully to substitute those images of being "broken into separate pieces" (p. 91) with complementary images of a bounded and stable habitat and with daydreams of a world immune to change. These are the first of Rhoda's dreams that actively turn toward a life in the outside world. Her dreams of an undifferentiated secret world are increasingly disrupted by intrusions of the real, which eventually change the status of her imaginary productions.[9] Instead of using her phantasies as a medium of dedifferentiation, she begins to use precise geometrical figures to project and stabilize boundaries. The image of an "oblong upon the square" (p. 139) symbolizes this development. Rhoda also extends her newly acknowledged need for boundaries to graspable forms such as a housing. Her body is no longer experienced as a prison, but as a container that protects her from dissolution.

Rhoda visualizes her emergence from within herself as a pilgrimage to Greenwich—that is, to ground zero of historical space and time. Unable ever truly to appropriate those codes and measures for herself, she turns them into a symbol of her desire to fit into the symbolic order. In these new dreams she encounters the once dreaded life through a sort of identification with her aggressor: what she had feared most she now seeks out with a grim determination. A thorough psychological reevaluation of her desires transforms her fear of being touched into an urge to throw herself at the world and her fear of losing herself in contact with others into a desire to be devoured: "Now I will relinquish; now I will let loose. Now I will at least free the checked, the jerked-back desire to be spent, to be consumed" (p. 140).

Rhoda's figures of speech, however, reveal that her ambivalent emotions have only inverted the relationship between what can be admitted into and what must be repressed from her consciousness. Behind her desperate embrace of life lurks a hidden death wish. All the symbols she chooses contain both ideas: to merge with the world also means to be devoured by it. Rhoda's gift of herself to the world or to others is also a sacrifice. Her change only reveals the other side of her unbounded and disembodied subjectivity. Realizing that her willful turning toward the world remains an empty imaginary act, Rhoda, in looking back at her life, reactivates her early symbols. Her wish to be housed in the world expresses only a transitory sense of self, and offers her no real chance of escape from her isolation. While the pilgrimage to Greenwich was supposed to carry her to ground zero of space and time, this ground proves to be identical to the edge of the world, from which she fears falling into nothingness. Thus her most consuming desires again coincide with her deepest fears, which ultimately converge in her death wish. By taking her own life, Rhoda realizes the final contradiction of her ambivalent desire to be consumed and dissolved.

Percival as the Imaginary Other

While Rhoda is destroyed by her lack of boundaries, the other characters profit from their temporary fusion with others. For Rhoda's friends, the dissolution of self-boundaries remains partial and transitory, and therefore they can realize an otherwise unattainable potential for self-experience. Experiences of temporary fusion or dissolution, rather than being a threat, provide access to an alternate state of consciousness that momentarily transcends the decentered position of the subject.

Through its nonreferential images, poetic speech in *The Waves* renders visions of such unbounded states. Many of those visions are centered around one character, Percival, who does not have his own voice in the text but who nonetheless becomes one of its crucial symbolic figures. Like Woolf's nonreferential images, the absent character of Percival is conceived as a textual strategy that counteracts the polarization or, as Ehrenzweig calls it, the "horizontal division" of the subject. Percival incorporates the desire for a mystic expansion of consciousness. The characters' fantasies of fusion culminate in their collectively shared imaginary relationship with Percival. At the same time, however, Percival also represents unattainable otherness. He symbolically fills a deeply felt lack and holds the promise of mystic wholeness. His absence generates a collective myth shared by all the characters. Since he resides in India, his friends endow him with an aura of Eastern thought, projecting onto him a vision of personal wholeness in cosmic transcendence. This turns him into a sublime figure who comes to represent the unrepresentable ground of subjectivity. *The Waves* reaches its compositional peak when the characters' poetic speeches evoke a mystical experience of collective fusion during one of their gatherings, engendered by the felt presence of the absent Percival.

Despite Percival's central role, his status in the text is rather ambivalent. He not only functions as an organizing principle for the textual transgression of boundaries between the characters, but he also embodies the textual heritage of a romantic character. But Percival's impersonation of a romantic myth of transcendence appears as the effect of an impossible idealization by his friends. The more the characters project themselves toward this myth, the more it collides with the hard edges of their normal lives. Finally Bernard, in his last monologue, demystifies Percival by showing that he was, after all, just one of them. The romantic myth of transcendence embodied by Percival appears as a mystification created by nostalgic memory. Percival's mythologizing function is thus undermined by his textual conception. He represents a romantic heritage that can no longer be lived but cannot simply be discarded.

Still, it remains true that the very myth of Percival assumes a concrete reality for his friends, since it functions as a structuring device for their subjectivity. This becomes most obvious at the moment of his death, which only further radicalizes his paradoxical presence in absence. The way in which Bernard, the writer, reflects upon this function turns the aesthetic figuration of Percival into an object of textual self-reflection: "Here are pictures. Here are cold madonnas among their pillars. Let them lay to rest the incessant activity of the mind's eye . . . Mercifully these pictures make no reference; they do not nudge; they do not point. Thus they expand my consciousness of him [Percival] and bring him back to me differently" (p. 133).

Those "pictures without reference" that Bernard describes in fact form part of the basic aesthetic technique of *The Waves*. As we have seen, all the characters are depicted by individual nonreferential images whose poetic recurrence forms a leitmotif of their subjectivity: Louis's eyes are "green leaves, unseeing" and his roots go to the depth of the world; Susan is "tied down with single words"; Bernard is "making phrases"; and Rhoda is "outside the loop of the world" and "has no face." In their aesthetic abstraction of emotions and experiences, these images also recall the subject's entanglement in a network of imaginary representations.

As Stanislav Grof has shown in *The Realm of the Human Unconscious*, the formation of recurring images corresponds to the systematic repetition of certain psychosocial patterns, which are then internalized as systems of condensed experience.[10] The nonreferential images in *The Waves* not only provide a pictorial analogue to the repetition of similar patterns or subjective systems of condensed experience, they also reinforce such systems. The text translates the tacit mythologies that inhabit a character's self-image into poetic metaphors of subjectivity.

This function of mythologizing images is reinforced by Percival, who embodies the imaginary Other of his friends' imaginary selves. Percival endows the poetic presentation of the characters' interior lives with a new complexity. While all six characters use their inner speeches to dramatize the split between a true and a social self, the text insinuates that the very split between the two is already imaginary. Not only the social but also the true self and, even more important, the deeply felt opposition between them appear as social constructions. It would, however, simplify matters if one were to conclude that this social construction undermines the psychic reality of this opposition. The effects of the split between a true and a social self are as real as can be, and the textual function of Percival is to cause the clear-cut division between the real and the imaginary to crumble—if only to promote its re-creation along different lines. The characters' doubling by Percival as an imaginary Other results in a differentiation of imaginary functions. By exposing the imaginary constructions of subjectivity, the poetic speeches mark their distance from both the discursive construction of a social reality and the mythologies that the characters oppose to the social.

Centering the text around the figure of Percival creates a point of convergence for the characters' esoteric speeches. But the paradoxical effect of Percival is that, like myths in general, he contains the desire for unboundedness on both a psychological and an aesthetic level. Like Moby Dick, the character of Percival generates a myth of transcendence and wholeness. The passionate desire for transcendence in these myths is domesticated by the myth's form, which provides closure. This structural ambivalence of a bounded myth of unboundedness is repeated in the aesthetic form chosen for the presentation of Percival. The characters voice visions of unboundedness and mystic fusion with an imaginary Other; yet this Other, once it has become a myth, provides closure and centeredness.

More than any other device, the character of Percival marks the historical affiliation of *The Waves* with Romanticism. But it is a Romanticism in question, broken by the hard edges of the material world, its cruelties and trivialities. We thus experience a text whose characters retain a romantic desire for transcendence and unboundedness but whose literary devices challenge this romantic affiliation. The positioning of *The Waves* within the modernist imagination is largely due to its experimental and esoteric forms of poetic speech. This experimentalism accounts for the text's relevance in relation to later, more radical presentations of unbounded subjectivity in twentieth-century literature.

The Interior Dialogue

Poetic speech in *The Waves* establishes a highly unusual relationship between language and subjectivity. On the one hand, speech is commonly thought of as a mode of consciousness. Yet, on the other hand, the characters use the aesthetic stylization of speaking in "pictures without reference" in order to voice aspects of subjectivity that are usually left uncommunicated or remain unconscious.[11] In particular, the nonreferential images articulate poetic abstractions of each character's basic moods. This aesthetic device endows moods with a conscious, self-reflexive quality they usually lack. For example, after Percival's death, Neville indulges his pain in a way that is not uncommon as a mood, but rather unusual in its form of expression: "Come, pain, feed on me. Bury your fangs in my flesh. Tear me asunder. I sob, I sob" (p. 130). Equally striking is the poetic abstraction of Bernard's depressive mood: "I see what habit covers. I lie sluggish in bed for days. I dine out and gape like a codfish. I do not trouble to finish my sentences, and my actions, usually so uncertain, acquire a mechanical precision" (p. 158).

The translation into poetic images of moods that we commonly experience unconsciously is one of Woolf's central aesthetic devices. Moreover, she enforces this process by translating it into an intersubjective mode of communication between the characters. Since their voices are not interior monologues but strange forms of dialogue, we are confronted with a highly innovative literary subjectivity. The text generates the impression of a hypostasized poetic consciousness of characters, externalized in highly stylized speeches, which remind one of musical sextets. The sequences of speech do not form an explicit dialogue; rather, they take shape as literary forms of interior speech. Most critics have interpreted the characters' poetic speeches as interior monologues. But this categorization ignores the fact that the poetic sequences are explicitly intersubjective and are usually direct responses or resonances to the sequences of other characters. This can be seen when a character who is addressed by one of the speeches indirectly takes it up in the following sequence—not in the form of an answer, however, but in the form of a corresponding image or a reweaving of the same thought.

This exchange, then, turns out to be a form of "interior dialogue," which produces the curious effect of a transparency of thoughts or of a collective exchange of emotions at a subliminal level. Such interpersonal transparency or permeability of thought and emotion is unusual even in literature. Interior dialogue in *The Waves* doubles the fictional biographies of the characters with poetic dramatizations of the mental events and emotional turmoil that mark these biographies. At the same time, this interior dialogue creates an intersubjective internal drama that reveals a much stronger connection between the characters than that established through social relations.

This interior dialogue also constitutes a transgression of the familiar boundaries of subjectivity on a formal level. The poetic speeches fictionalize an intersubjective communication that takes place at an intrapsychic level. This form of interaction exceeds the logical boundaries of the subject. Multiple affinities and rhythmical symmetries across different scales of the interior dialogues suggest that the characters have access to a tacit knowledge about one another. On the formal level of poetic expression they share concrete images, rhythms, and vibrations. When Susan, for example, cries out her jealousy—"Now I will wrap my agony inside my pocket-handkerchief . . . I will take my anguish and lay it upon the roots under the beech trees" (p. 10)—she is echoed by Bernard: "Susan has spread her anguish out. Her pocket-handkerchief is laid on the roots of the beech trees" (p.11). This striking self-similarity of their inner speeches and nonreferential images suggests a transindividual affinity in deeper spheres of the characters' experience.[12] The boundaries of literary subjects marked by individual names are continually traversed within their interior dialogues.[13] The formal transgressions of boundaries within their speeches thus echoes the characters' desire to transgress the boundaries of subjectivity. Even though the romantic myth of a *unio mystica* is refracted by the characters' quotidian myths,[14] their poetic speeches retain the impression of a deep structure of collective experience on a formal level. From this perspective, the multiple fantasies of fusion may be seen as figural representations of an unconscious interpersonal connectedness. It is crucial to see that this connectedness is established at the level of the inner core of the self, which the characters themselves hypostasize as the "true self." The painful sense of isolation they voice is not only isolation from others but also isolation from their own core.

The interior dialogue in *The Waves* can thus be read as a stylized poetic speech that not only transgresses the boundaries between characters but also exposes the inner core of subjectivity. Outside of aesthetic experience this inner core is accessible only through tacit knowledge. As a fictional communication about tacit knowledge, the interior dialogue fulfills, on an imaginary level, what Winnicott described as a wish "to be found in one's inner core" without having to expose it directly. Aesthetically, this interior dialogue about the core of subjectivity is reflected in the fact that the exterior form of the speeches is solipsistic, not addressed to anyone in particular, while the internal images and rhythms of this dialogue resonate with each other. From this perspective, even the voice of the anonymous narrator, who identifies the speeches for the reader with "said Bernard" or "said Susan," can be read as a suggestion that interior speech, too, is always directed toward, taken up by, and resonated by an Other even when no explicit dialogue is taking place.

This imaginary Other is further elaborated by Percival as an absent third agency of the dialogue. In this context, Percival can also be seen as a symbolic externalization of the imaginary Other toward which the interior dialogues are directed.[15] Poetic speech thus communicates aesthetically about the inner core of subjectivity without violating the taboo placed on such a communication in everyday life. We remember that Winnicott claimed this as one of the basic functions of literary communication in general. *The Waves* brings this function to the surface: its characters communicate about this inner core in the form of dialogical exchanges. While on the level of literary presentation, these exchanges function as an aesthetic equivalent of unconscious communication between the characters, for the reader they appear nonetheless in a medium of conscious expression. Conceived in this fashion, the interior dialogue is also a form of aesthetic reflection about tacit interpersonal communication. Without necessarily reaching a conscious level, such a communication doubles all speech and action. Just as subjects communicate with each other through their unconscious, so do they communicate with each other through tacit knowledge. On this level, a successful communication would consist in a tacit recognition of the inner core of subjectivity. The interior dialogue in *The Waves* can be read as an aesthetic stylization of such a tacit communication. It thus resonates with the fulfillment of the wish "to be found in one's inner core." This communication momentarily suspends not only the boundaries between I and Not-I, but also the boundaries around the inner core of subjectivity. By establishing an explicit form of transitional speech within its fictional world, the interior dialogue reflects intermediacy as a basic aesthetic function.

This implies that the characters' poetic speeches not only simulate unconscious, transsubjective, or tacit forms of knowledge, but also generate an increased reflexivity. The characters internally articulate, comment upon, and analyze whatever they perceive and experience— often the most trivial things. Next to the nonreferential images, this self-reflexive doubling of all events is another characteristic feature of poetic speech in *The Waves*. As hyperconscious and hypersensitive as this constant reflection makes the characters appear in their dialogues, it remains amazingly inconsequential for their everyday lives, which continue to be highly conventional and limited. It seems as if their distant self-reflexivity and their imaginary reshaping of experience operate independently from the everyday life functions of their consciousness. Tacit or unconscious dimensions of subjectivity seem to emerge in their interior dialogues without ever really interfering with their social sphere. The formal level of poetic speech in *The Waves* even integrates modalities of experience that are conventionally conflictive and competitive. Moreover, because the characters have a tacit knowledge of what happens at remote places and times, one might read their interior dialogue as the literary fiction of a utopian unbounded consciousness. This consciousness ignores the exclusions, incompatibilities, and spatial and temporal boundaries of traditional consciousness. The aesthetic intermediacy in *The Waves* thus enacts a playful change of the conditions of decentered subjectivity.

The Ironic Gaze

If the consciousness of the characters in *The Waves* were as integrated on a psychological level as it is on the formal level of aesthetic presentation, the characters would be presented as truly unbounded subjects. Unboundedness would then no longer be a threat but a utopia. Such a utopia, however, is only realized at the formal level of poetic speech in *The Waves*. The characters are not really able to integrate their desire for fusion and transcendence but instead remain caught up in a dichotomy between their bound identities and their states of unboundedness. On a formal level, this tension is presented by a narrative that runs counter to the poetic figuration of an unbounded consciousness. Without completely undermining this poetic figuration, the narrative prevents the characters' poetic speeches from ever freezing into an ideology or a myth of unbounded subjectivity. Full of textual irony, the narrative creates a decisive countermovement to the poetic and mystical aura of the text.

What can irony achieve in a highly poetic, mystical text that is supposed to be "eyeless" and free from reality? Irony in *The Waves* mainly operates through breaks in a character's perspective or through images that convey a clash of mystic experience with the banalities of daily existence. The ironic image of a bee, for example, disrupts the festive aura of the college graduation ceremony: one of the characters imagines that it stings Lady Hampton, the general's spouse, on the nose. Such ironies unsettle the mystic poetics of the text and prevent it from becoming "eyeless" to material realities. Far from mystic detachment and relaxation, irony also reveals the disturbing mannerisms of a hyperconsciousness that pedantically meditates upon trivialities.

Similarly, irony intrudes when simple activities like eating are conveyed with poetic reflexivity: "Instinctively my palate now requires and anticipates sweetness and lightness, something sugared and evanescent; and cool wine, fitting glove-like over those finer nerves that seem to tremble from the roof of my mouth and make it spread (as I drink) into a doomed cavern, green with wine leaves, musk-scented, purple with grapes" (p. 118). While Neville, the pedant, comments about his meal, the text's ironic gaze reveals the bathos of his stylization of the trivial. In similar passages, the characters themselves establish an ironic distance from the ordeals of daily existence in order to make the reader an accomplice to their own questioning of their social identities. Often, however, irony is directed against the characters from an outside perspective, thus creating a distance toward their poetic self-stylizations and rationalizations. The hyperconsciousness that creates these stylizations is shown to live under the constant threat of self-mythologization. Trapped in a narcissistic aggrandizement of the trivial, the characters at times indulge in a self-celebratory artistic rhetoric. Their narcissistic entanglement culminates in the aesthetization of their own self-image. As a result, self-deceptions and private mythologies dominate their dialogues. On a rhetorical level, the mythologizing function of consciousness manifests itself through the recurrence of clichés—as simplifying images and as an unconscious repetition compulsion.[16]

As an implicit critique of consciousness, textual irony in *The Waves* also challenges the boundaries of constructed identities. It is mainly directed against conscious activities through which the characters project self-images in order to secure a sense of identity. The textual irony reveals how, under the pressure of individualization and identity formation, the characters continually project new fictitious self-boundaries. A similar irony exposes their signatures as illusory acts of identification.[17] Louis's pathetic apotheosis of his identity through the mechanics of signature lays bare a consciousness that has to secure its identity artificially: "I have signed my name," says Louis, "already twenty times, I, and again I, and again I. Clear, firm, unequivocal, there it stands, my name. Clear-cut and unequivocal am I too." (p. 142).

Significantly, textual irony in *The Waves* does not completely undermine the poetic and mystic aura of the characters' speeches; rather, it punctuates the ambivalent status of self-stylization. It is no coincidence that the only character who escapes the sharp bite of textual irony is

Rhoda, who lives without the comforting sense of identity. The fact that irony is directed against the unifying and mythologizing functions of self-images establishes within the text an implicit differentiation of the capacities for self-representation. Just as the experience of the body needs a framing body image, self-experience in general needs a frame of self-projections and images. *The Waves* polarizes experience and its imaginary mental adaptations, including those adaptations that make use of primary processes and tacit knowledge, in order to extend the boundaries of subjectivity. In their speeches, the characters dramatize a split in their subjectivity arising from the conflict between their public lives and their inner sense of themselves. Their interior dialogue can be read as a form of working through of this split. Against the reductive forms of their social selves, their dialogue hypostasizes a true self to which they have only sporadic access, through the experience of mystic epiphanies. This true self escapes the confines of a self-image and has to be withheld from explicit communication. In order to represent it at all, mentally or verbally, one needs to develop specific, indirect forms of representation and communication.

When Louis distinguishes his syncretistic experience of a true self from his integrative but latently paranoid representation of a social self, he uses the metaphor of a shattered mind: "This will endure. From discord, from hatred . . . my shattered mind is pieced together by some sudden perception. I take the trees, the clouds, to be witness of my complete integration. I, Louis, I, who shall walk the earth these seventy years, am born entire, out of hatred, out of discord" (pp. 32–33). There seems to be a strange ambiguity—if not a paradox—at work in those stylized self-relations. While the "shattered mind" produces the undifferentiated or syncretistic forms of a holistic vision, the paranoid delimitation from the other produces an ambivalent, if fragile, sense of unity. The metaphor of the shattered mind presents a mental analogue of the phantasm of the fragmented body. Just as phantasms of the fragmented body retain their ambivalent fascination after the formation of a body image with stable boundaries, undifferentiated forms of primary experience retain their validity after the consciousness of a bounded I is formed. The complementary desires for fusion and transgression of self-boundaries seek out those undifferentiated forms for their representation.

This polarity allows one to see the problems of representation that *The Waves* poses in sharper profile: in order to voice experiences that are hardly ever brought to consciousness, one has to find a speech that is qualitatively different from discursive speech. The esoteric poetic language of *The Waves* can be read as an attempt to voice areas or dimensions of subjectivity that can no longer be grasped by representations of a consciously delineated identity.

Aesthetic Effects and Responses

Shifting the representation to unconscious areas of subjectivity goes hand in hand with increasingly emphasizing the form and materiality of language. *The Waves* no longer draws its main effects from its narrative, which only serves as a background for inner events. The appeal of this text stems largely from what exceeds the bounds of narrative and consciousness. While the dramatic suspension of a narrative setting and the esoteric language initially hold the reader at a certain distance in relation to the characters, this effect is counterbalanced by the poetic aura of the text, its musicality, and the suggestive power of its imagery, all of which are precisely attuned to its sequential formal constructions and rhythms.

Nothing is static in this text: images have no sharp contours, noises are rhythmical and flowing, objects are transparent and vibrate with the play of light and melting shadows. In one of her diary entries about the style of *The Waves* Virginia Woolf says, "It is now so fluent and fluid that it runs through the mind like water."[18] Like impressionistic music, the artistic poetic composition uses material and formal elements in a dynamic balance. This fluidity is echoed in the textual play of light and shadow, in the precisely crafted recurrences of non-referential images, and in the network of reiterated themes and musical sounds of words and sentences.

The introductory sequences that create the aura of each chapter momentarily contain this textual flow within a painted scene or a still life of emotional rhythms. The passage introducing the first chapter, for example, resonates with the merging musicality of daybreak, the melting together of sea and sky, the movement of the waves, the transparent luminosity of the leaves, and the unconscious breathing of the sleeping children. Recalling primary modes of childhood experience, these stills of flowing processes elicit the unconscious responses of a syncretistic reception. Together with the interior dialogue, these flowing images and rhythms ground the characters' desire for fusion in the formal structure of the text. Language in *The Waves* is full of the traces of primary processes or of the effects of what Kristeva calls the semiotic. The text appeals to our latent fascination with modes of undifferentiated or primary-process experience: it not only reinforces these modes on a thematic level but also materializes them in its form.

The appeals to primary-process experience are complemented by an emphasis on abstraction and self-reflection. The way in which *The Waves* mediates the specific interaction between these two poles affects the reading process. During the course of the novel, the lyrical images and rhythms are increasingly embedded in discursive, often analytical, and sometimes very prosaic passages. These passages break the musicality of the text to the extent that they disrupt the reader's unfocused attention. Yet, they never succeed in pushing the reflexivity to a level of intensity or sophistication that could create a productive counterbalance to the appeals to unconscious reception. As we have seen, these textual strategies are used mainly to expose the negative effects of a hyperconscious aesthetisizing of one's life. For example, if Louis exclaims in a restaurant "I am conscious of flux, of disorder, of annihilation and despair" (p. 80), his abstract rhetoric not only marks him as a character who records his own life with aesthetic distance, but also keeps the reader from becoming too closely involved in either the events or the character himself.

This distancing of the reader follows a double strategy. As we have seen, the characters often voice with astonishing matter-of-factness the secret areas of their tacit knowledge. The reader could react with empathy to this revelation by mobilizing his or her own tacit knowledge. The artificial and abstract forms of presentation, however, work against such an empathetic reading. In a similar way, abstraction and reflexivity counterbalance the textual musicality and the nonreferential images that appeal to primarily emotional, if not unconscious, reactions. In the characters' dialogues the overly abstract passages indicate their efforts at integrating, if not neutralizing, their desire for unbounded subjectivity and fusion with others. In a similar way, the formal abstractions in the text integrate or neutralize an unfocused or unconscious experience of reading. In both cases, reflexivity is used to restabilize boundaries and to neutralize desires for fusion and dissolution.

In general, literary texts that appeal to the unconsious—and any textual transgession of boundaries of subjectivity necessarily entails such an appeal—cannot avoid deploying some kind of double strategy. They have to make sure that their traces of primary material and their solicitation of unconscious responses are transposed into a communicative structure; but they also have to stay within the boundaries of what passes the restrictions of censorship. Regarding censorship and the respective formation of formal and representational compromises, textual strategies are faced with a task that can be compared with that of dream-work—with the additional requirement that what escapes censorship has to be accessible to literary communication.

It is not only through its strategies of reflective distancing that *The Waves* addresses the problem of censorship. Even its poetic and lyrical modes of presentation reveal traces of representational compromise. The highly structured and bounded composition guarantees a formal integration of the dissolution and transgression of boundaries. Syntactic and semantic functions of language remain intact. And even though the narrative only serves as a background for the characters' inner drama, it nonetheless releases coherent life stories. Moreover, the poetic rhythms and forms of the interior dialogues lose their exotic aura while they assume increasing familiarity during the reading process.

The Waves is thus far from being a radically decentered or unbounded text. Since its desire for unboundedness remains formally bound, its appeals to the unconscious are not disruptive. Far from unsettling unconscious fantasies or formal configurations stimulated by primary processes, the harmonious musical rhythms of poetic language in *The Waves* are comforting in their appeal and transported smoothly to the unconscious. The textual strategies thus work toward a temporary permeability of the polarized modes of experience and play across the split within decentered subjectivity, while refraining from challenging this polarity. Though the text conveys the ambivalent fascination of a desire for unbounded subjectivity, its language and its formal composition do not require a new conception of the subject. Poetic language in this context fulfills a double function. While it appeals to the unconscious, at the same time it retains the boundaries between the conscious and the unconscious by formally incorporating primary-process material. A shifting dynamic of closeness and distance mediates between the dichotomous spheres of decentered subjectivity while leaving the dichotomy itself intact.

Subjectivity in *The Waves* therefore remains grounded in a binary,

dichotomous model. Social boundedness and imaginary unboundedness form incompatible poles of subjectivity, impermeable to each
other except in rare epiphanies or moments of ecstatic fusion. In this
model of binary opposition, social integration always implies a loss of
what the characters perceive as their true inner selves. Yet the refusal
of social integration entails the risks of a complete disconnection from
the outer world: it drives Rhoda into fierce isolation and suicide.

As we have seen, the characters' interior dialogue does mediate
between these two poles. But these dialogues do not provide a quasi-
realistic rendition of the characters' subjective condition. Rather, they
are conceived as an artifice that poetically expresses the characters'
unrealized potential. Since this expression does not change their conventional social lives, the characters' subjectivity in *The Waves* retains
a dichotomy that is already surpassed by the aesthetic medium in
which it is voiced. With its tension between the subjectivity of characters and their modes of expression, this novel prepares the way for
later, less dichotomous presentations of subjectivity.

The Final Chapter

The previous observations about the productive tension within the
modes of presentation in *The Waves* would suffice were it not for the
last chapter, which is voiced by Bernard, the writer. Though it introduces a completely new tone and compositional structure, this chapter
has either been given little special consideration or been taken almost
too literally as the authoritative voice of the writer among the characters. A close reading, however, reveals an astonishing break with the
previous textual conception.[19] The interior dialogue is replaced by the
voice of a single character, Bernard, who narrates the story of the six
friends to an anonymous stranger—an absent character who, like Percival, figures as an imaginary Other. Surprisingly, Bernard's discourse
falls back onto a conventional form of narration that had been left
behind in the earlier chapters. This discourse not only recalls the main
events described in the previous chapters, it also provides concrete
background information for the poetic interior dialogues. The enig-
matic scene at the beginning with the interior dialogues of the children, for example, receives a fairly unpoetic explanation: awakened by
the breaking of a huge wave, the children voice their first impressions
of the day.

Such explanations function as an anticlimax: they retrospectively rob the mysterious interior dialogues of their fascination. It feels as if, after the fact, Bernard must demonstrate *ex negativo* why the text had to renounce a conventional narrative presentation. His narrative destroys the atmosphere and mood conveyed earlier through the interior dialogues. Because Bernard is all too aware of his shortcomings as a writer, one might be tempted to read his final speech as a form of textual self-reflexivity. But though this might be justified from a conceptual point of view as a demonstration of the failure of conventional narration, it is hard to integrate from an aesthetic perspective. How can we justify Bernard's explicit rejection of linear consciousness and discursive narratives when we consider the fact that he voices this supposed rejection in the very form he rejects? And how does Bernard's narrative at the end relate to the composition of *The Waves* as a whole?

Bernard once again laments his failure as a writer. Writing for him has always been an attempt to establish continuity and identity, but now, retrospectively, he distances himself from both. Linking his discursive narratives with the conventional, myopic restrictions of quotidian life, he now sees these narratives doomed to fail when it comes to expressing what lies beyond these boundaries. Writing, moreover, was for him an aestheticization of his own life, and he now rejects this aestheticization as inauthentic. Ironically, he cannot prevent himself from aestheticizing this new rejection in turn: "Standing by the window looking at a sky dear like the inside of a blue stone, 'Heaven be praised,' I said, 'we need not whip this prose into poetry. The little language is enough" (pp. 225–226).

Bernard's narrative about his own failure as a writer is full of stylistic awkwardness (if not clumsiness), verbal clichés, and empty pathos. His reiterated phrases reveal more than ever that he verbalizes his self for the gaze of the Other. But it is precisely these linguistic "failures" that give Bernard's final speech a secondary relevance within the composition of the novel. One could even be tempted to read the gaps and breaks within his speech as aesthetic slippages. When, in the midst of his most inauthentic self-stylizations, Bernard dreams of "broken words, inarticulate words," he inadvertently names what would be a more adequate form of articulation. Thus his discourse assumes a kind of secondary authenticity. The inconsistencies and contradictions and the bathos in Bernard's story of past failures insert a new instability into the aesthetic balance of the text as a whole. The poetic speeches are affected retrospectively by the weight of a self-conscious linear narration. But at the same time the character of Bernard gains a complexity and plasticity that he lacked previously. It is precisely the slippages in his discourse that release him from the firm grip of mere textual ironies. Undermining the leveling and, in a sense, unifying force of ironic distance, Bernard's slippages drive the text of *The Waves* beyond its own boundaries. The "aesthetic failure" of Bernard's discourse disrupts the well-constructed but instable balance of the textual composition so profoundly that it appears as if the character Bernard frees himself from his aesthetic conception and breaks through the figural and formal boundaries that confined him in the previous chapters.

Recalling the blind security of unconscious productions, the "failures" of Bernard's speech anticipate the direction pursued by later fictional presentations of unbounded subjectivity. These later texts renounce the comforts of harmonious aesthetic composition and stable literary characters in order to explore with even more radical disruptions of narrative a poetic language of the unconsious. The aesthetic slippages in Bernard's speech may be an involuntary manifesto of modernism announcing the dissolution of stable literary characters and rounded aesthetic compositions. With its broken and inarticulate words, Bernard's speech strives to articulate a dimension of experience that has its roots in the phantasms of the fragmented body, for which Louis coined the metaphor of a shattered mind. It is not without irony that *The Waves* has Louis, the bureaucrat, as the one who hallucinates an early form of postmodern schizophrenia and Bernard, the unsuccessful writer, as the inadvertent proponent of postmodern pastiche. Is Rhoda, then, the intrusion of the real?

5

"I, a Self the Sign": Language and
Subjectivity in *Finnegans Wake*

Creativity remains closely related to the chaos of the primary process. Whether we are to experience chaos or a highly creative order
depends entirely on the reaction of our rational faculties.
—*Anton Ehrenzweig*

In the buginning is the woid, in the muddle is the sounddance.
Instead of the sentence, the sounddance.
—*James Joyce*

Logopoeia: "When Language Celebrates, the Words Dance"

The epigraph taken from *Finnegans Wake* may initiate us into a reading that does not begin with a word, but with a "sounddance." The
dynamic movement of a dance replaces the relative stasis of a word,
and the sonorous quality of sounds supercedes the eye's silent capture
of a written sentence. But the epigraph also reminds us that such a
reading leads through a muddle of sounds, which at the beginning
feels much like undifferentiated noise devoid of meaning. Upon first
encountering the *Wake*'s singular use of words, readers, though be-
wildered, immediately direct their attention toward the materiality of
language. Once we have acquired the culture of the written word, it
becomes hard for us to respond to the immediacy of archaic sound-
dances. They slip away from our conscious attention and appeal to us
unconsciously. In a sense, we have to reverse the direction of our
acculturation into language in order to open ourselves to *Finnegans
Wake*. Only if we are willing to suspend cognitive understanding as a

95

condition of reading can we gain immediate access to this text. Deprived of any spontaneous constitution of "surface meaning,"[1] the reader's eye traces unfamiliar wordshapes that capture the ear more often than the eye.

Still, the text resonates with enough familiar sounds and words to entice us into trying to decipher it. The interest that the growing international Joyce community invests in *Finnegans Wake* can perhaps best testify to the extent to which this obscure text engenders both pleasure and pain. It has produced a whole body of reader's guides, concordances, and annotations. The *Wake*'s history of reception discloses a symbiosis between the text and its secondary literature. But strangely enough, even though such production of "semantic crutches"—to recall Samuel Beckett's term—may render the text more understandable, it does not make it more readable. And paradoxically, in deciphering this obscure text, Joyce's critics usually do not emphasize the singular process of Joyce's textual production but, on the contrary, invert it by reconstructing familiar and conventional roots of Joyce's new forms of speech. The reception of *Finnegans Wake* has thus for a long time been marked by a curious regression. Like the first sentence of the *Wake*, the flow of critical commentary moves against the current of Joyce's narrative time. This may indicate that reading *Finnegans Wake* should not be reduced to mere attributions of semantic meaning. Joyce's text deploys a spatiotemporal economy that differs from both the temporality of linear narration and the architectonics of a closed spatial form. The text's aesthetic potential seems rather to emerge from a space of difference between signification and sense, a difference that suspends the constitution of meaning according to a linear temporality. Meaning is shifted from the signification of decipherable words or word fragments and word conglomerations to the process and experience of their spatial condensation and mutation.

If the pure construction of possible meanings amounts to an effort that can at best supplement a textual dimension other texts seem to presuppose, the very status of interpretation becomes problematic. For example, interpretations that merely restitute a narrative, which the text itself seems to contain but resists unfolding, may be extremely helpful textual archeologies, but they fail to account for the experience of reading the *Wake*, in which the inability to focus on a narrative is crucial. The tireless deciphering passion of the Wakeans results from our clinging to those very historical habits of reading that the *Wake* itself challenges in order to initiate a completely new type of reading. We thus have a choice: to open ourselves to the flood of associations and the suggestive power of this text, or to become a kind of speech detector who roams through the caves of this "book of kills" in search of buried corpses of language. If we follow the clues hidden on the surface of Joyce's text, we can identify those corpses as victims of a symbolic order that rise to a carnivalesque dance of words, a "logopoeia" engendered by Joyce's celebratory anarchy of poetic speech.[2]

Joyce's sounddance engenders a condensed aesthetic experience of endless mirrors and echoes of literary, biblical, historical, geographical, cultural, and philosophical allusions. During the process of reading, earlier parts of the text assume ever more connotations and the network of possible meanings becomes denser and denser. The overflowing richness of the retrospectively growing connotations of the first sentence, for example, has been widely documented.

> riverrun, past Eve and Adam's, from swerve of shore to bend of bay, brings us by a commodius vicus of recirculation back to Howth Castle and Environs.[3]

"Riverrun" flows into a torrent of speech, which in its last sentence reverts back into itself. This recursive loop carries all the connotations of an eternal return of histories, texts, and readings. Endlessly spiraling loops bring everything into eternal motion—from the shapes of words to the space, time, and characters created by them. Words that spill over into other words invade the boundaries of familiar systems of order. As Joyce critics have shown in their meticulous accumulation of ever more possible meanings, the first sentence alone alludes to a whole network of textual and intertextual strands. "Riverrun" refers to Dublin's river Liffey, which flows past a church named "Adam and Eve's" and will transform into Anna Livia Plurabelle, the symbolic river woman. Mediated through the identity of names, Dublin's geography links the beginning of *Finnegans Wake* with the beginning of Genesis. If we follow this connection we can already name the central themes of the text: paradise as the archaic space before human history, the creation of the word/world, the fall of mankind, and the polarity of gender.

"Commodius vicus of recirculation" offers another typical network of condensations. "Commodius," a combination of "commodious" (large) and "commodus" (comfortable) also alludes to the Roman Commodus, whose name in turn evokes the downfall of Rome. This association further extends the motif of the Fall—"Eve and Adam's"— to the fall of an ancient civilization. "Vicus," on the other hand, which can mean village, street, or path, first alludes to Vico, whose metaphysics of history inspired *Finnegans Wake*.[4] "Recirculation" resonates with "recorso" and enforces the Viconian figure of a cyclical recurrence—just as the recursive flow of speech suggests a backwards-flowing time. "Howth Castle and Environs," the legendary site in Dublin, has been compared to the skull of the legendary giant Finn Mac Cool, whose belly carries the city of Dublin.[5] Joyce's own disclosure that *Finnegans Wake* renders the thoughts of the dying giant Tim Finnegan, links Finn Mac Cool with Tim Finnegan, both of whom henceforth appear as condensed characters. Historical associations enlarge the network of references. Finn Mac Cool's guards were posted on the very same highland on which, hundreds of years later, after the Anglo-Norman King Henry II had subjugated the island, the conqueror Sir Almeric Tristan built Howth Castle. The subsequent sentence makes this historical link explicit: "Sir Tristram, violer d'amores, fr'over the short sea." "Howth Castle and Environs" also gives the initials of Humphrey Chimpden Earwicker (HCE), thus commencing the innumerable mutations of this central character, who materializes in ever new shapes through his initials.

The entirely unusual and innovative language games in *Finnegans Wake* immediately exert a diffuse fascination. Familiar words are clad in alien shapes. Well-known historical, mythological, and bibilical figures populate the textual universe, cast in and defigured by poetic speech. Sir Tristram is joined by Tom Sawyer (topsawyer, 3.7), Isaac (3.11), the giant Finnegan (3.19), and, echoing his fall, Humpty-Dumpty (humptyhillhead . . . tumptytumtoes, 3.20–21)—to name only those who present themselves immediately to the eye or the ear. Collected throughout centuries of history, this exotic cast of characters-in-language entices the reader into deciphering hieroglyphics and identifying defamiliarized shapes.

Apart from containing multiple meanings in each of its words or phrases, *Finnegans Wake* also retrospectively engenders ever new meanings. Joyce's strategy of condensing multiple words and languages has even affected the future: due to the chance operations that allow one to generate new connotations and meanings of condensed words, it appears as if the *Wake* contains resonances to words that have only been invented after its publication. The potential for deciphering and the possibility of finding new readings of the *Wake* are, in other words, infinite.

But the text not only invites a variety of possible meanings; it also calls for different modes of reading. In addition to inviting its readers to become word *bricoleurs,* the *Wake*'s rhythmical and sonorous language appeals to the ear and makes one want to read it aloud. Initially, the aesthetic experience of the *Wake*'s soundshapes is diffuse. Motivated by direct sensual stimuli to the eye and the ear, the reader may receive the text with undifferentiated attention and scan it unconsciously instead of trying to decipher its meaning. The two forms of reading, the focused activity of deciphering and the unfocused, syncretistic perception—follow two basically different strategies of communication in *Finnegans Wake,* but both result from the singular use of language with its condensations and overdeterminations.

These bipolar appeals engage completely different receptive faculties. On the one hand, Joyce uses aesthetic devices that require a high degree of attention and reflexivity, as well as a large corpus of knowledge and an exceptional memory. On the other hand, his text exerts a strong sensual appeal, eliciting both the pleasure of the eye as the reader perceives unfamiliar configurations of words, and that of the ear as the reader takes in the rhythm and music of the language. However, it is impossible simultaneously to perform these two modes of reading—the deciphering of condensed or transfigured words and the syncretistic reception of the sounds and shapes of words. Since aesthetic experience cannot be focused and unfocused at one and the same time, the *Wake*'s double appeal requires a series of successive and partial readings.

Condensed Dreamtextworlds

With its condensed words and sounds, *Finnegans Wake* probes the limits of representability. Within literary history, Joyce's linguistic experiments can, of course, be affiliated with the modernist movements of the surrealists and the symbolists, and with imagistic poetry. Mallarmé, Pound, and T. S. Eliot are powerful intertextual figures among the modernists, but the *Wake*'s affiliation with their work is embedded in resonances with other poets from various centuries and cultures.

We also find implicit reflections on theoretical issues as well as references to a wide range of culturally diverse philosophies. Theories of
music, painting, and theater figure as prominently as theories of language and literature.[6] Ironic allusions to current debates—especially
those about Freud, Jung, and the worldwide impact of psychoanalysis
as the new science of dreams—flavor a text whose implicit critical
challenge of contemporary epistemologies, aesthetic conceptions, and
cultural and moral values is far from exhausted even to this day.

The history of the early reception of *Finnegans Wake* is characterized
by tireless attempts to provide frames of reference that determine the
text's true object of representation. A frenzy to penetrate this obscure
gestalt took hold of critics, who studied the roots of Western and
Eastern cultures in order to unearth the collective memories accumulated in Joyce's monumental dream of language. The *Wake* became
the white whale of literary criticism—its impenetrable surface prom-
ising a sublime object of desire. Passionate attempts to hunt down
Joyce's word-monster, to find what is hidden in its depths, dominated
this early form of reception. It was also, in a way, an imperial hunt,
an attempt to domesticate the monster by turning into civilized language what had grown wild in this text. Ironically, this gigantic critical
endeavor inverted the Joycean process of production. Critics reassembled the fragmented body of a narrative scattered all over the universe
of broken and disfigured words. They restored the separate entities of
what had been condensed into one word and supplied the missing
links and referents. They translated the eternally flowing sounddance
into a city of words with clearly delineated architectural shapes.[7]

The dream seems to provide an exemplary frame of reference for
this cryptic text, especially since Joyce himself suggested reading the
Wake as a dreamtext. Once the dream was established as a model for
the text's mode of literary production, the interpretation of dreams
became a model for its reception. And yet, the literary presentation
of Joyce's nocturnal "wake" is very different from a quasi-realistic
fiction of dream-consciousness. Among critics who embrace the notion of a dreamtext, the disputes about the identity of the dreamer
reveal an all too literal use of the dream metaphor. Clive Hart's
Structure and Motif in Finnegans Wake introduced a seminal new
approach when it appeared in 1962.[8] Hart differentiates between
dream cycles, dream levels, concrete dreams, and dreamers within
dreams, as well as quoted dreams or mutations of famous dreams and

dream theories, among which—apart from the more familiar dream theories of Freud and Jung—the dream theory of the Upanishads figures most prominently. Highlighting Joyce's multiple use of the dream—as leitmotif, structural principle, mental or linguistic form, literary quote,[9] and object of different theories—Hart abandons mere equations of the text with the stream of consciousness of a dreamer. This is a decisive critical move, because even the most basic affinity of *Finnegans Wake* to the dream—namely the primary-process structure of its language—reaches far beyond a mere representation of a dreamer's consciousness. Formally, the effects of the primary process are produced by Joyce's complex condensations of words and structures, which govern the text on both a micro and a macro level. These condensations exert a tremendous power and generate semantic and structural overdeterminations that expand the linguistic universe far beyond the relative privacy and idiosyncracies of the dream. But the *Wake* shares with the dream its atemporality and nonhierarchical order. Rather than being fixed with clearly defined boundaries, time and space in *Finnegans Wake* are flowing and malleable. Unlike more directed forms of conscious memory, Joyce's presentation does not order objects according to different degrees of relevance, but endows them, as does unconscious memory, with the effects of a nonhierarchical presence and actuality. The *Wake*'s affinity with primary processes and the dream is further intensified by its rhythmic sonority, and particularly by alliteration, assonance, and other soundplay. Both the condensed forms of the primary process and the musicality in Joyce's text thus encourage unconscious reception. If a reader follows these textual appeals, the focus of meaning becomes less consciously determined than that of a text that emphasizes secondary processes. In addition, a language that relies heavily on primary process is harder to remember and less liable to generate the affective cathexis of a narrative. Signification becomes more open as the text offers multiple frames of reference and an unlimited pool of possible associations. Some of these associations may remain unconscious, since the whole process of signification remains so close to the primary processes.

This poetic use of primary processes pursues a goal different from that of either dream or myth, both of which focus on the shaping of what Freud has called unconscious material. In *Finnegans Wake*, primary processes operate through their surface structure and as decidedly linguistic qualities. The opening of language toward the unconsious is not mediated through unconscious material but structurally through literary stylization of primary process language. The text's relationship to the unconscious is therefore very different from that of a dream. In a dream, unconscious material is shaped according to the requirements of censorship; by contrast, in *Finnegans Wake* it is not the unconscious material but the shape and structure of primary processes that take priority. In other words, the *Wake* generates the effects of primary process not by shaping unconscious material but by mimicking the structural qualities of unconscious production. *Finnegans Wake* thus reaches beyond the use of primary process as a mere mode of representation.

Polylogue and Family Romance

This emphasis on structural effects has decisive consequences for the subjectivity manifested in this form of literary production. Subjectivity can no longer be located mainly in literary characters. Nevertheless, critics of the *Wake* have reconstructed the complex narrative of a family whose traces are disseminated throughout the whole text.[10] The characters of this narrative—Humphrey Chimpden Earwicker, Anna Livia Plurabelle, their sons Shem and Shaun, and their daughter Isabel (Issy)—do not, of course, attain a psychological profile comparable to that of characters in a psychological novel. They appear instead as effects of linguistic condensations and cultural or literary resonances. Because they appear as linguistic traces of archetypal characters, their psychological profile becomes secondary. Even their archetypal shaping remains a surface phenomenon, since the archetypes are mere linguistic evocations. They function as empty foils,[11] and their appeal to the unconscious is therefore different from that of conventional archetypes in mythologies or literature. Rather than being an effect of fictional psychological or historical destiny, their profile is carved out through the rhythms or intonations peculiar to a specific character. We could say that their subjectivity appears as an effect of language—yet not in the general sense in which this is true for all literary characters, but in the very specific sense that the linguistic expropriation of psychological density puts them on the same level as other linguistic material.

The number of historical, mythic, or literary characters that can be identified through allusions or transfigured traces of names in *Finnegans Wake* amounts to several thousand. Without becoming the carriers of a narrative or an elaborated fictional identity, they appear as empty characters borne out of language games or, as Adaline Glasheen called them, mere tropes.[12] This is even true for the members of the Dubliner family romance, who bear the traces of innumerable family romances since Adam and Eve. Allusive linguistic equivocations evoke mirror images of other characters within the language subjectivity of the Dublin protagonists and thus generate a condensed historical conglomeration of the tradition of family romance as such. Different characters with the initials of HCE and ALP continually appear. Boundaries between characters, as well as between characters and landscapes, between the animated and the nonanimated, and between texts and intertexts, are fluid. The links between them are linguistic affinities. HCE is Everybody—Here Comes Everybody, He'll Cheat E'erawan, Earwig, Homfrie, Haromphrey, honophreum, Humpopolamos, Humperfeldt, and other similar mutations. HCE's shapes range from an African lake (into which another lake, which is associated with Anna Livia Plurabelle, flows) to Humpty-Dumpty (to whom he is linked through the Fall and the myth of the cosmological egg) to Perce O'Reilly *(perce-oreille),* Finn Mac Cool, and Tim Finnegan and finally to the biblical Adam. These characters traverse the text as structures of personalities that overdetermine the character of Humphrey Chimpden Earwicker.

A similar fluctuation marks the character of Anna Livia Plurabelle. She figures as a river (the Liffey) and as an archetype of the feminine (as Eva) or an incorporation of the Great Mother. She appears as Annah the Allmaziful, the Everliving, the Bringer of Plurabilities, Amnis Limina Permanent, Annushka Lutetiavitch Pufflovah, Appia Lippia Pluviabilla. Her language subjectivity is merged with that of her daughter, Issy, who combines past and future, the daughterwoman on the hills, ready to replace her aging mother. Issy is Isabel and Isolde, a symbol of the erotic female and an archetype of the father's seduction. If Anna Livia recalls female unity, Issy stands for multiplicity. She is associated with the multiple personalities of schizophrenia or spiritual dissociation, the myriads of drifting minds, and is linked with the legendary seven rainbow girls and the twenty-nine leap year girls. She has, moreover, a mirror-sister who doubles her various manifestations.

All this indicates that, despite their fluctuating language subjectivities, the characters are decidedly individualized. But even though they may be described as characters, they are not described in a conventional way. They obtain their characteristics by way of the connotations associated with their archetypal grounding and the acts of naming and renaming. A specific rhythm of speech attributed to each of the main characters helps further to individualize them. These rhythms convey emotional dispositions or stages and moods beyond semantic signification. Like reminders of a rhythmic experience that psychogenetically precedes the acquisition of symbolic functions, those rhythms embed the characters in the archaic modes of experiencing language through sounds, rhythms, intonations, and modulations of voice. Language in *Finnegans Wake* is, in other words, a figuration of what Kristeva calls the realm of the semiotic. The characters gain profile not only through their associations with various mythological, legendary, and literary narratives, but also through differentiations within this semiotic space.

All the devices used by Joyce to create literary characters—condensation and overdetermination, displacement and substitution, shifts in temporal and spatial boundaries, archetypal affiliations, and recurring rhythms of speech—extend and transcend the boundaries of individual characters. At the same time, however, the characters in the *Wake* are different from decentered subjects[13] in a psychological or psychoaesthetic sense. Their multiple subjectivity[14] is not one induced by depersonalization or alternate consciousness. Transgressions of the boundaries of subjectivity in Joyce's *Wake* are not, as they are in Woolf's *The Waves*, figured as a character's desires or as a utopian expansion of consciousness. Any equation with familiar models of decentered subjectivity appears reductive in relation to characters who only emerge temporarily out of linguistic shapes in order to redissolve into new mutations and permutations. Thus released from allegiance to individual characters or voices, the *Wake* oscillates between the extreme notions of a universal consciousness[15] and a speech without subject.

The transgression of subjectivity through language in *Finnegans Wake* makes this text attractive for theories of language and subjectivity that emphasize the textuality or determination of the subject by the symbolic order. Joyce has become a favorite paradigm for poststructuralism, and since the late sixties we have witnessed an increasing trend in literary criticism to link Joyce with the theories of Lacan, Kristeva, Cixous, Derrida, and Deleuze and Guattari—who have themselves all written on Joyce.[16] In 1982, after more than twenty years of "deferral," Derrida "rewrites" two words of Joyce as the

Other who haunts his theories before their time: "setting up a hypermnesiac machine, there in advance, decades in advance, to compute you, control you, forbid you the slightest inaugural syllable because you can say nothing that is not programmed on this 1000th generation computer—*Ulysses, Finnegans Wake*."[17]

Far from reading Joyce with some of the poststructuralists as recording the "perpetural flight of the subject and its ultimate disappearance,"[18] I am, rather, interested in inverting this perspective. The language subjectivity of the *Wake* is a colossal language game that generates not only literary characters endowed with subjectivity but also a new form of subjectivity proper to language alone—that is, a subjectivity that cannot occur beyond language, but that is made imaginable through language and experienced as subjectivity. In this respect, it is closer to Derrida's textuality than to Lacan's subject of the symbolic order. The point to emphasize in respect to this textuality is, however, that subjectivity is not at its vanishing point but, on the contrary, at the point of its emergence as a form of language. My use of the term *language subjectivity* refers therefore to a form of textuality that no longer produces subjectivity as a mere referent or effect of language but as a quality residing within the formal aspects of language. And despite its thoroughly textual nature this subjectivity is endowed with an unconscious—the textual unconscious of *Finnegans Wake*, which Hélène Cixous emphasizes in "Joyce: The (r)use of writing."[19]

This peculiar textual subjectivity is generated at a moment when the historical interest in language and its boundaries challenges conventional assumptions about the relationship between language and the subject. Subjectivity in *Finnegans Wake* playfully inverts the function of language in the constitution of the subject. Instead of shaping the boundaries of subjectivity, language in the *Wake* destabilizes them in order to create a subjectivity in hitherto unknown forms that can emerge only from language. For this purpose, the *Wake* uses primary processes to provoke effects similar to the dream's dissolutions of the boundaries of subjectivity and language. Emptied of psychologically motivated characters, however, the *Wake* generates an intermediary language game aimed at challenging not only the boundaries of subjectivity but also familiar uses of language.

Even though the *Wake* presents the most radical challenge to the boundaries of language, each level of linguistic manifestation deploys its own dynamic of drawing and lifting boundaries. Joyce's linguistic artifices break through all affinities with models of linguistic transgressions as we find them in daily life. Language in the *Wake* differs from all other primary-process-oriented forms of speech, such as the language of dreams or the speech of early childhood, as well as so-called alternative or pathological forms of speech. All those forms are quoted in the *Wake*, but at the same time they are melted into a new textual form that reveals a highly differentiated inner composition. This enfolding of the linguistic transgressions into an encompassing order that presupposes familiarity with the ordering principles of the secondary processes generates a formal counterbalance to the linguistic dissolutions. Poetic speech in the *Wake* thus transgresses the boundaries of the symbolic order not so much for the sake of anarchy, dissolution, and disintegration as for the sake of new compositions of sound and sense.

The formal integration of primary processes into the communicative structure of a literary text has important consequences for the reading process. The reader must temporarily suspend the boundaries of the symbolic order. But rather than merely effacing those boundaries, the *Wake* seeks to render them more flexible in order to expand them. This expansion of the boundaries of language is one of the crucial historical functions fulfilled by *Finnegans Wake*. Its effects reach much further than a mere language game. Each poetic practice that pushes language beyond the boundaries of symbolic or literary convention also implies an expansion of subjectivity. *Finnegans Wake* transcends the conventional literary presentation of subjectivity from within the logic of language. Once speech becomes the driving force for transgressing the boundaries of subjectivity, it can no longer fulfill its conventional function of stabilizing the boundaries of subjects within speech. This is one of the ways we may understand the modernist dictum "I am spoken by language." Joyce's practice of poetic condensation becomes crucial for this inverted relationship between speech and subject, with all its ambivalences.

Language can tolerate only a certain amount of overdetermination before it loses its communicative function. When overdetermination becomes the structuring principle of poetic speech, it generates a decisive instability with regards to the speaker. The question "Who is speaking?" has haunted the experimental literature of this century. But it is too easy simply to dismiss this question with a narrative of the loss of the subject. *Finnegans Wake* has not lost its subjects or its subjectivities, precisely because its overdeterminations are integrated within a formal and structural composition that can be experienced and reconstructed in the reading process.

The ways in which *Finnegans Wake* integrates its transgression of language and subjectivity into a new form of ordered composition is, however, highly peculiar. The ordering principles are not compatible with any single preexisting order but generated from within the text. Once again, overdetermination becomes the dominant ordering device. Joyce imports ordering principles from various cultures and texts into *Finnegans Wake*. By superimposing them onto each other, he creates overdetermined layers of order. Since this overdetermined order of *Finnegans Wake* does not correspond to any of the orders that have inspired the textual composition—be it the Viconian circles, the aum of the Upanishads, or the different foreign languages and cultures that overdetermine the *Wake*'s English—the text begins to assume the quality of an artificial symbolic order. Seen from a different perspective, we may say that *Finnegans Wake* gradually creates its own code and its own rules of reading. Even though the various orders upon which the text is modeled originally pertain to the symbolic orders of various cultures, their condensation in the *Wake* reconfigures their specific structuring principles.

By creating an artificial symbolic order of its own, *Finnegans Wake* uses the potential of the transitional space of literature in an extreme way. The overdetermination of language and subjectivity in the *Wake*, in fact, combines all the ambivalences and paradoxes of the transitional space. It results from a language game that, like the early games in the transitional space, structures, dissolves, and reorganizes the boundaries of subjectivity. According to the multiple coding of the text, the aesthetic experience of this language game oscillates between the extremes of an unfocused attention to the soundplays on the one hand and of a reading based on deciphering possible meanings on the other. But this aesthetic experience also stimulates an imitative productivity documented in the *Wake*'s history of reception, which ranges from the first wave of mimicking letters to Joyce to such intertextual responses as Arno Schmidt's *Zettels Traum* or Derrida's *Glas*.

Decentered Orders

The transgressions, dissolutions, and condensations of the *Wake* undoubtedly elicit the atavistic pleasures of chaos. But as we have seen, the history of its reception also documents the desire to appropriate the otherness of the text, or to experience it, like an ethnographer, as a foreign system of order. Joyce's critics have untiringly constructed orders of *Finnegans Wake* that are anything but chaotic. They have identified a highly complex and differentiated macrostructure in which multiple meanings are assigned to each segment of the microstructure. Such constructions of order, however, reveal principles of textual composition hardly accessible in a simple reading. The same is true for the network of intra-, inter-, or extratextual references, which grows with each reading and is potentially endless. Joyce, of course, already amused himself by thinking of the unlimited potential of interpretation enfolded in the *Wake*.

But we have to define more clearly what is specific to the *Wake*'s unlimited potential of interpretation. The fact that literary critics reveal principles of composition or allusions that remain latent or unconscious during the reading process is true for every text, just as it is true that every text is potentially open to future interpretations. One of the distinguishing features of the *Wake* is its peculiar relationship between parts and whole. While reading, one gains the impression that the parts refuse to be translated into a whole that contains them. Rather, they generate a network of wholes, which manifest themselves in a condensation of different macrostructures. Before it becomes perceivable, this condensation must be translated into conceivable layers of order. The network of fragmented and layered traces of an immense pool of narratives that are either encapsulated in the etymological history of certain words or generated by the abundant mirroring and echoing devices can be ordered according to a multidimensional system of axes. Each signifying element occupies numerous spaces on the axes. Moreover, the different axes themselves relate to each other in various ways without allowing one to subsume them under one metaorder. This whole system of order, however, can hardly be experienced and consciously identified during a regular reading.

For a long time, conventional narrative has been grounded in a relative continuity of time, space, action, and character. Each element of such a narrative order is in principle able to form a verifiable temporal or spatial relationship to the other elements. On this basis, literary characters generate the effects of bounded subjectivities. The spatial, temporal, and personal axes allow for a meaningful relationship between the parts and the whole. A reading of *Finnegans Wake* cannot rely on such narrative conventions. The reader is not only faced with an inscrutable density of newly coined, alien, polyphonous, and polylingual words, but also with highly suggestive disruptions within words, syntax, and semantics. Moreover, these fissures and fault lines in the familiar grounds of our reading practices may not be sutured from a macrostructural perspective because the ordering principles of the *Wake*'s condensed macrostructure do not disclose themselves in the reading process and can at best only be reconstructed with an intense amount of intellectual labor. Order as such becomes a problem in the reception of *Finnegans Wake*. It also functions as one of its basic themes. At stake is not only the order of the text, but also the order of language and the world, and the relationship between words and worlds, as well as the conditions for the production and experience of order as such. The textual transgressions of the *Wake* thus cannot be reduced to experiences of chaos or anarchy, even though this experience is essential to the reception. The transgressions also function as ordering perspectives that complement, challenge, reorganize, and condense existing orders, thereby increasing their complexity and potential range. The pleasures of chaos and anarchy are counterbalanced by the pleasures of order and complexity.

This balancing device becomes crucial for the aesthetic experience of the *Wake*. If its linguistic transgressions were mere dissolutions of differentiation, we would be faced with textual entropy and/or a complete contingency that would leave us indifferent. In order to generate the energy that has accompanied the reception of *Finnegans Wake,* textual transgressions and dissolutions of order must draw from a different source of appeal or offer alternate differentiations. Apart from the archaic pleasures released by the network of textual condensations, the *Wake*'s suggestive power resides above all in its multiple mirroring and echoing devices. Binary opposition is among the few ordering principles of the *Wake* that are immediately accessible to aesthetic experience. Similarity and opposition, the two basic modes of relating, stimulate processes of selection and combination in the reader. Joyce has, in other words, retained those categories of order that Ferdinand de Saussure saw as the basic constituents of linguistic value.[20] Doubled figures of speech that mirror each other through similarities or oppositions provide a powerful organizing principle in the *Wake*. Its characters, too, are grouped in couples, siblings, doubles, or opponents who incorporate archetypal oppositions such as the masculine and the feminine, the polarization of generations or cultures, and the complementarity of twins or of a mirror self that functions as a double.

Binary oppositions in the *Wake*, however, serve less to emphasize contrasts or incompatibilities than to produce new syntheses. Hermetic or alchemical philosophies that assume the existence of a *coincidentia oppositorum* between microcosm and macrocosm are quoted in order to support this synthetic vision. Vico, Bruno, and Boehme, as well as the Upanishads and other Eastern philosophies, are evoked in a playful use of language magic. Mirrored in all great philosophies, these allusions, however, ironically produce the *coincidentia oppositorum* as "the antithetical meaning of primal words" *(Gegensinn der Urworte)*.[21] Often these magic correspondences in the *Wake* produce comic effects by using the old comic device of combining the sublime with the trivial. The endlessly repeated pattern of rise and fall, for example, places the biblical Fall on the same level with the different falls of the giant Finnegan, Humphrey Chimpden Earwicker, Satan in *Paradise Lost,* and even Humpty-Dumpty. This de-hierarchizing effect is only one of many in this gigantic language game, which divests all quoted philosophies of their exclusive or hierarchizing characteristics. The most basic effect consists in dissolving the two parts of a binary opposition into a myriad of different shapes so that they become submerged into the flow of language and begin to reflect the uncountable shapes of water rather than the two distinct shapes of binary opposites.

As we have seen, the various systems of order that underlie the macrostructure of *Finnegans Wake* lose their original organization during the process of their condensation. Condensing different systems of order inverts their ordering functions. In general, order reduces complexity and contingency. By contrast, the condensation of different systems of order in *Finnegans Wake* increases both complexity and contingency. The text fictionalizes the totality of human history by condensing histories and languages from all over the world, including their competitive philosophies and systems of order. The *Wake*'s macrostructure resists being read as a structure. Only if one interprets textual allusions to extratextual philosophies or systems of order as signals for the text's own organization can one actually project those orders back onto the macrostructure of the text. This is the only way in which *Finnegans Wake* incites a (re?)construction of macrostructural systems. Even though such projections help to order the text retrospectively, they produce a problem for the aesthetic experience. Reading as such cannot convey the macrostructural order, and yet the cultural or aesthetic appropriation of *Finnegans Wake* seems to depend on the plausibility of such an order. The cryptic character of this text, in fact, increases the need for establishing an overall perspective, a retrospective glance from a bird's-eye view.

The first major critical work that presented *Finnegans Wake* as a major work of construction containing a precise and elaborate macrostructural system of order was Clive Hart's 1962 book, *Structure and Motif in Finnegans Wake.*[22] Hart's analysis is especially interesting on the issues of textual boundaries, transgressions, and dissolutions, because all of the macrostructural models identified by Hart deal with dissolutions of order. Following Hart's description of the *Wake*'s organization into four books with different cycles of rise and fall—four dream cycles, four Viconian cycles, and the five cycles of the Upanishads—we could say that the *Wake* grounds its textual dissolutions and transgressions in different cultural models or philosophies in which the cycle of construction and dissolution is crucial as both a concept of historical change and as an organizing principle. According to Hart, the composition of each of the four books follows the pattern of construction, while the ending of each book (as well as of each chapter) simulates the dissolution of order necessary to the beginning of a new cycle. Seen from this perspective, the *Wake*'s macrostructure performs its transgressions of order not as a celebration of chaos; rather, it simulates chaos as a necessary phase in a cyclical process of continuous reshaping or renewal of order.

The Indian philosophy of the Upanishads assumes a special status in Hart's analysis of the structure of *Finnegans Wake.*[23] He reads the four chapters in analogy to the Ur-sound "om," which, in the Upanishads, symbolizes the path to cosmic transcendence. The Upanishads reveal the meaning and power of the sacred syllable "om," which as Ur-sound is composed of four constitutive elements, namely the three mores *a, u,* and *m* as well as *laya,* a coda whose figuration of dissolution and silence symbolizes the interaction of individuality and universality as well as the dissolution of opposites. Since "om" and "aum" as well as other Sanskrit words are evoked throughout *Finnegans Wake,* Sanskrit figures as one of the Ur-languages of the text. Like the *Wake,* Sanskrit is supposed to contain the whole universe and all other languages. The allusions to the Upanishads and the Ur-sound "om" evoke notions of cosmic transcendence. But, like all other philosophies, the Upanishads, too, are subsumed by the fluid textual form of the *Wake*. They lose the character of a model able to explain the universe of the *Wake*—without, however, losing their suggestive analogical power.

The same is true for the Viconian cycles, which also contain dissolutions integral to their processes of renewal. The mystic cycles of growth, decay, and renewal in Vico's philosophy of history repeat the archetypal structure of cosmologies in which dissolutions or destructions are the condition of the emergence of a new order. In the Viconian cycles, the three ages of the Divine, the Heroic, and the Human all end with a period of dissolution, the *recorso*. During the *recorso* the established order falls temporarily back into chaos. A new order is then required to continue the cycle. As Clive Hart has pointed out, Joyce's chapter endings, as well as the last chapters in each book, put much more weight on the dissolutions of the *recorso* than does Vico's own model.

The first book ends with the famous Anna Livia Plurabelle chapter, in which two washerwomen gossip about HCE and ALP. As darkness falls, they slowly turn into an elm and a stone. The river continues their murmurings, and the flow of language becomes oblivious to meaning, ebbing into rhythms and sounds. The penultimate chapter of the second book prepares its final dissolution with a gigantic carnivalesque language game. A dense entanglement of carnivalesque speech fragments and hybrids of different languages, styles, and dialects suggests festive activities in HCE's tavern. The "conversation" of the guests is intermingled with radio broadcasts and with the story of the Flying Dutchman, which in turn mirrors the story of HCE. We may infer that toward the end of the festivities, HCE, drunk and proven guilty, begins to dream the last chapter. His dream contains a vision of the emerging quarrel of the brothers, in which the dissolution of characters reaches its culmination. Stretched out on a mountain ridge, like the body of the giant at the beginning of the text, Shaun's body dissolves while spouting out alien voices that unite him with a whole genealogy of characters from Adam and Tim Finnegan to HCE. In oscillating linguistic figurations, Shaun evokes not only the history of Ireland but all of human history. His unbounded, wild, blasphemous, and contradictory speech mirrors that of the dying giant Finnegan and, since the whole text at one level is Finnegan's wake, turns into another miniature of the textual universe.

The last book consists of only one chapter, which figures as the *recorso* of the whole text. The increasing textual dissolution releases new characters, while the perspective slowly narrows down from the time of the druids to the present. *Finnegans Wake* dissolves into the long monologue of Anna Livia, which bespeaks a universal desire for dissolution. The river wants to break through its embankment in order to flow into the ocean. As abrupt as the awakening from a dream, the text's ending appears like the end of a dream, which brings about a new awakening that flows back into the beginning of the text: "A way a lone a last a loved a long the . . . riverrun . . ."[24]

All these patterns in *Finnegans Wake* suggest a new perspective on what we call order. The fact that order is conceived in cyclical rather than linear terms affects both Joyce's narrative time and the experience of reading. Since the text is not teleological or directed, one can traverse it without being bound to one specific direction. The lack of a clearly defined boundary for any ordered material in *Finnegans Wake* allows readers to shift between various possible orders. For the sake of readability, they have to make pragmatic and heuristic selections among them. But even when, like Clive Hart, we make a concrete macrostructural projection, we cannot simply say that this macrostructure contains the various microstructures of the text. The boundaries between the whole and the part are so unstable that we may be lured into believing what the *Wake* suggests—namely, that the whole is in each part or that each part *is* the whole. And yet, this collapse of clear boundaries hardly prevents us from trying out more of the constructions of order implicitly evoked in the text. The *Wake*'s stereoscopy of multidimensional orders thus depends upon an ordering gaze of the reader, which means that the order/universe of the text includes the reader.

Polylogicity

A single language appears more and more contemporaneous: the one which would be, after more than thirty years of distance, the equivalent of *Finnegans Wake*.

—*Julia Kristeva*[25]

The condensed forms of the *Wake* have far-reaching cultural implications, because the technique of using primary-process condensations opens the text not only toward the unconscious but also toward an inter- and multicultural field of global extension. Joyce's linguistic condensations are a form of cultural contact[26] capable of activating a very specific "political unconscious."[27] His condensed words often invoke vanished or repressed forms of language or popular knowledge and thus allude to the domination or colonization of one culture (especially the Irish one) by another. Moreover, on a larger scale, Joyce's condensations invoke multiple cultural and historical contexts whose unusual proximity or simultaneity opens up new flashes of insight.

Critics have interpreted Joyce's expansion of language in space and time—including the enfolded timelessness of the unconscious—not only as the fiction of a collective dream but also as that of a cosmic consciousness. This fiction condenses the most diverse times and spaces, cultures and styles, languages and philosophies along with the sacred and the profane, the abstract and the concrete. It establishes intertextual relations with other literary texts as well as intercultural relations with vastly different languages and cultural communities. The cultural implications of this inter- and multicultural "polylogicity"[28] seem nearly inexhaustible. It is true that the tight network of condensations, at times, threatens to exceed the boundaries of intersubjective communicability. But it also opens up a space of multicultural associations that reaches far beyond the English language and the Irish culture that form the core of the text. This core is to be understood as material rather than dominant, because specific cultural references are defunctionalized and thus set free to assume new meanings in contact with other languages, literatures, and cultures.

In her analysis of polylogicity, Julia Kristeva argues that each practice of signification, from the most archaic to the most artificial or experimental postmodern, also manifests itself as a form of subjectivity. For Kristeva, the multiplication of languages emerges as the only acceptable "positivity" in the signifying practices of a global culture. From this perspective, *Finnegans Wake* appears to be—as Kristeva and numerous other critics have claimed—one of the most radical paradigms of contemporaneity. But this claim only becomes interesting if we understand this contemporaneity as an effect of the peculiar timelessness of Joyce's text. The *Wake*'s process of signification creates a global synthesis of languages, codes, genres, styles, epochs, and cultures. Instead of using them as authoritative discourses, Joyce uses them as cultural materials, which undergo a thorough linguistic transformation and assume their own expressive power without ever falling prey to the temptations of totalization. This process also removes the fixation of cultural allusions and quotations to any specific historical context. Thus opened up to potentially endless new combinations, associations, and contextualizations, they become indeed both timeless and contemporaneous in the sense that they simultaneously establish associative links with many different cultures and historical times.

One cannot reduce Joyce's abundant use of some forty foreign languages to a mere phenomenon of polylingualism. All these languages evoke their own cultures and thus produce a paradoxical effect of extratextuality that by far exceeds the limits of cultural or linguistic competence that can be expected. But if we raise the question of the *Wake*'s readability, we have to consider the fact that this multiculturalism assumes a specific linguistic form. The *Wake* as a linguistic melting pot textualizes the foreign cultures so that multiculturalism appears as an effect of intertextuality. Despite the fact that language in the *Wake* has reduced its referential qualities to a minimum, the text paradoxically evokes an implosive quantity of possible referential languages and cultures. The following sentence illustrates how the *Wake*'s referential density severs the ties to one specific culture or historical time: "He would preach to the two turkies and dipdip all the dindians, this master the abbey, and give gold tidings to all that are in the bonze age of anteproresurrectionism to entrust their easter neappearance to Borsaiolini's house of hatcraft" (483.7–11). In one sentence, Joyce here invokes the times of religious imperialism and missionary colonization, the division of Turkey into a European and an Asian Turkey, and—mediated through the pun "dindians" which contains *dinde,* the French word for turkey—the baptism of the Indians (dip), the age of Japanese buddhism (bonze) condensed with the "bronze age" and Joyce's own "Italian time," marked by the Borsalino hat fashion and the culture of little pickpockets *(borsaiolini).* The condensation of multiple cultural and historical references prevents their convergence into a fiction of one stable historical world, with the effect that Joyce's universe appears as peculiarly worldless, a mere spectacle of textual effects. This paradoxical worldlessness generated by the condensation of all possible worlds inverts the familiar topos of language's eternal nostalgia for presence and its failure fully to grasp the world. Instead of speech becoming speechless in the face of the world, the world becomes worldless in the face of speech—paradoxically producing the effects of more worldliness than linear referential equations could ever produce.

This playful inversion of the topos of the failure of language to contain the complexities of the world can be traced on different levels of presentation. Foreign languages, for example, lose their primary meaning as foreign languages once they are melted into the text of the *Wake*. The criteria for their selection do not primarily reside in their foreignness nor in the signification of their words, but rather in their proximity to or resonance with English as the maternal language of the *Wake*. The artful construction of systems of linguistic correspondence on the levels of sound, rhythm, etymology, or meaning weaves the foreign languages so seamlessly into the text that they acquire new levels of signification generated by similarity and association. During this process of approximation, the famous "Wakisms" change the sign value of their assimilated signifiers in a way that the quoted cultural systems lose their conventional philosophical or ideological implications or effects. Like everything else in the text, cultures are turned into linguistic raw materials. The *unio mystica* between different philosophies or cultures is materialized as a mystical union of language games. Merged with each other and displayed on the surface structure of language, different cultures, languages, and literatures relativize each other and undermine the historical relations of power and domination while, at the same time, quoting them. The emphasis is shifted from mystic correspondence as a worldview to the process of generating mystic correspondances within and between different languages, literatures, mythologies, and cultures.

This demystifying effect is characteristic of the *Wake* in general. Within the melting pot of its condensations, this text draws upon the effects of a Bakhtinian carnivalization of language. Joyce quotes an arsenal of various popular carnivalesque practices. Legendary or fairy-tale characters, such as giants, the rainbow and leap-year girls, the four allegorical old men, and characters from nonsense literature, such as Humpty-Dumpty, are mixed with the burlesque characters of everyday Dublin. Evocations of eating, drinking, sexuality, fighting, blasphemies, insults, and curses—even the classical satire of academia—add to the carnivalesque effects. A whole range of other devices—the transformation of names into nicknames, the playful use of dialect, the aesthetization of gossip (especially over the incident in the park), travesties, parodies of grammar and rhetoric, and linguistic nonsense—all use the resources of grotesque realism in the disguise of linguistic condensation.[29]

In the popular carnival culture, laughter is commonly used to transgress cultural boundaries. According to Bakhtin, its basic functions are to violate taboos, to subvert established conventions and orders, and to destruct all static boundaries. A playfully self-ironic distance is often part of carnivalization. *Finnegans Wake* does all this within the linguistic transgressions of its carnivalesque language games. With its reaching toward a universal language able to voice the hidden unity of all humankind, the amalgamation of all possible foreign languages into the *Wake*'s maternal language can be seen as a self-ironic performance of a grandiose game of creation played by a narcissistic artist-god. But wherever God is evoked in the text, he does not appear as deus ex machina but, to use Jean Michel Rabaté's formulation, as "lapsus ex machina."[30] The very notion of a *unio mystica* or of a divine presence functions as a mere carnival mask without any pretensions toward totalization. This carnivalesque subversion of quoted mythologies also includes the romantic myth of the poet as the one who represents human totality.

Joyce's experimental radicalization of aesthetic freedom transgresses the framework of Bakhtinian carnivalization. Like all the cultural traditions quoted in the text, the various traditions of popular carnival cultures, too, function as elements of an artificial order of language. Joyce's highly artificial carnivalization of language nevertheless retains what Bakhtin sees as the most basic function of carnival, namely the restoration of an "active, accumulated memory."[31] *Finnegans Wake* cumulates a fictional memory of all languages. Containing traces of a historical or simply imagined past, present, and future, it gains the status of a privileged paradigm of global culture. Resistant to all normative restrictions, this "memory of language" merges disparate, contradictory, and incompatible elements. It brings to life whatever does not fit into any symbolic order. According to Bakhtin, breaking grammatical, syntactical, and semantic conventions is a precondition for the process of carnivalization, which subverts the norms of an epoch, establishes an interchange with other realities, and breaks the official, direct, and proprietary surface of the words.

By radicalizing all these functions of carnivalization, *Finnegans Wake* opens itself up not only to other languages and textual cultures but also to pretextual, or oral, cultures. The text condenses the arsenal of nonliterary, vernacular speech and popular culture and brings together early oral traditions with the classical forms of literary tradition or other "high" forms of speech. It thus challenges, as Ihab Hassan has argued, the very modernist notion of high literature by anticipating postmodern contaminations with pop culture on the one hand and a new gnosticism on the other. This new gnosticism combines the old gnostic dream with a new technological dream[32] in order to produce what Derrida calls a "supercomputer beside which the current technology of our computers and our microcomputerified archives and our translating machines remains a *bricolage* of a prehistoric child's toys."[33] The written and the oral, *écriture* and speech, are brought into a dialogical relationship that shuns the conventional boundaries between the two modes of language. Moreover, the text gives life to what commonly resists speech and breaks through what Bakhtin calls the "dead external layers" of conventional forms of discourse.

Here Joyce's strategy of inverting the flow of time also affects the history of linguistic forms. Joyce's condensations evoke a time before the Renaissance and before the invention of printing, which has forced languages to be unified into authoritative forms and systems. At the same time, Joyce's condensations also reach into the future by parodying in advance new forms of speech or technospeak with what Harriet Weaver called a "wholesale safety pun factory." This literary inversion of the historical development of languages and speech unearths a whole etymology of archaic meanings. It uses the liberties granted within the transitional space of poetic language in order to anticipate new connections, affinities, mutations, and transmutations that affect not only the words but also the reader: "Change, transubstantiation, the metamorphosis of gods, men, animals (especially insects), protean transformation affect the words as well as the reader, the contents of whose mind are also subject to change."[34]

Voicing the Text

Far from offering the lure of a return to the paradise of voices before the fall of language into writing, Joyce's condensation of sounds and signs explores the potential of sounds within signs and, vice versa, of signs within sounds. The conventional distinction between writing and speech is challenged in this text, which wants to be read aloud *and* to be perceived. The *Wake* is thus a writerly and a readerly text at one and the same time. Numerous Wakisms emerge from the sound of spoken words and thus appeal more to the ear than to the eye, while other effects are transmitted by the written signs of the text. Thus silent reading reverberates with the effects of a spoken text, and reading aloud resonates with the effects of a pictogram. More radically than any other text, *Finnegans Wake* transgresses the boundaries between writing and speech in a form of presentation that the text itself, emphasizing its tripartite focus, most adequately calls "verbivocovisual." Stephen Heath rightly insists on the necessity to read and hear the text simultaneously: "This 'soundscript' is not the reproduction of speech, but the ceaseless confrontation of writing and speech."[35]

This procedure clearly inverts the primary cultural modes of language usage. Since the invention of writing and printing, the functions of sign and meaning have dominated the cultural uses of language, and this dominance is reinforced psychogenetically by the cultural practices of language acquisition. Against this trend, *Finnegans Wake* reactivates the sensual dimensions of language, the materiality of speech/sound and writing/script, that is, the body of language in the largest sense of the word. Using Kristeva's notion of polylogue, one could say that Joyce privileges the semiotic over the culturally dominant symbolic functions of language and thus emphasizes the whole range of unconscious semiotizations.

Since in patriarchal cultures the formation of the semiotic occurs at a time when the mother figures most prominently in the infant's life, Kristeva desribes the semiotic as the space of a linguistic inscription of the maternal. Many French feminists, from Cixous to Irigaray, perceive the fluidity and openness of the semiotic as characteristic of their notion of an *écriture féminine* and celebrate Joyce as one of its proponents.[36] Joyce himself has clearly marked Anna Livia Plurabelle's rhythm as feminine speech, invoking the fluidity and uncountable shapes and murmurs of rivers. Throughout the *Wake*, he ironically opposes the mobility of women to the stasis of men: "woman formed mobile or man made static" (309.21–22).

At the same time, *Finnegans Wake* is also a text that resists what Derrida criticizes as "phonocentrism," that is, the privileging of the voice as an instrument of the self-transparency of meaning.[37] Derrida has, of course, paid careful attention to Joyce's textual play with voice and writing. In his words, "Now despite the need to 'phonetize,' despite this book's appeal for reading out loud, for song and timbre, something essential in it passes the understanding as well as the hearing: a graphic or literal dimension, a muteness which one could never pass over in silence."[38]

Joyce also inverts the conventional functions of language as defined by Husserl. For Husserl, the form of expression is not present to the experience during the constitution of meaning.[39] In order to experience the form of expression, one must consciously direct one's attention toward the materiality of language. According to Husserl, the constitution of meaning *(Bedeutungsvollzug)* and the constitution of sign *(Zeichenvollzug)* form a phenomenological unit, but the constitution of meaning is primary, since consciousness is normally restricted to it. Husserl also speaks of a "life within meanings." From this perspective, the act of reading would privilege the meaning of a text and its affective cathexis.

The cryptic form of the *Wake,* however, creates other conditions for reception. By refusing any "automatic" (Husserl's term) constitution of meaning, it confronts one with the materiality of the text. Instead of a life within meanings, the *Wake* requires a life within the body of language. The *Wake* does, of course, allow for partial constitutions of meaning and for the immediate realization of a pun or condensation. These partial meanings, however, do not spontaneously fall within an overall pattern of understanding the text. Whatever we can constitute as meanings in the *Wake* requires working through a resistant materiality of the text. On the other hand, this materiality is capable of eliciting numerous rewards, such as the pleasures of nonsense or surprise, of association, or of rhythmic, sonorous, or musical effects. The sound qualities do not simply complement or replace the constitution of meaning, but rather become an integral part of it. One could, of course, say that Joyce only radicalizes a common function of the sound qualities of poetic language in general. But within the genre of the novel—in which most readers include the *Wake*—the musicality of a text only rarely becomes a focus of reception. Here again Joyce plays with an inversion of a culturally dominant receptive disposition. Inversion, however, does not mean here that Joyce simply privileges voice and sound over writing and script, but that he overcomes their cultural polarization.

If we agree with Jacques Derrida that phonocentrism is a humiliation of writing by speech and a cultural repression of *écriture*,[40] we could say that *Finnegans Wake* by contrast performs an explosive increase in the potential space and a new valorization of *écriture*. But Joyce avoids any hierarchical revaluation. The celebration of *écriture* is not grounded in a respective devaluation of the phonetic but, on the contrary, in a parallel reinforcement of phonetic potential as well. *Finnegans Wake* increases the expressive potential of both *écriture* and speech by undermining the linearity of writing along with any linear concept of speech. Multidimensional notations as well as the simultaneity of primary-process condensations expand a one-dimensional line. The linear "grammatology" is turned, as Derrida says, into a "homography,"[41] or, as one could even say with regard to the tripartite "verbivocovisual," a hologram in which each element obeys a new holistic order.

In fact, the notion of a holographic order is evoked throughout the text. As we have seen, Joyce builds his project of writing the textual memory of an accumulated history of humankind on the structural idea of a representation of the whole in each of its parts. A symbol of this holographic order is the Great Letter. *Finnegans Wake* is figured as a text that enfolds within itself the whole universe and all other texts, while being itself enfolded within the Great Letter. Deposited in a mud-hill, this Great Letter is supposed to reveal the guilt of the eternal scapegoat HCE, which has been passed on to his sons. The origin and calligraphy of the Great Letter introduce the fifth chapter of the first book: the Letter is a miniature that mirrors the universe of *Finnegans Wake*. Belonging to many times and places, the Great Letter is highly overdetermined and assumes multiple meanings during numerous metamorphoses. Dictated by Anna Livia Plurabelle and written by Shem the Penman (or one of his historical predecessors), it evokes the revelation of Godfather by Mother Nature through the different stages of its fragmentary tradition in literature and myth.

The Great Letter replicates the tension between boundaries and unboundedness characteristic of the *Wake* in general. As a reservoir of all signifiers it forms a bounded unit; and yet, like *Finnegans Wake* itself, the Great Letter resists the confinements of a written document.

It subverts the rules of documentation and codification in an attempt to generate a language game that records what cannot be coded, thus posing as a rival to the history of written documents. Similarly, textual experience rivals lived experience, trying both to contain and outdo it. But, at the same time, the text also evokes the idea of a cryptogram with a secret code, or of the Great Letter as a hologram that contains—like *Finnegans Wake*—all other letters in each of its parts. The Great Letter contains the utopian notion of a form of written presentation that transcends the linear order of language and writing toward a simultaneous fiction that is freed from close ties to temporality. In competition with the conventional norms and rules of writing, *Finnegans Wake* creates a graph of its own that challenges the boundaries of phonetics, syntax, and semantics.

In this respect, the simultaneity of *Finnegans Wake* not only reflects the timelessness of the unconscious—a metaphor that itself basically refers to an alternative relationship to time—but it also reflects the time of writing as such. Joyce reflects a situation in which, due to the conditions of a global media culture, the readability of the world begins to assume new forms, according to which the time of writing might seem uneconomical. Joyce's own economy of signs and hieroglyphs explores the limits of readability in general. From a different perspective, it also exposes the decreasing readability of the world for the common reader. Due to the explosive potential of new communication technologies and new modes of information, this decrease, however, goes hand in hand with an increasing readability for the specialist. The difficulties in reading *Finnegans Wake* and the respective appeal to specialists thus only mirror a historical change in the readability of the world in general. From this perspective, *Finnegans Wake* can be seen as an early reaction to the threatened economy of the book in the face of increasing pressures toward simultaneous computation of the most diverse spheres. As a response to this challenge of writing, Joyce performs a language game that, instead of repressing writing (in Derrida's sense), expands the notion of writing and develops the dream of a written hologram that—like the Ur-sound "aum" or the Ur-writing of the Great Letter—is able to store in its unlimited memory all sounds and writings, past and future.

Ultimately, the empowering effects of the holographic model are based on the idea of an Ur-writing at the time of its technological reproduction. This Ur-writing reflects the multiculturalism and poly-centrism of a global culture and stimulates a syncretistic perception of all the languages and sounds condensed in it. Thus the *Wake*'s poetic language requires the reader to reactivate those faculties of syncretistic perception that have atrophied during the long historical period that saw writing reduced to phonetic writing. By breaking through grammatical, syntactic, and semantic rules, *Finnegans Wake* allows for an experience of writing that cannot be reduced to semantic information. On the contrary, by refusing to release enough semantic information, writing in *Finnegans Wake* draws its effects from the communicative potential of its materiality. The text thus induces an aesthetic experience of the asemantic body and the material order of language.

If we read the Ur-sound "aum" and the Ur-writing of the Great Letter as allegories for an implicit order of the text, they suggest a holistic notion of language that transcends our conventional uses of language. "Aum" and the Great Letter both evoke the idea of a holographic and holophonic textual order. Such an order activates functions of consciousness that transcend the structures of what we commonly associate with verbal thinking. In *Languages of the Brain,* the neuropsychologist Karl Pribram writes, "My hypothesis is that *all* thinking has, in addition to sign and symbol manipulation, a holographic component."[42] This component is grounded in an experience qualitatively different from a speech-oriented one. Usually, it is described as a syncretistic apperception comparable to unconscious or intuitive experience. As we have seen, Ehrenzweig's notion that unfocused attention and unconscious scanning are necessary components of aesthetic production and experience presupposes a similar holistic conception.

One of the cultural functions of *Finnegans Wake* consists in playing with the possibility of a holistic experience of language. If we assume with Wittgenstein that the boundaries of our language mark the boundaries of our world, we could say that *Finnegans Wake* draws its powerful effects from the seeming paradox that it uses the medium of language in order to transcend the boundaries of coded language(s). We can therefore say that the *Wake*'s poetic language explores a new way of exceeding what specific cultural codes define as the boundaries of language.

Eareye and Phonoscript

What can't be coded can be decorded if an ear aye sieze what no
eye ere grieved for. (482.34–36)

The idea of a "holistic reading" of *Finnegans Wake* does not seem so
farfetched if we recall that the presence of the whole in the part is
one of Joyce's favorite ideas. About *Ulysses* he supposedly said, "I
should like it to be possible to pick up any page of my book and know
at once what it is."[43] The sentence from *Finnegans Wake* used as the
introduction to this section can be read as reflecting an implicit holistic
aesthetic of the text. It refers to the *Wake*'s specific relationship between voice and script and calls for a new type of reading that focuses
on both aspects simultaneously. Since such a condensed reading is an
entirely unfamiliar and somewhat paradoxical aesthetic experience,
Jean Michel Rabaté rightly speaks of *Finnegans Wake*'s "performative
utopia."[44]

"What can't be coded" cannot be communicated as a message. Its
articulation requires an unbounded speech manifested in a singularity
that resists any code. What can't be coded also belongs to the unconscious of speech, which, like the Freudian unconscious, cannot be
subjected to the common historical erosion of codes, because it is
excluded from the symbolic order. However, the uncodable "can be
decorded." As a condensation of *decoded* and *recorded*, "decorded"
suggests that, paradoxically, the uncodable can be deciphered as well
as recorded. Once recorded, the uncodable would be preserved in a
way that resembles more the knotting or weaving of strings, or *cords*,
to form texture (French: *la corde, recorder*) than inscription in the
sense of writing. But at the same time, "de-corded" also implies an
unraveling, untangling, or unknotting of strings, which dissolves or
eliminates what had its form in the texture. The uncodable thus
follows the familiar Joycean pattern of "weaving, unweaving."[45]

The record of an event is, however, also its historically or legally
recoverable testimony. Decording the uncodable therefore renders
accessible what has been excluded from the official coded history. But
how does this decording tie into official history? The French word
recorder enriches the semantic field with the notion that the official
history can be "tied back" to the unofficial history, which has not
been coded but can be remembered (the Italian word *ricordare*), or

simply recur in the sense of a Viconian *recorso*. The unofficial history, in other words, recurs in the uncodable language of *Finnegans Wake*. Given their common etymological reference to the Latin *cors* (heart), *recorder* and *ricordare* also retain a sense of interiority. What is woven into texture forms a core and can be recorded in one's heart (Latin *cors*). But "de-corded" adds an element of repression or forgetting, so the text keeps an ambivalent balance between remembering and forgetting.

Musical connotations extend this spectrum of verbal associations. Beyond the more obvious connotations of a phonographic recording and a flute, the word "chord" offers a wider perspective. "Chord" refers both to the strings of a musical instrument and to the simultaneous sounding of notes: an accord that can be concordant or discordant. If the ear's activity deserves to be called "dec(h)ording" rather than "decoding," it can grasp ("an ear aye sieze") the audible materiality of sound. What an ear can grasp ("an ear aye sieze") are the sound qualities of language, which express themselves beyond the phonetic qualities—namely pitch, duration, timbre, intonation, volume, and spectrum. These qualities appeal to an auditive reception supplementary to the one stimulated by the phonetic dimension. Because these sound qualities do not function as carriers of semantic information, they usually do not become the object of decoding.

Our common reception of language seldom focuses on this kind of sound perception. "Dechording" will occur only if an ear can grasp particular sound qualities ("*if* an ear aye sieze"). The contrasting final part of the quoted sentence emphasizes this: Dechording can occur if the ear grasps what has escaped the eye. The eye is—at least in our visually oriented culture—the agent for perception of sharply delineated figures that, when focused, stand out against a background and catch the eye. After we have learned to read, the delineated figures of written language that the eye identifies come also to govern the aural perception of language.[46] Uncontaminated by the eye, the field of aural perception would be continuous and polyvalent. Once the eye imposes its own perceptual habits upon the ear, its divisions and decisions establish a dominance of the univocal and discontinuous. The eye decodes; the ear can "dechord" the uncodable only if it can gain access to sound that is not encased in the structure of linguistic entities. Such access is facilitated to the extent to which a text like Joyce's inverts the habitual hierarchical relationship between eye and ear. Instead of an eye dominating the ear—"eye ere"—the ear gains temporary priority over the eye—"ear aye." If the eye no longer determines the ear's perceptual figures, the reader will be freed to read "the ear seizes the eye" in Joyce's phrase "an ear aye seize." Because we are accustomed to read with our eyes, an order that "no eye ere grieved for" escapes our attention. Once we learn to pay more attention to the ear, we can grasp additional meanings. Then we will, in fact, be able to perceive what "no eye ere grieved for"—namely, what the symbolic order represses or deems uncodable. This is how Joyce's sentence recalls a forgotten history that cannot be experienced as long as the eye remains the dominant medium of linguistic codes.

Apart from being supported by the antiquated "aye" and "ere," the notion of a forgotten history can also be found in the larger context of the quoted sentence. It is present and yet absent in allusions to Irish place-names that have been anglicized in the course of history. This colonization of language, which has effaced the Irish roots from the official codes of spoken language, has also buried a part of the history underlying this colonization. They now emerge again in the poetic language of *Finnegans Wake*. Derrida analyzes Joyce's play with a hegemony of the English language in the *Wake*, "a *war* in which English tries to erase the other language or languages, to colonize them, to domesticate them, to present them for reading from only one angle."[47] This "contamination of the language of the master by the language he claims to subjugate"[48] is one of the core strategies of Joyce's carnivalization. Like the lost histories that reemerge in *Finnegans Wake*, its own language does not obey any master code. Historical words and meanings—"aye ere"—reappear as poetic ones. The old "counterpoint words"(482.34), enfolded within the new Wakisms, also allude to buried histories. As Sean Golden has argued, the effaced Irish place-names have, so to speak, slipped into the anglicized forms and become submerged in them. They are part of what the poetic language of *Finnegans Wake* brings to the surface again: "If the spelling of these anglicized placenames is ignored so that the pronunciation suggests the original Irish words, then the original meaning, in Irish, of anglicized placenames can be discerned ("if an ear aye sieze what no eye ere grieved for"). The result will be a simultaneous apperception of two names, sometimes with two different meanings, for the same place, in two languages."[49]

Place-names in *Finnegans Wake* are thus more than proper names for places. They are a space for the etymological storage of repressed Irish history and culture. They can be perceived at the very moment when the ear seizes the text and releases its phonetic potential.

The unraveling process of my reading has thus far mainly articulated some of the potential meanings enfolded in the quoted sentence. This sentence voices what had been repressed but tacitly recorded and preserved in traces over centuries by "etymythology."[50] Through his carnivalized etymologies, Joyce releases the accumulated memory of all those cultures whose hybridized words have found access to the *Wake*. Words and counterpoint words carry with them whole histories, which, though never spelled out, can now be reconstructed by the reader. The *Wake* can be called one of the first truly multicultural texts of our century. Apart from Irish history and culture, *Finnegans Wake* draws—as we have seen—upon a whole arsenal of histories and literatures of all written cultures, including the sacred texts of the major world religions. The quoted sentence, for example, also contains an echo of the Bible, that other Book of Books with which the *Wake* enters into an ironic competition. In "Epistle to the Corinthians," we find the following verses: "But as it is written, Eye hath not seen, nor ear heard, neither have entered into the heart of men, the things which God hath prepared for them that love him. But God hath revealed them unto us by his Spirit: for the Spirit searcheth all things, yea, the deep things of God."[51]

While the Bible evokes a revelation beyond language, one that does not need to pass through the eye or the ear, but is inspired by pure Spirit, Joyce instead evokes a revelation brought about by erasing the conventional boundaries between the two senses that ground language. For him, too, the Word becomes flesh, yet not through the Spirit, but through the material senses.

The most radical implications of Joyce's language games with eye and ear stretch far beyond a mere etymological or intertextual play. They reach for a utopia of reading where eye and ear would come together in a completely new way. Readers would not construct meaning through isolating words and sounds. Instead, the activities of eye and ear would be condensed in one single act of reception. By suggesting such a condensation of eye and ear, the *Wake*'s "soundscript" (219.17) projects the utopia of a synaesthetic reading. A precondition for this type of reading is that the mind dissolves the written "ear eye sieze" and "eye ere grieved for" into their phonetic gestalt. Instead of forming a relationship of changing dominance, ear and eye melt into "eareye" and "eyeear." This results in two different combinations of the same perceptual apparatus. The point is not so much that what we hear can be experienced visually and vice versa, but that we perform a synaesthetic reception of linguistic material as such. Eyeear reads as it would hear, and eareye hears as it would read. The effects of such a condensed reading reside in what the written signs refuse to articulate: the truly uncodable, which cannot be discursively formulated.

It is not enough to call this reading simultaneous. Eye and ear do not really perform separate but simultaneous activities. Once they cease to function as separate channels, sounds and sense become inseparable, too. No wonder that, given the historical and cultural formation of our senses, such a reading ultimately remains a utopia. It can never completely preclude a less utopian, concrete reading, the frustration of which Fritz Senn describes: "A large part of the irritation about *Finnegans Wake* is the certainty that we shall always remain deaf and blind to a great many potentialities of the text."[52]

On the other hand, the reading I have just developed would not have been possible had Joyce not already treated his linguistic material according to this utopia. Writing has been read phonetically, and the effect has been retranslated into writing. This manipulation of language leads to the paradoxical result that one possible meaning of "ear aye sieze what no eye ere grieved for" consists in legitimizing the very reading that generated the sentence in the first place—namely one that tries to synthesize the functions of the eye with those of the ear. The retrospective constitution of meaning so typical in *Finnegans Wake* culminates in this temporal paradox.

This process of a retrospective accumulation of meaning gains new relevance in light of the poststructuralist challenge of theories of signification. Both Lacan and Derrida ground their theories on the idea of a retrospective determination of meaning. In his reading of the *Wake,* Derrida sees this process radicalized to the point of a double bind produced by Joyce as a revenge against the God of Babel: "I order you and I forbid you to translate me, to interfere with my name, to give a body of writing to its vocalization."[53] According to Derrida, the inverted temporal order also places the translation of the text before its reading: "Translation has begun with the first reading, and even . . . before reading. There is scarcely anything but writing in translation, as Genesis tells us."[54] Within the temporal paradox of *Finnegans Wake* the retrospective melts together with the actual perspective. Endless Viconian spirals present what is chronologically separate as simultaneous. And, as John Paul Riquelme has pointed out, this spiraling paradox repeats itself within the *mise-en-abîme* of the book itself: "*Finnegans Wake:* Joyce wrote the book whose teller describes a writer who reads a book that resembles a book that Joyce wrote."[55]

A similar paradox marks the reading process. Joyce's reflection on language in the quoted sentence surpasses all familiar paradoxes of linguistic self-reflexivity from the paradox of the Cretan liar to Russell's barber of the regiment. It uses the meaning of a sentence in order to produce a sentence that produces this meaning. One could also imagine a different perspective: only a reading that tacitly performs the utopia of the text can prepare the ground for an interpretation that discovers this utopia within the text.

But this reading is already a secondary reading. It has been decoding by following the oscillation between eye and ear along linear linguistic units and by analyzing this process conceptually. The quoted sentence instead suggests a utopian primary reading, which would allow for a completely new aesthetic experience of meaning. A truly audiovisual reception of language not only creates meaning along the vertical flow of language; it also stimulates a horizontal reception, which focuses on the condensed knots of meaning. Thus the process of reading would have to be vertical and horizontal at the same time. It cannot simply follow one voice or melody that tells a story with other voices or melodies in the background. Like polyphonic music, *Finnegans Wake* seems ideally to call for a horizontal listening that distributes its attention simultaneously among several voices that are condensed into one single linguistic gestalt. There is no hierarchy among these voices; they cannot even be clearly distinguished from each other. Like polyphonic music, the text thus resists any focused attention that would select only a single figure. In other words, the experience of reading suggested in the quoted sentence on the eye and the ear requires a receptive disposition that Anton Ehrenzweig has called "multiple attention" and that emerges in the *Wake* as "abcedmindedness."

"Abcedmindedness" is a truly ingenious pun, because it points to the very paradox that forms the core of the Joycean utopia of reading.

The emphasis on "abc" reminds us that we will never be able to read language just like music, since the alphabet has already contaminated our ears. But on the other hand, as soon as we can let go of our alphabetic minds, we can "absentmindedly" grasp what we could never see or hear by focusing on one activity alone. "Abcedmindedness," then, is more than a linear reading or a horizontal listening; it requires a combination of the two. Only a horizontal "listenreading" that simultaneously engages eye and ear can respond to the *Wake*'s sound-script. Such a reading is grounded in the paradox that the reader has to let go of semantic fixations, while at the same time remaining deeply embedded in a written culture's reliance on the alphabet, the "abc."

If we could develop such a paradoxical receptive skill, we would be less dependent on chronological, linear, and vertical orders of the text and grasp its deep structure, which contains the order of the whole in each of its parts. Just as the quoted sentence contains an implicit conception of the reading of the whole text, Joyce envisioned an order of the *Wake* in which the order of the whole text would recur in all of its parts. James Atherton writes in *The Books at the Wake*: "In *Finnegans Wake* words are constructed so as to contain within themselves sufficient data to allow the structure of the work to be deduced from any typical word."[56] This means, as Klaus Reichert once said, that in the *Wake* each part *is* a whole.[57]

When critics have commented upon this structure of the *Wake*, they have mainly focused on the activity of deciphering, which in principle does with a word what it does with the whole text. We can, in a sense, as Klaus Reichert points out, experience the whole of *Finnegans Wake* in an exemplary way by deciphering one of its sentences. Joyce's implicit utopia of reading, however, also envisions a different form of experiencing the whole in its parts. As I have argued, this experience would require unfocused attention and proceed through unconscious scanning.[58] In addition to the familiar pleasures of deciphering, the unfocused horizontal reading of the text would temporarily release the reader from the selective functions of conscious memory. Ehren-zweig assumes that "horizontal hearing is totally blank as far as conscious memory is concerned."[59] If horizontal reading could make us forget, for a while, our acculturation into a symbolic order governed by alphabetical signs and textual memories, it could perceive in each part of *Finnegans Wake* a different and undifferentiated order of the text. From a different perspective, such a horizontal reading would not only reconstruct the surface order of *Finnegans Wake* but unconsciously scan what David Bohm calls the implicate or "enfolded order."[60] It is this unconscious scanning of the *Wake*'s enfolded order that may help to turn our reading into an aesthetic experience of "ear aye/eye ere."[61]

6

Not-I Fiction of a First Person Narrator: *The Unnamable*

How to Proceed?

First I'll say what I'm not, that's how they taught me to proceed,
then what I am, it's already under way, I have only to resume at
the place where I let myself be cowed. (p. 53)[1]

"At the end of my work there's nothing but dust—the namable. In
the last book—*L'innomable*—there's complete disintegration. No 'I,'
no 'have,' no 'being.' No nominative, no accusative, no verb. There
is no way to go on." While this was Samuel Beckett's response to *The
Unnamable* in his interview with Israel Shenker in 1956,[2] the unnamable's last words appear as a scathing rebuttal to his author: "I can't
go on, I'll go on." More than thirty years after its publication, Samuel
Beckett's *The Unnamable* still marks the cutting edge of contemporary
explorations of language and subjectivity. He probes the very limits
of dissolution and disintegration while firmly rejecting a philosophy
of depravation. How can we read this exhaustion of literary subjectivity without reducing it to a mere phenomenology of decay?

There is hardly any contemporary conception of subjectivity—be it
literary, philosophical, or psychological—for which *The Unnamable*
does not present a challenge. Beckett's text has a striking capacity to
incorporate the most diverse theories and conceptual models without
remaining caught in any one of them. It echoes numerous other
literary texts—not the least of which are Beckett's earlier novels—as
well as centuries of philosophical thought, both Eastern and Western,
and finally contemporary, especially psychoanalytic, theories of lan-

guage and the subject. The subversive power of Beckett's intertextuality is rooted less in a practice of quotation than in a practice of deconceptualization. Indeed, one of Beckett's main concerns is to explore the limits of conceptualization. His texts, however—just as his characters—ultimately resist and mock all attempts at being swallowed up by any specific conception. "The thing to avoid, I don't know why, is the spirit of system" (p. 4), says the unnamable laconically, amid his endless series of hopelessly systematic self-conceptions, each of which he rejects as soon as they materialize. Alas, readers and critics face the same paradox as the unnamable himself: "What am I to do, what shall I do, what should I do, in my situation, how proceed? By aporia pure and simple? Or by affirmations and negations invalidated as uttered, or sooner or later?" (p. 3). Most likely, our response will echo his own: "I can't go on, I'll go on."

Literary Subjects, Empirical Worlds, and Philosophies

But can that be called a life which vanishes when the subject is changed? (p. 92)

The unnamable seems to mock literary fictions whose characters are built according to the conventions of literary realism by exposing them to the light of philosophical models of subjectivity. But the inverse is also applicable, for he forces the most basic philosophical assumptions to collapse by testing them within the concreteness of a fictional life. It is impossible to confine this protagonist to any clearly delineated fictional world or philosophical model, since he merely traverses them in order to play them off one another. By constantly contradicting his own utterances and self-projections, he evokes the fleeting notion of a subject at the vanishing point. The medium of fiction grants him a space for probing epistemologies and ontologies that would be unavailable to either an empirical or a philosophical subject. Having left behind a literary tradition that evokes the illusion of an empirical world with empirical subjects, his referential systems always retain a theoretical dimension. However, the theories evoked in *The Unnamable* are also embedded in the concreteness of a fictional world. The narrator thus gains the peculiar status of a literary subject located on the boundary between an empirical subject and a transcendental subject of philosophy.[3] He uses his fictional space for exploring the aporias of any imaginable concept of the subject. He blames anonymous others for implanting alien concepts of himself in his mind and for forcing him to speak about himself. But in so speaking, he endlessly asserts that he can neither speak of himself nor keep himself from speaking about himself. A never-ending chain of affirmations and negations withdraws the ground for any utterance at the very moment it threatens to become even minimally assertive. "If only I were not obliged to manifest," he says (p. 10). This statement names the desire of the unnamable's paradoxical speech acts. In order *not* to manifest himself, he would have to be silent, but since he cannot be silent, he needs to speak endlessly so that he can efface whatever becomes manifest. Speaking, the unnamable refuses the position of a speaker and denies the validity of his speech. From this perspective, the very notion of attributing an "I" to this speaker becomes paradoxical.

What type of subjectivity manifests itself in this speech—provided that subjectivity is still the right word? A striking feature is its hybrid quality, produced by the peculiar merging of empirical and theoretical perspectives within a literary fiction. From a logical perspective, *The Unnamable* simply commits epistemological errors by confusing different levels of abstraction—the empirical, the philosophical, and the literary. But at the same time, the text plays with such epistemological errors in order to challenge established epistemological complacencies. It is true that at one level of abstraction the unnamable's literary subjectivity gains a privileged status over empirical, philosophical, and psychological models of subjectivity. However, the literary subject constitutes itself precisely by undermining the conditions of subjectivity defined in philosophical theories and in psychological theories of empirical subjects. Literary subjectivity in *The Unnamable* thus constitutes itself by effacing precisely that level of literary abstraction that distinguishes it from other conceptions or modes of subjectivity evoked in the text.

Despite this deliberate conflation, it is nearly impossible for readers *not* to distinguish different levels in the unnamable's discursive self-projections. It seems hard to read otherwise, and yet we become increasingly aware of the fact that our readings move against the grain of the text. We may know, for example, after a few pages that our discoveries of familiar features in the unnamable's subjectivity—be it a Cartesian scepsis, an existentialist paranoia, or a Kierkegaardian sickness unto death—will lead us nowhere or, worse, be exposed to the unnamable's sarcastic practice of negation and rejection; yet we can hardly prevent ourselves from responding with delight to every new philosophical allusion we find. This might create a feeling that we are caught in discursive traps, if not double binds; but then we immediately realize that this is what the unnamable's discourse is all about. So we finally accept that, if we are willing to follow the maze of this narrator's mind, we have no choice but to proceed, like the unnamable, "by aporia pure and simple"—which means that we have to mobilize, against our better judgment, all available concepts of subjectivity in order to expose them to Beckett's challenge.

The unnamable's invocations of diverse philosophical conceptions of the subject are pointedly approximated to symptomatology. As Beckett critics have convincingly argued, the ways in which the unnamable projects himself as the subject of his imaginary world have strong affinities to psychological dispositions of ontological insecurity or even a psychotic disintegration of the self.[4] Translated into the textual world of a literary character, these dispositions, however, undergo decisive transformations. Features that remind one of schizoid or paranoid structures of experience emerge primarily when the unnamable speaks under the compulsion of negating each manifestation of his self. In speaking of himself, the unnamable must keep himself free from any positive attribution. Constant qualifications and negations of his own utterances initiate a dynamic of increasing disintegration in his discourse. This disintegration appears to go hand in hand with a disintegration of his self. Utterances that the unnamable constructs in order to empty out his self-projections and reverse all manifestations threaten instead to revert to manifestations of an empty self. One can hardly ward off the impression that a metaphysical *horror vacui* in the presence of the unnamable's own emptiness is what motivates his maniacal replication of self-images that have to be destroyed as soon as they are produced. An empty self seems to be as threatening as a full self. This is why he must produce ever new images at the same time as he prevents them from becoming stable or constant.

Two reasons move him to maintain this discursive strategy of accelerated negations: each act of negation is supposed to mark his unbridgeable difference from any self-image as well as to protect him from being appropriated by anonymous others who impose their own images on him. All these rhetorical gestures of withholding are supported by fantasies of being devoured, of intrusions by others, of implosions or petrifications of the self. Together they create the impression of a schizoid subject threatened by disintegration and loss of reality in a paranoid world. Obsessed with the idea that even his own speech has been disowned, the unnamable tries to escape all the alien voices that speak through him. In psychological theories the frantic production of imaginary bodies and selves is commonly interpreted as an effort to fight self-dissolution. However, the unnamable voices desire for dissolution and unboundedness. His discourse is motivated not by a desire for either stablization or disintegration, but for the constant oscillation between the two. By insisting on this tension, the unnamable produces a discourse that hurls itself against the boundaries of subjectivity.

These notions of a schizoid and paranoid subject are only partially related to psychological concepts of the subject. From the very beginning, they are infiltrated by philosophical concepts of subjectivity, which make them more than mere fictions of pathological subjects in an empirical sense. Some of these philosophies are drawn from conceptions that assume an absolute ground of being—such as Plato, Descartes, Leibniz, or Fichte. Others insist on the irrevocable contingency and embeddedness of all being in the world or in textuality—such as Hume, Wittgenstein, or Derrida. I do not mean to imply that *The Unnamable* was in any way directly influenced by these philosophical positions, simply that they correspond to those played through in *The Unnamable*. We can thus, for example, easily find striking affinities with Wittgenstein's *Philosophical Investigations* (which appeared in the same year as *The Unnamable*) or with Derrida's work, which Beckett seems to anticipate. *The Unnamable* shares with all those philosophies a problematic relationship between language and subjectivity. Am I what I say, or can I be outside of it? Playing upon diverse variations of this question, the unnamable insists on a fundamental undecidability between the two alternatives. Thus his discourse exhausts a whole tradition of metaphysical questions. Am I in my body or in my mind, and can the two be separated? Am I what the gaze of the Other wants me to be—be it the gaze of anonymous others or concrete others, like Basil? Am I a windowless monad? Does my individual substance encompass infinity such that it cannot be encompassed itself? Can I only be identical to myself in pure reason or in silence? Is individuality or mediated textuality the condition of my self-consciousness? Am I an endless process? Is my I generated by symbolically mediated interactions with others? Do I have to give up my particularity in order to conceive of myself as a timeless subject of pure reason, or does such a timeless subjectivity dissolve me into nothingness? Do I speak or am I spoken by others, or even by a language from which I remain alienated?

These questions form the philosophical horizon of *The Unnamable*. They emerge from direct allusions or quotations, or they are evoked by similar figures of thought. The unnamable seems to carry them around like a burden of his philosophical heritage. But while these questions resonate throughout his discourse, he can no longer pose them with philosophical earnestness.

What happens to all these philosophical conceptions of the subject in *The Unnamable*?[5] The narrator transposes them with a sarcastic sense of humor into the imaginary shapes of his own subjectivity, envisioned under conditions of a quotidian world that dissolves their rigorous philosophical shapes. Snatched away from the aloof abstractions of a philosophical system and translated into the fiction of an empirical world, the conceptual consistency of these philosophies often dissolves into absurdity. The unnamable's trick is to take literally philosophical conceptions such as solipsism, dualism, and monism, and such philosophical assumptions as the objectification of the subject under the gaze of the Other, the unrepresentability of a subject-in-process, and the self-transparence obtained through mystical silence. By taking these things literally, he exposes their deepest aporias. In subjecting philosophical abstractions to the conditions of empirical concreteness, he produces a literary subjectivity that is subversive to both philosophical and empirical notions of the subject. Not even a literary subject can incorporate a dualistic Cartesian subject or a solipsistic Berkeleyan subject under empirical conditions without getting into serious difficulties.

These difficulties strongly resemble the difficulties encountered by persons with disturbed individuation or schizoid dissolution. At times, it looks as if *The Unnamable* lays bare the inherent paranoia of our whole philosophical tradition. Allen Thiher has interpreted this coincidence as a trademark of the postmodern schizo-text: "This view of the separation of language and self is a schizo-comedy that takes desperate delight in its own impossibility. In this respect Beckett's work ushers in the era of the schizo-text that is perhaps the postmodern text par excellence."[6]

By merging the two horizons of philosophical conceptions and schizoid dispositions, the discourse of the unnamable equivocates the epistemological premises of our cultural heritage with the symptomatology of schizoid disturbances. Notions of a cultural schizophrenia come to mind, which at first glance seem to support readings that proclaim the death of the subject. But what exactly is the status of the unnamable's schizo-discourse? How can we describe its literary subjectivity?

As we have seen, the whole text is marked by tensions and fissures within a subject who suffers from an unwanted and imposed subjectivity, but who at the same time must continue to produce more and more imaginary configurations of subjectivity. From whatever perspective we approach this subject, its very disposition will inevitably entangle us in paradox. Often the same utterance appears either as the expression of a subject suffering from intolerable social and psychological conditions (if one chooses the perspective of an empirical subject) or as the willful play of a philosophical subject who roams through its cultural heritage in search of a fitting frame for its mock-projections of subjectivity. From a third perspective, one could even assume a literary subject whose ontological insecurity results from its fictional status, but who is free to use a whole heritage of philosophical models in order ironically to expose the cultural conditions of both philosophical and empirical subjects in relation to language. Or, to use another formulation by Allen Thiher: "The schizoid suspension of logic allows the unnamable to live his narrative project as an experimental critique of language theory."[7]

Even the setting of the rudimentary narrative echoes one of the great texts of our philosophical tradition. The beginning of *The Unnamable* is full of resonances with Plato's "The Simile of the Cave."[8] Like Plato's cave dwellers, the unnamable seems to live in a cavelike space, unable to move or to see his own body. Like them, he has to develop his conception of the world and the self under conditions of sensual deprivation. But in constrast to them, he has inherited the conception of a three-dimensional world. Given his philosophical erudition, we might even suspect that he knows Plato's simile and plays with it by questioning the adequacy of both a two- and a three-dimensional model of the world or the self. These abstract mind games reveal that he possesses a conceptual sophistication the cave-dwellers lack. But it is precisely this philosophical erudition that opens up the abyss of his ontological insecurity. This lack of ontological stability has epistemological rather than psychological roots. The categories the unnamable finds in traditional philosophies all presuppose the notion of a finite, spatiotemporal, causal world. Taking seriously his fantasies of an unbounded, infinite subjectivity would require a four-dimensional continuum of time and space. Without it, he, like the cave-dwellers, would lack the conceptual tools to describe his world. In both cases, this lack of tools accounts for the necessary aporias of all projections of world and self, aporias of which the unnamable is fully aware, since he suffers from hyperconsciousness and must continually expose the inadequacies of all available means of thinking and speaking.

It is tempting to link the unnamable's epistemology of doubt with the tradition of metaphysical philosophies. Since Aristotle, the infinite and the unrepresentable have appeared as negative metaphysical definitions of individuality. From this perspective, the discourse of the unnamable sounds like a postmodern version of voicing the paradox of individuality. The unnamable indeed evokes philosophical notions of a pure I that reach as far back as antiquity and mysticism. Such a pure I would be beyond space and time, but also beyond thought and speech. In playfully pursuing this notion, the unnamable effaces all traces of self-consciousness and challenges even the illusion of an I. Paradoxically, however, the very project of imagining oneself as a nonconceptual I is itself a new conception. As such, the project already contains its own failure. As soon as the unnamable finds himself entrapped in anything definite, he tries to undermine it. But each utterance leads to new definitions and differentiations and thus establishes new boundaries that subsequently must be removed. The unnamable remains caught in the paradoxes of endless affirmations and negations, until he begins to shake the foundations of language itself. Only a literary subject can incorporate such an epistemological position with self-reflexivity. The level of abstraction at which the unnamable performs his epistemological games makes it possible to imagine a purely literary or textual subjectivity, which figures as an ironic postmodern substitute for the old metaphysical notion of a pure I. This notion, however, seems as hard to conceptualize as the unnamable himself.

Never Born and Buried before Time

You'll never be born again, what am I saying, you'll never have been born. (p. 128)

I alone am immortal, what can you expect, I can't get born. (p. 134)

In principle, a purely literary subject could be imagined as completely freed of a body. And yet, the unnamable demonstrates how hard it is to maintain the notion of a disembodied subject. He finds it as impossible to sever himself from the notion of a concrete body as to invent himself as pure consciousness. "It is well to establish the position of the body from the outset, before passing on to more important matters" (p. 22), he declares after numerous unsuccessful attempts to do precisely that. He can neither take his body for granted, nor can he maintain an internalized body image. As a result, his own corporeality becomes an object of investigation to which the unnamable turns with the meticulous obsession and the fantastic inventiveness of a pedantic philosopher. Even the mere existence of a human form with familiar organs is questioned. Suspending the idea of a conventional body, he uses diverse and changing imaginary bodies as artifical constructs for temporary incorporations.

At first, the unnamable retains the notion of a stationary, semihuman form with rudimentary sensory organs whose existence he deduces by self-observation. Since he hears voices, he concludes that he must have some kind of auditory passage, and since he perceives his immediate surroundings, he assumes that he has eyes. He speculates that he must also have hands because he is writing, but, at the same time, he is convinced that he cannot lift them from his knees. Soon, however, he has worn out the reliability of feigned self-observation as evidence of the body and replaces it with deliberately unrestricted inventions of the most bizarre bodily shapes or functions. He muses about the disappearance of certain body parts and imagines himself without legs, nose, and sex: "Why should I have a sex, who have no longer a nose? All those things have fallen, all the things that stick out, with me eyes my hair, without leaving a trace" (p. 23). The body turns more and more into an elastic form that can be molded at will.[9] The unnamable hardly conceals an uncanny pleasure in fragmenting and recomposing his imaginary bodies or in presenting them as obscene objects, often afflicted by infirmities. Finally, he abandons anthropomorphic forms altogether and envisions his body in the form of geometrical abstractions.

These phantasms of the body, in conjunction with imaginary reorganizations of organs or projections of organless bodies, question the very conditions for representing the body in literature.[10] Often they even violate cultural norms—as, for example, when the unnamable indulges in artificial conceptions of intimate bodily acts or functions. He produces phantasms of insemination, incarceration in the womb, and incomplete birth. At the same time, he is obsessed with phantasms of amputated limbs, a decaying and decomposing body, and a premature burial. These images are interspersed with de-eroticizing descriptions of the sexual organs and functions of the body, or with neutralizing abstractions of the common affective cathexis of bodily functions. Like the Lacanian phantasms of the fragmented body, the unnamable's imaginary bodies abound with severed limbs and reconstructed body parts or organs that have become autonomous. He even envisions an organless hearing and speaking: "Without an ear I'll have heard, and I'll have said it without a mouth" (p. 134). By transcending any notion of a functioning human body, these geometrical abstractions or condensations of bodily shapes, along with their vanishing, decomposing, and recomposing organs, evoke the notion of a literary subject who freely disposes of a series of highly artificial bodies. There is, of course, a whole literary tradition of carnivalesque literature that uses grotesque bodies to violate taboos regarding the human body. From this perspective, the phantasmatic bodies in *The Unnamable* appear as postmodern descendents of the grotesque bodies in carnivalesque cultures. But their bold conceptualization reaches far beyond a mere violation of cultural taboos. Rather than fantasizing bodies as grotesque distortions of empirical bodies, the unnamable tries to break with the notion of a given empirical body altogether. By stylizing grotesque bodies as literary phantasms (such as an organless ball that speaks without a mouth or a flat surface without interiority or emotions) he carnivalizes phantasmatic bodies. Instead of directly exposing or subverting social codifications of bodies, Beckett thus aims his literary images at the unconscious effects of such codifications, which may be traced in the multiple phantasms of the body. The carnivalization of social conventions of the body is replaced by a carnivalization of an unconscious spectacle of the body whose actors are imaginary bodies and body phantasms.

Deleuze and Guattari have read Samuel Beckett's characters as models of the schizo.[11] They see the organless bodies in *The Unnamable* as resulting from a sort of autopoiesis, a self-production that disturbs all cultural codes. They say that, like the schizo, the unnamable incorporates the illness of our epoch and figures as a universal producer, inseparable from his products.[12] Noncompletion is the imperative of this production, which is haunted by the fear of closure. Accordingly, the goal is no longer to produce a product—for example, the I—but rather to produce a dynamic of endless production. Without the illusion of an identity, the agent of this production continually reproduces himself in moments of pure intensity, void of any formal definition. Unwilling to assume the balance of a systemic entity, he traverses an unlimited number of stationary, metastable positions in which the distinctions between I and Not-I or inside and outside are no longer meaningful.

Undoubtedly, the unnamable voices similar dispositions. But rather than reproducing the basic features of a schizo, the unnamable seems to amalgamate the philosophical concept of the schizo as one among many other philosophical concepts in order to reveal its internal aporias. The unnamable projects his humanoid as well as his organless bodies without turning them into a foundation for a subjectivity—not even for the unbounded subjectivity of a schizo. To the extent that he empties his imaginary consructions of the stereotypes of human corporeality, his principles of forming and shaping become more and more autonomous. "All that matters is that I am round and hard, there must be a reason for that" (p. 306), he remarks, then wishfully assumes the form and consistency of an egg, or indulges in the fantasies of being a big talking ball, a cylinder, or simply a geometrical surface: "Perhaps that's what I am, the thing that divides the world in two, on the one side the outside, on the other the inside, that can be as thin as foil. I'm neither one side nor the other. I'm in the middle, I'm the partition. I've two surfaces and no thickness" (p. 134). Playfully mirroring, once again, in abstract form the conditions of Plato's cave-dwellers, the unnamable projects himself as a two-dimensional geometrical border creature within a three-dimensional space—a surface without outside, inside, or depth. By now, we have become used to the fact that, in *The Unnamable,* such fantasies are always open to multiple frames of reference. Apart from the Platonic allusions, this vision of the narrator also recalls numerous other philosophical conceptions such as the traditional theory of two worlds (Decartes and Kant) or the notion of the self as a worldless boundary (Husserl and Wittgenstein). At the same time, it also brings to mind psychological notions of the self as depth, and of the I as a surface—as in Freud's formula of the I as the projection of a surface.

From a psychological perspective, geometrical phantasms of the body are understood as creative artifacts produced by the I in order to ward off its dissolution.[13] The recourse to a simple order is commonly interpreted as an attempt to contain the onslaught of a complexity that threatens to revert into chaos. By creating very simple geometrical shapes as self-figurations, the subject tries to regain control by reducing unbearable complexity to primary structures. The image of the I as a surface, for example, neutralizes a depth that threatens the subject from within. Without interiority, the I can maintain itself as the projection of mere surface.[14] If one adapts this perspective to the conditions of literature, one could also say that the unnamable envisions himself as surface in order to neutralize the symbolic depth of a literary character and thus to assert the two-dimensionality of a textual being. While his early fantasies about his body are still inspired by stages of the decay or mutation of a conceivably empirical human body, the geometrical phantasms play with intricate imaginary equivocations between body and self. For the unnamable, such geometrical shapes must be especially attractive because of their seemingly inherent neutrality. They can either work against the dissolution of the I or prevent the stabilization of a definite form of the I. This irreducible ambiguity is fundamental for shaping the literary subjectivity of the unnamable. His imaginary bodies can function against tendencies of stabilization as well as against tendencies of dissolution, depending upon whether or not the unnamable assumes or rejects the notion of a formed I as the starting point. Shunning the conventional forms of the human body, these imaginary bodies also refuse the illusion of a physical ground for an I. We are thus faced with the paradoxical result that even though the delineated geometrical forms provide the clear boundary of a material shape, the unnamable prevents them from ever becoming reliable projections of either his body or his self.

This, however, brings us back to the disposition of a schizo. As Melanie Klein and others have convincingly argued, a very similar dynamic steers schizoid and schizophrenic productions of mechanistic or geometrical body images. The body as machine or simple form expresses the ambiguities of a psychotic disintegration and a "will to form" that tries to counteract it. Undoubtedly, the images of the unnamable often recall the conditions of psychotic disintegration. His concrete projections, however, complicate and transcend this framework. In the unnamable's discourse, the multiple phenomena of dissolution generally result from the explosive complexity of his ever changing provisional creations of body and self. This implies that they are not induced by a lack or a decrease of differentiation, but, on the contrary, by overdifferentiation. This explosion of complexity is a function of the narrator's rejection of any stable form or conceptualization. For the unnamable, even the most minimal notion of a bounded body or self appears as too much of a fixation. He therefore does not use his imaginary bodies to ground a self, but to ground the paradox of the impossible, yet inevitable, manifestation of an I.

Released from the fixations to an organic body, the first person narrator thus projects himself on the boundary between I and Not-I. But a subject without a self and a body cannot project an imaginary life because the very categories of birth, life, and death seem to depend upon the notion of an embodied subject. This is why the unnamable also projects himself on a boundary that marks neither life nor nonlife, death nor nondeath: he envisions himself as "unborn, yet buried before his time." For one never born, it does not make sense to project a life between birth and death. Endless fantasies of one who has never been born and therefore cannot die—interspersed with images of a prenatal or postmortal existence—engender the unnamable as a fictional character beyond those boundaries of a lifetime. "I can't get born" (p. 134) is the underlying theme of numerous fantasies, such as those of a dry sperm freezing in the linen of a bed, a lifeless creature who yearns for his impossible ending, or a fake human upon whom others try to impose the status of a living being in order to expect his paradoxical death. Other fantasies evoke the notion of "one buried before his time" (p. 149). A paradoxical dynamic of endless autogenesis, maintained only by continuing dissolutions of every manifested form, creates a paradoxical existence in which it is impossible either to live or to die. Imaginary self-figurations become the representational analogies of an unlimited nonbeing. Yet, at the same time, they assume changing and provisional, but nevertheless concrete, forms. They may, for example, temporarily materialize as a new character named Worm, who is born out of a condensation of prenatal and postmortal phantasms. Worm is an atavistic creature without being, or, as Ruby Cohn has said, "a larva conceived but not quite born, a maggot buried but not quite dead."[15] The unnamable describes him as follows: "He the famished one, and who, having nothing human, has nothing else, has nothing, is nothing. Come into the world unborn, abiding there unliving, with no hope of death, epicentre of joys, of griefs, of calm . . . On the outside of life we always were in the end" (p. 82).

Worm himself is, however, only one of many immortal frames for the nonselves that temporarily assume form in the discourse of the unnamable. Paradoxically, its form is formless. As a nothing on the outside of life, Worm does not appear to have a body, even though his name links him with the unnamable's prenatal and postmortal phantasms. If we can talk about the form of Worm at all, it is only in the sense that the unnamable creates a discursive form for him by naming him and speaking about him. But even this cannot be stated without qualifications, since it never becomes clear in the text if or when the unnamable is speaking about Worm or about himself. To use the name "Worm" would logically presuppose a minimum of difference between the two, but the unnamable performs his discourse about Worm as such a mirror reflex of his own situation that the logic of difference crumbles under the nauseating spirals of his reflections: "I'm like Worm, without voice or reason, I'm Worm, no if I were Worm I wouldn't know it, I wouldn't say it, I wouldn't say anything, I'd be Worm. But I don't say anything, I don't know anything, these voices are not mine . . . Who make me say that I can't be Worm, the inexpugnable . . . Who make me say that since I can't be he I must be he" (pp. 83–84).

Paradoxes of an Impossible and Unavoidable Subject

he who I know I am, that's all I know, who I cannot say
I am . . . (p. 161)

If we follow the unnamable's assertions that his I can no longer be
grounded in a body or a self while he nevertheless continues to say
"I," one question becomes more and more urgent: the question of
the possibility or impossibility of the I as pure textuality. How can
one talk about oneself without presupposing a speaking I? "I, say I.
Unbelieving" (p. 291) is the unnamable's very first utterance. Is this
an utterance about himself? Or does the unnamable put into question
that he possesses a core of unchallenged certainty about himself, a
so-called epistemic self-consciousness?[16] Does he merely doubt the
linguistic function of the personal pronoun of the first person singular?
The sober, analytic language philosopher would, of course, just diag-
nose a wrong use of language, arguing that "when the word 'I' is
used significantly it is not possible that the entity referred to does not
exist"[17] or "since I cannot doubt in my own case that I employ the
word 'I' significantly, the self-evidence from which Descartes pro-
ceeded arises—*cogito (loquor) ergo sum*."[18]

The unnamable's post-Cartesian mediations, however, start with
suspending any evidence of a *cogito (loquor) ergo sum*. The utterance
"I, say I. Unbelieving" is both a problem of language and a problem
of subjectivity. What kind of subjectivity and what use of language do
we have to presuppose, if we want to understand the unnamable's
discourse as meaningful?[19] Benveniste insisted on the close link between subjectivity and the functioning of pronouns in a linguistic
system. At times, the unnamable's discourse sounds like a literary echo
of such linguistic theories. But at other times he seems to parody the
general skepticism toward pronouns in contemporary theories of language, found not only in Benveniste, but also in de Saussure, Levi-
Strauss, Lacan, and Barthes: "It's the fault of the pronouns, there is
no name for me, no pronoun for me, all the trouble comes from that,
that, it's a kind of pronoun too, it isn't that either, I'm not that either"
(p. 164).

There seems to be a widespread theoretical consensus that subjectivity is linked to the functioning of the I within discourse. But in *The
Unnamable* an I speaks about itself and establishes so much distance

to itself within its discourse that it doubts the very possibility that the pronoun "I" could refer to a speaker or express a self-identification. The I itself becomes a paradox. Since the unnamable uses the pronoun not only to refer to himself but also to mark the distance to himself, the linguistic I is simultaneously a Not-I.[20] This is another dimension that the analytic language philosopher would have to exclude from the sphere of meaningful communication: "The talk of a 'not-I' is an absurdity, since as Aristotle already pointed out singular terms cannot be negated."[21]

Samuel Beckett, however, not only uses the term, he also develops a philosophy of the Not-I. Paradoxical formulations such as "I seem to speak, it is not I, about me, it is not about me" (p. 3) or "one who is not as I can never not be" (p. 16) or "where I am there is no one but me who am not" (p. 94) are typical of this paradoxical discourse, which tries to establish itself on a boundary between I and Not-I. From time to time, the unnamable intimates that all these boundaries on which he moves without acknowledging them—be it the boundary between I and Not-I, life and death, differentiation and undifferentition, or self and other—are produced as an effect of self-reflexive discursive acts without ontological foundation. The self-relationship of the unnamable thus turns increasingly into a problem of speech. Or, more precisely, the problems of this speech seem to result from the deliberate confusion of different levels of self-reference. The unnamable feigns the unhappy consciousness of a language philosopher who knows that the pronoun "I" only refers to the speech act in which it occurs, and who therefore pursues the paradoxical project to speak an I beyond language—which, in turn, keeps him imprisoned in unending self-reflexive spirals. If the use of "I" alone is already a self-referential speech act, the unnamable exaggerates this unwarranted self-referentiality by reflecting the difference between the pronoun "I" and the I of the speaker—thus building an abysmal self-reflexive distance into his own discourse. But since the difference between the pronoun "I" and the I of the speaker results from the abstract quality of linguistic signs and syntactic functions, the unnamable must undermine the foundations of language if he does not want to be trapped within a merely rhetorical problem.

As a consequence, the relationship between language and speaking subject itself becomes paradoxical. The unnamable rejects both the idea of a subject outside of discourse and the notion of an identity between speaking subject and discourse. This impasse remains deliberately unresolved in his discourse. How can a speaker mark the difference between himself and his speech without at the same time constituting himself *ex negativo* on a different level of abstraction as the one who marks the difference? How can one document one's absence from one's own speech without saying "I"? It seems impossible to speak of oneself without assuming the position of an I. The unnamable's willfully helpless attempt to blame everything on the pronouns and subsequently to avoid the pronoun "I" demonstrates all the more clearly that this is no option. "I shall not say I again, ever again, it's too farcical," he declares—only to end up with the very same problem of differentiating between I and Not-I on a higher level of abstraction. The pronoun "he," which he decides to use instead of the "I" soon becomes indistinguishable from the he that he had reserved for others such as Worm. The threat of forming with those others an unwanted identity—even if only the identity of a shared pronoun—eventually drives the unnamable back to using the "I," which then breaks forth in his discourse with a vengeance. Thus the paradox of an impossible and unavoidable I also founds the conditions of speech in *The Unnamable*.

Inventing and Being Invented

He speaks of me, as if I were he, as if I were not he . . . (p. 163)

Without a clear distinction between I and Not-I, it is impossible to establish a relationship to others. And yet the unnamable tenaciously clings to a notion of anonymous others who force him to speak of himself, who determine the rules of his language games, who impute a self and a voice on him, and who want to define him as a living being. At times, he fantasizes that he is indebted to them, expiating a crime unknown to him. There are also concrete others, characters from the earlier books of the trilogy. At the beginning, he describes how Malone passes by him, though not without immediately qualifying that it could also be Molloy with Malone's hat. Since he mistrusts his sensory organs as instruments of reality testing, he also doubts if these characters even exist outside of his imagination. He remains equally undecided about whether a cry he hears comes from himself or from another "definitely not human" creature.

At that stage he still perceives others as figures who are at least temporarily differentiated from him. But the same dynamic that marks his self-relationship also marks his relationship to others. As soon as the pure form of an other manifests itself, he must efface it again. His constant oscillation between differentiation and dedifferentiation erodes the boundaries between different characters. He even inverts the logical possiblity of understanding the whole textual world as his own projection by claiming that he has been invented by the other characters. For him, the boundaries between inventing and being invented no longer pertain.

The most tangible modes of relating to self and other are also the most extreme poles: paranoid rejection on the one hand, and dedifferentiating fusion on the other. In the case of the unnamable, even the latter is marked by paranoia. His fusions are never symbiotic unions that create a primordial oneness, but involuntary fusions induced by the logic of his own discourse or calculated acts of mimickry intended to deceive the others: "I'll put myself in him, I'll say he is I" (p. 159).

The process of this self-undermining genesis of self and other is intrinsically endless. Any self-genesis requires the differentiation of self and other. The unnamable, however, also acts under the compulsion retrospectively to negate any form of differentiation. The emergence of other bounded characters would be tantamount to the respective delineation of himself as a bounded character. This is why he must maintain the uncertainty of boundaries between himself and all other provisional characters. While his discourse begins formally as an impossible linguistic self-definition of a first person narrator, it moves toward a universal dedifferentiation of imaginary subjectivities. Once again, the unnamable moves along a boundary: he remains between self and other or differentiation and undifferentiation without ever being one or the other.

At the most simple level of textual self-reflexivity, the diffusion of boundaries between self and other appears in the form of a question of who invents whom.[22] Hyperconscious of his own fictionality, the unnamable long ago left behind any historical convention of distinguishing between the real and the imaginary. And yet, the question of the real seems to reappear through inversion when the unnamable begins questioning the fictionality of fiction. The fictionality of the real is one of the most powerful contemporary epistemological configurations, and it affects all disciplines, including those beyond the humanities. Beckett's insistence on questioning the fictionality of fiction adds an unsettling dimension to this episteme. While most contemporary theories tend toward challenging strict distinctions between the real and the imaginary, Beckett's diffusion of boundaries is more radical. Instead of simply assuming a dissolution of boundaries and a respective revaluation of the real as an "absent cause" (Althusser/Jameson), as an "effect of structure" (Lacan), or as a "simulacrum" (Baudrillard), Beckett's texts suggest a complete reorganization of the relationship between reality, fiction, and subjectivity on a different level of complexity and abstraction. The virtuosity with which the unnamable ultimately avoids the differentiation from as well as the fusion with others, and the definition of his fictional status as either real or imaginary indicates that instead of passively suffering from a diffusion of boundaries, he actively practices and reflects such a diffusion. He makes an art of inventing ever more complicated diffusions in order to subvert traditional epistemologies, not just to reverse or reject them. At the same time, he probes the possibilities and limitations of higher and more complex differentiations.

And yet, even though from the very outset everything is staged as a problem of discourse and textuality, the necessity of differentiating between reality and fiction is not removed, because it reappears on a higher level of abstraction as a problem of the reality of fiction within fiction. One of the most cherished poststructuralist rhetorical figures, the *mise-en-abîme*, is here not the end point but the starting point of a discourse that, instead of eliminating the questions of reality, the subject, and individuality as waste products of a humanistic heritage, grounds them differently by forcing humanist traditions from Cartesianism to existentialism beyond their own boundaries.

The *esse est percipi* serves as a starting point for endless fictions of subjectivity. Basil, for example, under whose gaze the unnamable seems to assume the form that Basil has invented for him, embodies the persecuting and petrifying gaze of the Other. Basil mobilizes the unnamable's existentialist heritage. In trying to escape Basil's gaze, the narrator traces the self-referential spirals of a Kierkegaard, a Sartre, or a Laing—including the postexistentialist spirals of a Lacan—to a point where they disperse under the illusion of infinity.

The determination of the subject by the gaze of the other/Other is, however, only a starting point. Translating this problem into its textual equivalent—the determination of the subject by the voice of the Other—the unnamable envisions speaking in alien voices. Yet it remains unclear whether others have disowned his voice or, vice versa, he has disowned the voices of others. He keeps inventing literary characters who seem to speak from within him, or whose voices he speaks—and whose invention he might be. The inversion of the creative act, in which characters invent their author—a core problem of literary self-reflexivity explored in its most simple form by Pirandello and Borges—is brought to its extreme in *The Unnamable*. A simple inversion would still maintain the boundaries between I and Not-I. This is why the unnamable must problematize the inversions as such. The problem of inventing or being invented no longer obeys a logic of "either . . . or" but a paradoxical logic of "both . . . and." The unnamable stylizes himself as the creator of literary characters who invent him.

This telescoping of inverted acts of invention ultimately feigns the disowning of another voice: that of the author, Samuel Beckett, who by inventing the unnamable is in turn invented by him. One must only prolong this endless perspective of inversion far enough back into the past to arrive at an ironic invocation of the God of the Old Testament as the original creator. The unnamable, or course, immediately rejects the idea of such a creator god as another perspective imposed by others: "They also gave me the low-down on God. They told me I depended on him, in the last analysis" (p. 13).

The God of the Old Testament who, like the unnamable, refuses to be named, possesses the very self-identity of an "I am who I am" from which the unnamable removes himself further and further in his discursive spirals. Absolute self-identity with one's own speech, without *différance,* is, however, the Other of the unnamable's discourse, its tacit obsession.[23] Due to the paradox of feigning absolute self-identity as the Other, the unnamable transforms the "I am who I am" of the Old Testament into his endless chain of paradoxical counterformulas such as "I am he" or "Where I am there is no one but me who am not."

Self-identity or fictionality of the subject, differentiation between the real and the imaginary, speech as a medium of realization or fictionalization of the subject—these are the obsessive questions that over and over again force the discourse of the unnamable back to reiterating the old metaphysical questions and their reformulations in contemporary theories of language and subjectivity. The unnamable shows how, driven toward their extreme implications, they can only be reformulated as a paradox. While he probes the paradoxes of both absolute self-identity and self-presence of the subject in discourse, at the same time he indirectly questions the possibility that a literary subject can ever *not* be identical with its discourse. Deliberate shifts between the positions of a philosophical versus an empirical versus a literary subject inevitably create epistemological ambiguities and paradoxes. If a literary subject tries to feign the same status in relation to its own discourse as if it were an empirical subject, while, at the same time, insisting on its pure fictionality, it becomes entangled in the paradoxes that result from the confusion of different levels of abstraction. On the other hand, this is only true if one assumes that the literary subject differs from the empirical subject because of its pure textuality. With deconstruction, however, we have become familiar with a new convention of defining subjects in general as pure textuality. Textualists conceive subjects in ways that resemble the fantasies of the unnamable—as, for example, when they insist that subjects have no depth or metaphysical dimension, and that they can only be experienced as textualities.

Beckett, however, poses a problem for this position, too: he posits a literary subject as textuality that posits itself as transtextual and thus generates an epistemological problem, which adds a new dimension to the philosophical controversies. Recent textualist theories have rejected the idea of a subject that could situate itself outside its own discourse. The unnamable, however, organizes his whole discourse precisely under this premise. He aspires to the philosophical notion of a unity of self and universe while, at the same time, insisting on their irreducible difference. He draws on a long philosophical tradition that has defined such a unity as the ineffable. Following this tradition, the unnamable sets out to demonstrate that the paradox of representing the unrepresentable is the ultimate paradox of subjectivity—for empirical, philosophical, and fictional subjects alike. At the same time, however, he refuses to let go of the notion of absolute self-identity. In fact, he demonstrates that it is intrinsic to the notion of unrepresentability, since only the dream of an absolute identity of the subject with its self-representations can engender the notion of unrepresentability.

But this awareness leads to yet another manifestation that inverts the premises: the more he refuses any illusion of representability, the more he indirectly asserts his singularity and individuality. They appear as what is truly unnamable but, at the same time, as what determines the very forms of his discourse. As Manfred Frank has argued, individuality in this sense would be without its double, it would not know any interior alterity.[24] From this perspective, one could interpret the unnamable as a literary character who produces his paradoxical discourse because he tries to do the impossible, namely to name the unnamable, the ineffable. What comes out at the other end of his paradoxical spirals of thought is an increasing awareness that because absolute self-presence in discourse is impossible, the subject is faced with the choice of either continually producing new self-projections or renouncing every attempt at self-presentation. The choice of endless self-productions leads to a hermeneutic of the subject; the choice of renunciation, to a mystic philosophy of the subject.

The unnamable moves between these two poles—between the extremes of an endless hermeneutic circle of self-production and an unattainable self-presence through mystic silence, between absolute and irreducible individuality and an existence beyond individual forms. His discourse settles for neither the one nor the other, even though he extends it toward both extremes. "*The Unnamable*," writes Ulrich Pothast, "has left individuality as a form of 'life' behind."[25]

But one can also argue that, for the unnamable, attaining individuality in his discourse is as impossible as attaining mystical self-presence in silence. Contemporary literature and theory share a desire to open language toward both extremes. If we take modern and postmodern attitudes toward language seriously, we must assume that the dream of metaphysical presence is over. Following a logic of "imagination dead, imagine," the unnamable, however, is haunted by the old dream in his eternally self-negating autopoiesis.

The two poles of discourse, endless self-exegesis and mystic silence, both maintain the notion that there is something beyond language. If one understands irreducible individuality as what is unrepresentable and cannot be translated into meaning, the movement of hermeneutic self-interpretation would strive toward a form of representation beyond meaning. But this would also mean a movement against the philosophical conception that argues we cannot meaningfully speak about what resists meaning; the unnamable rather demonstrates that we cannot meaningfully silence what resists meaning and that we therefore must voice it in paradoxical speech acts. The spiraling discourse of the unnamable thus constitutes less a Sartrean hermeneutic of silence (which could still be understood in existentialist terms) than a hermeneutic of paradox within which categories such as absolute individuality and irrevocable mediatedness, I and Not-I, and subject and object seem to collapse into each other.

Speaking toward Silence

My mind at peace, that is to say empty. (p. 31)

Even though the unnamable can never embrace the notion of mystical silence, his spirals of representational negativity seem to imply a secret teleology of ultimate silence. Silence forms an imaginary end point, if not the last myth, of this tortured discourse. But to reach mystical silence, it would not suffice simply to stop talking. The unnamable intimates that a mere renunciation of speech would not grant the peace of an empty consciousness; rather, it would provoke a metaphysical *horror vacui*. Silence in *The Unnamable* appears as the only possible space of an impossible self-presence. While speaking, the difference between the subject and its speech cannot be transcended. Only silence could possibly erase this difference. Since a first person narrator is, by definition, condemned to speak, he can at best use his discourse to project himself toward silence.

With this project, the unnamable follows the traces of Kierkegaard's sickness unto death. In his speaking toward silence the unnamable seems to be afflicted by all three variations of the Kierkegaardian sickness at once: he is "in despair at not being conscious of having a self" (Kierkegaard's "uneigentliche Verzweiflung," translated as "Despair Improperly So Called"), "in despair at not willing to be oneself," and "in despair at willing to be oneself."[26] The Kierkegaardian subject is a self-conscious synthesis of finality and infinity, and the sickness unto death is an imaginary despair of infinitude. "Imagination is the reflection of the process of infinitizing," according to Kierkegaard. "The self is reflection, and imagination is reflection, it is the counterfeit presentment of the self, which is the possibility of the self."[27] The unnamable, who cannot define himself between the boundaries of life and death, reveals obvious traits of a reflection that creates infinity.

Endlessly dealing with ending and not being able to end, his "speaking toward silence" moves toward an "evaporation in the infinite."[28] "The self thus leads a fantastic existence in abstract endeavor after infinity, or in abstract isolation, constantly lacking itself, from which it merely gets further and further away."[29] The infinite discourse of the unnamable is stylized as the speech of a nonliving being who fantasizes mystic silence as an unattainable teleology: "Strange task, which consists in speaking of oneself. Strange hope, turned toward silence and peace" (p. 31).

The infinite spirals of discourse reveal the structure of a secularized, profane negative theology. Just as negative theologies attempt to clear consciousness of every trace of a representation of God in order to approach God as pure nothingness, the unnamable tries to clear his consciousness of every trace of a representation of his self in order to experience himself in silence as pure nothingness—hence his dream of ultimate silence and an "empty mind at peace." His dilemma, however, seems to result from the compulsion to put this attempted progression toward silence into language. To speak of himself while at the same time obliterating every trace of the self, becomes a paradoxical task that resembles solving a koan in Zen Buddhism. In fact, the unnamable deliberately plays with such affinities to mysticism and eastern philosophies. His desire for a complete emptiness of mind and his fantasies of death and rebirth have adapted some of their assumptions to his own cultural situation and heritage.[30] Yet to adopt positively a mystic philosophy would mean for the unnamable to define himself in a way he tries to avoid. He thus evokes notions of mysticism only to assert that they remain as alien to him as all the other philosophies that have imposed their traces on his mind.

Silence and infinite discourse are the two poles of a contemporary obsession with transcending the conditions of representation and the symbolic order. Negatively or positively, all these attempts rely on the figure of self-presence and struggle with irreducible difference and imaginary self-formation. The dream of a pure speech that would allow for self-presence while retaining absolute individuality has a long tradition within mysticism. We find it, for example, in the notion of an Adamic language in both Christian and Jewish traditions. Contemporary philosophies revitalize this notion as a problem of self-realization versus mediation or self-alienation by the symbolic order. The unnamable shifts the focus from the phenomenon of self-presence within discourse to the paradox within the notion of self-presence as such. If the experience of self-presence is ineffable, its philosophical representation is haunted by paradox. The unnamable, however, shows that such a paradox is necessary and relevant for any self-reflexive presentation of subjectivity.[31] Instead of cherishing a new myth of absolute self-presence, the unnamable rather reveals the roots of those contemporary philosophies in which the mythology is still operating. The dream of mystic silence is therefore not an end point, but an unattainable counterpoint of his discourse.

Since the unnamable takes it for granted that he can neither be silent nor attain self-presence in speech, he performs a paradoxical act of speaking against language. This seems to be the only way of speaking while avoiding any manifestation of the subject within speech. In order to speak against language, he tries to empty language of its semantic content. The changes in the forms of his discourse might be read as a progressive fulfillment of this program. Since the unnamable negates all self-determination in speech, we are reduced to focusing on the ways in which he materializes himself in the forms of his discourse. What happens to this speech, once the unnamable withdraws more and more semantic crutches? At times, it seems as if he won a new freedom from those symbolic mediations he had rejected as impositions from anonymous others. But then again, it seems as if the singularity of his speech catches up with him and makes him assume an unwanted identity. Or does he find a way also to establish distance from the *forms* of his speech?

Discourse and Form

it drags on by itself, from word to word, a labouring whirl, you
are in it somewhere, everywhere (p. 161)

The compulsive structure of negation that marks the unnamable's discourse increasingly reduces what can still be said, and, at the same time, requires ever more complex forms of negation. Initially, this discourse still obeys the basic rules of secondary-process speech. Moreover, the richness and eccentricity of the unnamable's vocabulary, as well as his abundant philosophical allusions and the complexity of his reasoning, testify to an unusually high linguistic competence, a solid and broad education, and a hyperreflective mind. However, the very rules of discourse and the philosophical erudition he displays so eloquently belong to a symbolic order and a cultural tradition he rejects.

Given its intrinsic complexity, the discourse of the unnamable seems to unfold at the opposite pole from the primary-process language of *Finnegans Wake*. But the structure of negation indirectly subverts the conceptual organization of speech. The constant use of negation indicates a hyperactive function of judgment,[32] but this function is driven to such an extreme and to such a level of philosophical abstraction that its practical effects are undermined. From a purely linguistic point of view, the use of negation would indicate a speaker who can distinguish between I and Not-I and whose discourse operates within the symbolic order. Primary process does not know a logic of negation. The unnamable, however, inverts the original function of negation. While psychogenetically negation provides the basis of the capacity to say "I," the unnamable uses it to undermine this capacity.

This strategy reveals a general tendency of the unnamable to draw subversive energies from within specific norms of speech or traditions of thought. By driving a certain cultural or linguistic practice to its extreme, he generates paradoxes that are latent, but immanent, within the system. Ultimately, this strategy of subversion undermines the very means it uses. "Yes" and "no" are commonly used to stabilize a discourse and to exclude contradictions, but the constant oscillation between affirmation and negation in *The Unnamable* produces the opposite. A consciousness whose function of judgment is so exaggerated that it subjects every experience to the most scrupulous epistemological and ontological doubts can no longer work with a binary logic of affirmation and negation. It will instead maintain an undecidability and an insistence on paradox and contradiction. Instead of revealing that he lacks critical judgment, the unnamable demonstrates that the extreme use of it disperses all those propositional certainties that usually ground what we call self-consciousness. By driving his self-projections to the extreme, the unnamable loses any ground that would allow him to distinguish between self-consciousness and fictions of the self.

The structure of negation also has formal consequences. Since the whole discourse circles around the problem of I and Not-I, the negations of the unnamable inevitably and repeatedly return to the very premises he had previously rejected. But as the discourse keeps spiraling around the same problems, its rhythm accelerates centripetally—

with the effect that the spirals become narrower and narrower. Despite its general tendencies toward dissolution, the discourse possesses a precise inner structure, which at first follows the dynamic of a hyperactive mind, but then assumes more and more an internal dynamic of accelerated speech. The traditional function of negation—namely, to provide a criterion for judgment and differentiation—is discredited. Instead, negation is used to subvert the very foundations of language and subject. "With the yesses and noes it is different, they will come back to me as I go along and how, like a bird, to shit on them all without exception" (p. 4). The subversion has a double edge: by negating the very strategy of negation, the unnamable performs a double negation, which ordinarily converts into an affirmation. His negations, however, operate at different levels of abstraction, and therefore fail to be affirmative. Instead they become the basis of a self-reflexivity that uses the most basic operations of speech in order to put the subject in question. This has the paradoxical effect that, on a merely formal level, the unnamable indeed circumvents complete absorption by his speech. In other words, he escapes what postmodern theories describe as a disowning of the subject by its speech.

At the same time, as we recall, he formally maintains the incompatible norm of self-presence. His insistence on these two incompatible attitudes toward language makes it nearly impossible to define his relationship to his discourse without becoming entangled in contradiction or paradox. One possible resolution is to read the formal qualities of discourse as symptomatic of the status of the subject. The high degree of reflexivity alone can be taken as a signal that the unnamable does not simply succumb to a regressive dissolution of speech—not even when, toward the very end, he increasingly abandons the discursive mode in favor of sounds and babbles, which remind one of the primary-process speech of early childhood.

But instead of resulting from a regression to linguistic undifferentiation, these dissolutions turn out to be a product of the most extreme differentiation. With the ever more complex refinement of his thoughts, the unnamable has reached a point where further differentiation can no longer be translated into greater precision.[33] The loss of precision creates the impression of secondary undifferentiation. Instead of founding an I, which, for the unnamable, would require a reduction of complexity, the unnamable performs an implosion of complexity, which results in a diffusion of the I. But instead of passively succumbing to primary process, he radicalizes this mode of speech by generating it from within the secondary processes. The goal, as Floyd Merrell writes, is not an archaic pleasure in using primary process, but a secondary pleasure in controlling it: "Beckett goes a step further; he desires to bring the primary process under his domain, to make words, creativity, laughter, and *aporia* possible when two or more ordinarily incompatible domains are intersected."[34]

Speech in this process remains irreducibly ambivalent: on the one hand, the unnamable denounces it as an instrument of reducing complexity; on the other hand, he uses language against the conventions of speech in order to increase complexity. If language can ground the subject, this function can also be inverted. The unnamable produces paradoxes of subjectivity from within the dynamic of speech to subvert both language and the subject. After all, we need language even to think the paradox of "I am Not-I." For the purpose of probing this paradox in all its possible implications, the unnamable performs the most complex operations of language and exaggerates this performance to a point where language itself becomes paradox. This enables him to develop a subtle critique of language within his speech. But, at the same time, nearly inadvertently, the difference between subject and language begins to vanish more and more. The unnamable pushes the assumption of a subjectivity beyond language *ad absurdum,* since he produces his paradoxical subjectivity from within language. It would be simply inconceivable without the very language he deems so inadequate. The result is a different kind of language subjectivity than the one produced in *Finnegans Wake.* Instead of announcing the end of the subject, *The Unnamable* reveals the insistence of the subject in language—albeit against its own will.

For the unnamable, the unavoidable subject effect of language appears as a coercion—an imposition of a symbolic order that is Other. But, as J. E. Dearlove has shown, such a rejection of the power of language can only be motivated if we concede that there is a nonverbal core of the self: "On the one hand, he [the unnamable] is the formless, fluid speaker who rejects all that is alien to the nonverbal core of himself. On the other hand, he resides in the fixed shapes and external orders of his spoken words."[35]

It is precisely this tension between a subjectivity of language and its nonverbal core that drives the unnamable to invent himself as a paradox in language. Far from effacing the words and silencing the voices in order to reveal a subjectivity freed from language—the non-verbal core of his empty mind—the unnamable develops a hermeneutic of paradox in order to document his inseparability from language at the precise moment when he attempts to locate himself outside the symbolic order. Instead of dissolving his subjectivity into nothingness, he infinitely expands it through operations based solely on language. In light of the unnamable's paradoxial discourse, the notion of a subject freed from language appears as reductive as the notion of a language freed from the subject.

Rhythms of Emotions in Language

nothing but emotion, bing bang (p. 170)

Since the unnamable can become neither identical with nor different from his discourse, he oscillates between the complementary fictions of a nonverbal core subjectivity and a discourse without subject. This oscillation regulates the shifting distance to his own utterances as well as the rhythm and affective dynamic of his discourse. As all fictions about ourselves, the fictions of the unnamable, too, reveal an intense affective cathexis. It is difficult to decide how much affective distance the unnamable really possesses to his own discourse. It might indeed even seem impossible to decide when the unnamable is controlling his discourse and when he is losing himself in it. This distinction, however, becomes crucial for interpreting his subjectivity. *The Unnamable* reiterates the complex dynamic between master and slave (which commonly characterizes the relationship between Beckett characters) as a dynamic between language and subject. As we have seen, the unnamable uses negation to prevent himself from being subsumed by language, but the further he drives this process and the more complex it becomes, the more he is in danger of becoming identical with his discourse. Negation turns into negative fixation.

This dynamic can be traced within the rhythms of speech. Initially, his discourse remains segmented by passages with short sentences that obey conventional rules of grammar and punctuation. Even the spirals of argumentation can be followed without too much difficulty. Increasingly, however, passages of speech and sentences dissolve into rhythmical fragments. Ever longer, uninterrupted sentences finally merge into a flood of mere parataxes. The affective cathexis of speech seems to increase proportionally to the decrease in its designative or semantic definition. This much, at least, we could conclude if we read the formal and rhythmical elements as affective expressions. We would notice the accelerated rhythm, the repetition of highly affective core words such as "silence" or "I," and the emancipation of formal qualities from semantic connotations, often exaggerated to the point of linguistic nonsense. The more the discourse begins to resemble primary processes, the more its energies seem to increase—which would confirm Freud's hypothesis of a decrease of energy in secondary processes.[36]

But things in *The Unnamable* are never as simple as they at first appear. If there was indeed an increasing affective cathexis of language, it would indicate decreasing distance between the unnamable and his discourse. Initially, this is still countered by increasing assertions of a complete nonidentity between speaker and speech. We could, of course, interpret such assertions as a defense. But even then they show that, for the unnamable, reflexivity as a medium of distancing begins to erode and collapse into entropic diffusion. This collapse of reflexivity happens at precisely that moment when the unnamable reacts by deliberately activating primary forms of distancing in his regressions to linguistic nonsense: "I'll laugh, that's how it will end, in a chuckle, chuck, chuck, ow, ha, pa, I'll practice, nyum, hoo, plop, pss, nothing but emotion, bing bang, that's blows, ugh, pooh, what else, oooh, aaah, that's love, enough, it's tiring, hee, hee . . ." (p. 170). Such an asemantic conglomeration of sounds recalls the spontaneous production of so-called glossolalia—a form of linguistic nonsense that is supposed to indicate a breakthrough of the pleasure principle in language.[37] But the unnamable only mimics this original discharge of affect. In announcing his glossolalia as "inarticulate murmurs, to be invented" (p. 170), he reveals a fully conscious and intentional utterance. If he has to "invent" archaic forms of language, their function does not unfold spontaneously. Instead, they are used in a calculated way to void the semantic content of discourse. The assertion "I'll practice" makes it clear that the unnamable does not produce linguistic nonsense in a spontaneous game with words and sounds. Rather, he uses nonsense as one of the possibilities to subvert his discourse even further and to enhance his paradoxical pleasure of controlling the pleasure principle.

He practices yet another form of regression when he uses foul language to spice up the phantasms of his body. The sarcastic pleasure he takes in obscene and scatological fantasies also enhances their ability to undermine the potential philosophical gravity of his reflections. Significantly, these interspersed vulgarities emerge whenever his discourse threatens to assume conceptual density or reach a level that smacks of philosophy. He particularly likes to fall back on them when his hyperconscious reflections collapse under their overcomplexity. As in the case of the glossolalia, the affective cathexis of these obscene images of the body is broken. They are not, as one might expect, used as a spontaneous assertion of the pleasure principle against the dominance of the reality principle and the cultural exclusion of the organic drama of the body from language. Rather, the unnamable uses artificial phantasms and obscene images of the body in a calculated way as an aggressive rhetorical strategy against the civilizing forces in language. Once again, his subversion is not figured as a spontaneous regression or a lapse into anarchy, but as a reflected and controlled act of speech.

On one level, the recourse to nonsense or to the obscene is just a further step in the unnamable's resistance to philosophical conceptualization. The dynamic of form in his discourse is governed by shifts in rhetorical strategies. Such shifts are necessary because the unnamable wears out each strategy by overusing it. The strategy of negation, for example, threatens to become a systematic philosophy of negativity, but for the unnamable, the "thing to avoid is the spirit of system" (p. 4). A philosophy of negativity could be interpreted and ideologized as the negative self-definition of a paradoxical subject forced to reject any self-manifestation.

We can thus conclude that, paradoxically enough, the unnamable deliberately uses rhetorical strategies like nonsense or obscene language not only in order to mock reflection and self-consciousness, but also to defer the failure of his self-reflexive spirals. He has it both ways: he undermines conceptual self-definition, but at the same time he neutralizes any traceable affective cathexis of his discourse. What appears at first glance to be linguistic traces of affect turns out to be only a willfully deceptive mimicking. His disguised affective abstinence then becomes just another strategy of speaking without manifesting himself.

This, of course, counteracts the initial impression of an increasing affective cathexis of language. Since, at the semantic level, affects are only mimicked, the last resource for measuring the unnamable's distance toward his speech is its changing rhythms. There are no signals in the text to indicate that the unnamable deliberately controls these rhythms. One could therefore assume that the more he tries to distance himself from all semantic manifestations, the more he inadvertently inscribes himself into the rhythms of his speech. This perspective would account for the increasing formal dissolution of language. Due to longer and longer paratactical sentences, speech becomes more and more leveled. Repetition of core sentences, words, and syllables makes the whole discourse more rhythmical but also more monotonous. The rhythm of speech begins to dominate over the semantic content, especially since its increasing uniformity and redundancy undermines the sparse reminders of narrative tension. The text eventually gains a stronger equilibrium toward the end, but it appears to result from textual entropy rather than from the narrator's mental balance. The unnamable seems to have eventually succeeded in emptying language of semantic content, but this does not help him in finding the "peace of an empty mind."

With his repetition of sounds and rhythms toward the end of his discourse, the unnamable activates an ancient technique of separating language from meaning, which has been used for centuries in the most diverse cultural contexts. Children love to keep repeating a word until its meaning disappears behind the sound. Eastern meditative practices use the repetition of internally spoken mantras in order to transcend consciousness. All these practices use sound and rhythm in order to detach language from meaning and endow it with magic or spiritual power. Evidently, however, the unnamable does not use language like a mantra or a playful nonsense game. Despite his dream of the meditative peace of an empty mind, his frenzy to avoid semantic manifestation ties him negatively to semantics. His hypersuspicious awareness of the semantic traps of language is maintained until the very end. Instead of moving toward silence, his discourse moves away from it. After a deceptive transitory period of rhythmic stabilization, his rhythms become increasingly hectic and ruptured. As Bruce Kavin writes, "The literature of the ineffable, in contrast to the language game of OM, accepts the conditions of time and fragmentation."[38]

We can conclude that even the ultimate recourse to rhythm and sound is marked by the unnamable's fundamental ambivalence toward language and subjectivity. The rhythms of speech form a countermovement to silence and reveal, behind all suspicion, a deeply rooted negative fixation to language. If the unnamable's speech were indeed a speech toward silence, its emptiness would have to be both semantic and affective. The forms of discourse, however, reveal how silence is at best a superficial teleology, an impossible dream performed by the unnamable in full knowledge that it can never be attained. Silence as the declared goal of speech is counteracted by the practice of speech. This tension is also mirrored as a tension between syntax and semantics. The further the unnamable proceeds in dissolving syntactic units, the harder it becomes semantically to evoke the cherished notion of silence: "I want it to go silent, it wants to go silent, it can't, it goes for a second, then it starts again, that's not the real silence, it says that's not the real silence, what can be said of the real silence . . ." (pp. 170–171).

The unnamable, who never wanted to occupy a space within language, seems to dissolve into the forms of his discourse. He, who wanted to renounce the use of the pronoun "I" in order to destroy the illusion of an identity with his speech, ends up producing a discourse more prolific in "I's" than any other conceivable text of the same length. *The Unnamable* ends as it began: with a paradox. The dream of silence, dream silence, generates an encompassing spiral of utterances that leads the speaker back to the impossible origin of his unending speech: "Before the door that opens on my story, that would surprise me, if it opens, it will be I, it will be the silence, where I am, I don't know, I'll never know, in the silence, you don't know, you must go on, I can't go on, I'll go on" (p. 179).

Aesthetic Experience

then it must be murmurs, and listening, someone listening, no
need of an ear, no need of a mouth, the voice listens (p. 171)

The fundamental ambivalence toward the spirit of system in *The Unnamable* also marks its aesthetic experience. Samuel Beckett's texts fascinate and threaten with experiences of primary undifferentiation. They elicit in the reader deeply rooted, often unconscious memories of such experiences. The fact that *The Unnamable* deploys such a high level of self-reflection without succumbing to the traps of consciousness and is also so close to primary processes without becoming entrapped by the unconscious accounts for this text's insistent effects on both a conscious and unconscious level.[39] This also accounts for its inherent openness, its seemingly endless number of possible interpretations, and its resistance to being understood from any one philosophical or theoretical perspective.

It is the dissolution of language and subjectivity in *The Unnamable* that has provoked the strongest reaction in readers and critics of this text. Its reception has been marked by our cultural ambivalence toward dissolutions of order and transgressions of boundaries, and especially toward primary processes, experiences of undifferentiation, and dissolutions of the self. But the cultural artifices of the unnamable, his unbounded imagination, his hyperconscious abstractions, his black humor and biting self-irony or his pleasurably pedantic obsessions all remove this dissolution of the subject from its archaic ground. Familiar psychological configurations are turned into abstract figurations of subjectivity.

These figurations unfold their conscious and unconscious effects simultaneously but at different levels. At a conscious level, the reader must follow all the paradoxical reasonings of the unnamable as he performs his tightrope walk on the boundary between I and Not-I with the artistic skill of a pedantic perfectionist. The more the first person narrator undermines the notion of an I, the more the reader, in order not to lose all imaginary ground, feels compelled to cling to whatever becomes manifest of this narrator. This produces the paradoxical effect of a loss of distance in the reader. It seems impossible to maintain an aesthetic distance in relation to a text which, like its narrator, cannot ever really be grasped. The absorption of the reader by the text becomes a condition of its reception. Whoever resists this dynamic will not be able to follow the unnamable into the abyss of his dedifferentiations. The pains and pleasures of this first person narrator might truly overwhelm the reader in an initial attempt to follow his acrobatic mind games. One can hardly avoid the full force of this text's explosive complexity, which always threatens to fall into a secondary undifferentiation. For these initial effects might all of a sudden mutate into their opposite: the pleasures or pains of order might turn into pleasures or pains of chaos—which appears as the inverse of pedantic order. By generating chaos from within order and order from within chaos, the unnamable polarizes them to a point where the difference between them is harder and harder to discern.

As we have seen, he also collapses other deeply ingrained cultural oppositions, such as that between I and Not-I or self and other. Ultimately, as Floyd Merrell has shown, even the very difference between "I am I" and "I am Not-I" is obliterated: "'I am I,' then, can be referred to *either* as *identity* or *difference*. It makes no *difference*. If *identical*, there is no discrimination—at one level—and if *different*, there is *nothing but* discrimination . . . Both 'I = I' and I # I are simultaneously right *and* wrong, at the deeper level."[40]

These plays with diffusions of boundaries, undecidabilities, and paradox provoke highly ambivalent reactions, since they break away from an order that defines opposites as incompatible with each other. As long as the unnamable oscillates between differentiation and undifferentiation, he cannot be perceived as a bounded literary character. He thus forces the reader also to follow the paradoxical strategies he uses to avoid the traps of subjectivity. The process of having to follow his self-reflexive flight from the self entangles the reader more intricately with the unnamable than if he were a bounded literary character. The diffusion between I and Not-I requires a closeness to the unnamable that results less from empathy or fascination with undifferentiatedness than from a loss of distance due to lack of orientation and certainty. The reader must at least temporarily adapt to the conditions of this text—with the hope of perhaps reducing its complexity retrospectively in a more distanced aesthetic reflection. *The Unnamable* thus produces its most profound initial effects more through its elaborate form than through the depiction of an imaginary world. Narrative voice and forms of speech counteract all semantic manifestations and prevent the reader from forming imaginary identifications. In other words, closeness is established as an effect of structure.

In fact, two different forms of closeness to the text need to be distinguished: one results from its hyperreflexivity; the other, from its affinities to primary processes and its respective appeals to the unconscious. But these two strategies of establishing a closeness between reader and text are inextricably tied to distancing strategies. The narrator's negations compel the reader to establish a self-reflexive distance in an attempt to determine the status of the fictional discourse from an outside perspective. One aesthetic device in *The Unnamable* particularly underscores this activity: the self-reflexive metalevel at which the text exposes itself as fictional with a fictional first person narrator. This metalevel grants the reader a certain distance from the overly complex reflections of the unnamable and allows him or her a certain reduction of complexity. But, at the same time, this metalevel shifts the focus from the subjectivity of the unnamable to the aesthetic devices that have produced this subjectivity.

The Unnamable engenders a peculiar aesthetic experience of the genesis of a literary character. As we have seen, the first person narrator performs his literary autopoiesis in contrast to the psychogenesis of the subject on the one hand and to philosophical foundations of subjectivity on the other. By fusing these two cultural formations of the subject, he creates a paradoxical subjectivity that can only be lived by a literary subject. His core problem, the relationship of the subject to its speech, changes with varying perspectives. The status of this relationship depends upon whether we assume that this subject is the fiction of an empirical subject, a philosophical subject, or the self-reflexive fiction of a literary subject. From a purely logical point of view, a literary subject cannot possess any subjectivity distinct from its textuality. In other words, a literary subject confirms undisputedly what theories of textuality claim in general: that there is no subjectivity beyond textuality. But we can just as easily read the whole discourse of the unnamable as an attempt to undermine this certainty along with all the others.

What is the aesthetic experience of the pure textuality of the un-namable like? As literary texts are concretized only in the reading process, the subjectivity of the unnamable is to a certain extent an effect of aesthetic experience. The unnamable can only constitute himself as a subject in interaction with a reader. But if we take this position seriously, he would no longer be protected from transtextual interferences—that is, from projections made by readers, those anonymous others from whom he is trying all along to escape. And what if he were conceived as a literary character whose subjectivity becomes manifest first and foremost in these projections, but who also tries continually to undermine them?

From this perspective, it becomes crucial to what extent the text allows for such projections and to what extent it tries to control or prevent them. One of the most striking characteristics of *The Unnamable* is that this text can be successfully linked with almost any philosophy or theory of the subject in relation to language. But as characteristically, it can never be completely subsumed by any one of them. As soon as we try to attribute a familiar subjectivity to the unnamable, we involuntarily assume the role of the anonymous others. Like them, we seem to disown him with our alien projections. Only by renouncing such unequivocal attributions can we escape the dubious role of the Other. But if we were capable of giving up such projections altogether, we would, from a cultural perspective, have overcome our habitual ethno- or anthropocentric patterns of appropriating otherness. In principle, those patterns can be activated in the reception of a literary text just as they are in the encounter with cultural otherness. The unnamable's insistence on his irreducible difference to all conceivable confining conceptualizations and the text's resistance to interpetive closure can thus also be read as a protection against the negation or appropriation of otherness.

The only problem with this perspective is that the text thus resists a basic operation of interpretation as such—namely, the hermeneutic mediation of otherness through familiar patterns.[41] With his insistence on irreducible otherness, the unnamable challenges the basic norms and conventions of interpretation. In resisting its appropriation of familiar terms, the text may convey the necessity of developing new modes of dealing with and retaining otherness. If we meet this challenge, the aesthetic experience of *The Unnamable* can indeed become a strong form of cultural interaction. The text would no longer be reduced to the status of a passive object used to confirm what we already assume about subjectivity in general. Reading would instead become an encounter with a true literary subject—character and text—able to challenge and transform our own subjectivity.

The Unnamable as a Transitional Character

perhaps that's what I feel, an outside and an inside and me in the middle (p. 134)

outside, inside, there is nothing but here (p. 173)

One of the most important cultural functions of the transitional space of literature is to transform the reader's subjectivity. In *The Unnamable*, intermediacy is also a central strategy of presentation by which the text deploys one of the most radical contemporary forms of literary subjectivity. The blurring of boundaries between I and Not-I, or the imaginary and the real, indicates a change in the transitional space of cultural objects and in the cultural formations of subjectivity. In tandem with a widespread cultural reorganization and theoretical revaluation of subjectivity, new forms and functions of literary subjectivity emerge. The vanishing of subjectivity under postmodern conditions ignites the controversial debates between those who celebrate its disappearance as the end of the bourgeois subject and those who see it as a further step in an overall cultural colonization of the subject.

The excruciating trials of subjectivity in *The Unnamable* address the core issues and epistemological implications of this debate. The literary subject of this text probes its resistance to cultural and textual appropriation. How can an invented literary subject assert a subjectivity against the author who invented it under the auspices of the literary canon and the rules of the transitional space? And how can this subject escape its appropriation by the cultural norms of the reader? From this perspective, the intermediacy of the subject functions as a privileged strategy of cultural mediation.

The unnamable's position between I and Not-I, life and death, body and disembodiment, time and eternity, speech and silence, reality and imagination in many ways resembles the position the subject assumes during the psychogenetic formation of the transitional space. From this perspective, we could see the unnamable as a transitional character par excellence.[42] Furthermore, if we define literature in general within the transitional space of culture, the intermediacy of a literary character would also entail a self-reflection of its fictionality. As a transitional character, the unnamable is a successor of the transitional objects in the transitional space. As such he also performs a literary equivocation of the basic function of the imaginary for the constitution of the subject. The tenacious insistence upon his own fictionality thus also reflects back on the imaginary constitution of subjectivity in general.

At the same time, however, the unnamable violates the taboo that regulates all activities in the transitional space: he asks the question of the real. According to Winnicott, the distinction between reality and fiction is temporarily suspended in the transitional space. "Do not challenge" is the most crucial attitude toward all activities during this transitional mode of experience. The unnamable clearly breaks this rule. His obstinate insistence on questions concerning the reality of events and observations, or the notion of a true self, works against this rule that is basic to the transitional space. It works equally against its aesthetic equivalent—namely, the convention of accepting the status of a literary character with willing suspension of disbelief. This violation of the rule, however, only illustrates the importance of the imaginary as a cultural force. The anthropological function of the imaginary in the transitional space and its contribution to the constitution of the subject—a function of which we commonly remain unaware—is brought to the surface of this fictional presentation of subjectivity. In this process, the function of the imaginary is simultaneously emphasized and problematized. The negated manifestations of subjectivity in *The Unnamable* reflect and deflect a social norm that requires the exclusion of the imaginary from one's relation to oneself. The text shows that even though it is impossible to fulfill this norm, it nevertheless brings about a split in the subject. The unnamable's feigned attempts to avoid all imaginary attributions always turn out to be the opposite of what they are supposed to be on the surface: instead of being an approximation to a hypothetical true self, they undermine its very possibility.

This epistemological skepticism of a fictional subject creates a conceptual affinity with contemporary theories that assume an imaginary and inaccessible dimension of subjectivity. As demonstrated in the unnamable's discourse, the process of voicing such a subjectivity depends upon facing the paradox of representing the unrepresentable. For this purpose, the unnamable chooses various forms of dedifferentiating language. This again recalls similar moves in theories that deal with the ineffable. Theoretically, dedifferentiation of language might be induced by a hermeneutic or a phenomenological model of reflection with the infinite regress of a self-reflexive hermeneutic circle. But another set of dedifferentiations similar to those in *The Unnamable* might be induced by either a poststructuralist model, like the Lacanian model, which follows the traces of the unconscious in the signifier; or a textualist model, which assumes the principal undecidability of linguistic disseminations. In all these cases the conventional forms of reading are questioned, if not overturned. Moreover, the development of new models of reading helps us to understand the implications of contemporary literary subjectivity and the cultural change in the status of the subject. Dieter Henrich, for example, interprets the self-reflexivity in contemporary fiction as a cultural reaction to the awareness that we cannot grasp "the ground of our own subjectivity."[43] While many critics focus on the effects of self-reflexivity, poststructuralism and deconstruction are more interested in the effects of the unconscious on speech that occur against the intention and beyond the reflexivity of the speaker.

The fact that *The Unnamable* encompasses both extremes—the unconscious as well as self-reflexivity—turns the text into a privileged paradigm of subjectivity in contemporary fiction. Self-reflexivity reveals the imaginary ground of subjectivity as well as its formal and material structures. The textual self-reflexivity in *The Unnamable* appears as an attempt to gain access to the inaccessible ground of subjectivity. The unnamable's relentless questioning of his own strategies of formal presentation—or what Dieter Henrich once called "the effort of form against itself"[44]—is the material condition for his speaking against an I. The form of this speech is turned against itself in order to prevent an I from stabilizing within a discursive formation.

We have seen how, as a transitional character, the unnamable challenges basic assumptions about subjectivity in our culture in such different spheres as literature, philosophy, psychology, and the empirical world. By using the energies and modes of production of the primary processes, *The Unnamable* plays across the boundaries between the conscious and the unconscious. Beckett has constructed a character for whom those boundaries are suspended, but who nonetheless sees himself forced to speak against his own alien discourse that presupposes them. In this sense, too, he is a truly transitional character. The transitional space of *The Unnamable*, in other words, circumvents the familiar dynamic between consciousness and the unconscious that is nonetheless inscribed in all the loops of its discourse. The paradoxical fictions of the unnamable draw on the imaginary, but can no longer be derived from it, just as his negations can no longer reduce uncertainty to doubt.

Beckett's transitional character is both an inhabitant of the new transitional space of postmodernism and a cartographer who draws its map across the boundaries of our cultural and philosophical heritage. Ultimately, the unnamable invites us to "grow new organs"[45] with him, organs adaptable to the conditions of the arid postmodern space beyond the illusory certainties of logical conclusions, binary oppositions, linear narratives, teleological trajectories, and bounded bodies or selves. He thus becomes the catalyst for traversals of ever more imaginable and unimaginable boundaries within the transitional space of contemporary culture—with all the ambivalence that those traversals entail. By pushing further and further the very limits of a literary mediation of subjectivity and language, the unnamable walks on a tightrope toward the impossible, suspended across time and space.

7

Carnivalesque Apocalypse of the Holy Text: *Gravity's Rainbow*

An Apocalyptic Metafiction

"Nature does not know extinction; all it knows is transformation. Everything science has taught me, and continues to teach me, strengthens my belief in the continuity of our spiritual existence after death." This quote by Wernher von Braun, which Pynchon chose as the epigraph of *Gravity's Rainbow*, marks the two thematic poles of the novel: apocalypse and transcendence.[1] Scattered scenes and fragmented stories from World War II, which appear in the text as a historical world theater, deal with dissolution and decay, transcendence and mystical worlds, disturbing the boundaries of subjects, systems, and language.

Despite its meticulous depiction of historical events that occurred during the final war years of 1944–45, Pynchon's fictional world remains remote and at times even surreal. Elements of various genres and styles are combined in a dense network of interwoven narratives. One may be reminded of a curious historical science fiction, a utopian novel with fairy-tale elements, a fantastic carnivalesque spectacle, or even a well-wrought pornographic novel spiced with spy stories. And amid all this, musical scenes erupt as the characters' comical self-stylizations. The multiple threads of narration are woven together in a seemingly contingent and somewhat elusive pattern. Pynchon often takes hundreds of pages to provide a context for his stories or to offer insight into the connections between them. Some four hundred characters appear sporadically, crossing each other and forming surprising connections in an obscure and frightening world that can no longer be comprehended by the logic of cause and effect. It seems nearly impossible to discern a coherent symbolic world from either a historical or a narrative perspective. Despite the return of history and stories and even a consistent narrator as an agency of order, the text remains as hermetical as the most esoteric experimental texts of modernism. *Gravity's Rainbow* thus raises the problem of order and chaos, sense and contingency through both its textual organization and its conception of history.

While all of Pynchon's main characters are affected by a widespread cultural and epistemological crisis of meaning, the narrator often parodies the ways in which they use this crisis in order to cover up the threats of a much more global destruction. At one level, *Gravity's Rainbow* questions the status of meaning in the face of total annihilation. But at another level, the text unfolds a critique of mythologies that exploit the characters' need for hope and a residuum of human values at the moment when humanity is threatened by self-induced extinction. Because of its aura of apocalypse and self-destruction, *Gravity's Rainbow* becomes an early apocalyptic fiction of the approaching fin de siècle.[2] Considering the global competition with atomic weapons and the exact calculability of their potential for destruction, such fictions can no longer be sufficiently explained by Frank Kermode's model of the so-called "concord fictions." According to Kermode, concord fictions render the moment between birth and death bearable by harmonizing the end with the beginning. Even though Pynchon's characters are highly susceptible to such forms of mythologizing, *Gravity's Rainbow* exposes their inherent denial of real destruction.

The characters create concord fictions and apocalyptic mythologies in order to ward off or deny their fear of the war. "Apocalypse is a part of the Modern Absurd," writes Frank Kermode. "If it becomes myth, if its past is forgotten, we sink quickly into myth, into stereotype."[3] Numerous characters in *Gravity's Rainbow* harbor a collective apocalyptic myth in which the Rocket functions as a medium of transcendence. Apocalyptic visions affect the very structure of their subjectivity. For the characters, apocalyptic visions hold a utopian promise of transcendence, which they enact in perverse rituals and through fantasies of rebirth from destruction. Symbols of transcendence, which pervade the entire text, not only center the private mythologies of the characters, but also form ordering devices for the narrator and lend structure to the textual composition. Originating from the most diverse mystical systems, these symbols of transcendence give the text an archetypal dimension. Cabalistic symbols from Judaic mysticism, mandalas from old mystic cultures, symbols of the Tarot, and even mythologized mathematical symbols all evoke a transcendent realm of mystical presence and fullness, as opposed to notions of a profane historical world based on cause and effect.

This polarization of two worlds corresponds to two forms of subjectivity: the bounded ego of a historically determined subjectivity and the unbounded and timeless subjectivity of an absolute here and now. In *Gravity's Rainbow* these polarizations grow out of "patterns of fear"[4] that the characters enact through the great myth of the Rocket. Rather than participating in this myth, the text critically reflects upon its effect on the characters and its ramifications in the social world. *Gravity's Rainbow* is thus less an apocalyptic fiction than an apocalyptic metafiction.[5]

Gravity's Rainbow may also be read as a "second-order semiological system" as defined by Roland Barthes. According to Barthes, such a self-reflexive construction of a mythological system reveals the potential meaning that has been disowned by the myth: "Truth to tell, the best weapon against myth is perhaps to mythify it in its turn, and to produce an *artificial myth:* and this reconstituted myth will in fact be a mythology. Since myth robs language of something, why not rob myth? All that is needed is to use it as the departure point for a third semiological chain, to take its signification as the first term of a second myth."[6]

The artificial myths in *Gravity's Rainbow* reveal what the characters try to repress in their own mythologies: the brutal reality of fascism and the threat of apocalyptic destruction. Pynchon's experimental myth of the Rocket, for example, is built on the historical knowledge of the Holocaust and culminates in an apocalyptic vision of total self-destruction. The real destruction at every level of history and the threat of a final global destruction are presented as a meaning encrypted within the mythologies of transcendence. The end of the novel parodies the impotence of apocalyptic myths by rehearsing an artificial apocalypse. Staged as a mock allegory, the fall of the Rocket over the *teatrum mundi* appears as a colossal show, which displaces the real destruction during World War II as well as the potential destruction, the arsenal of weapons, with which the readers of *Gravity's Rainbow* have to live.

Pynchon's novel challenges conventional apocalyptic fictions from a double perspective. By exposing the dangers of an apocalyptic myth—including the pleasurable cathexis of apocalypse with notions of mystic transcendence—the text establishes a metacommunication about its own modes of presentation. It raises the question of how to avoid the traps of representation or, more concretely, of how to present historical myth without in turn mythologizing history and thereby enforcing the catastrophe to be represented. Despite this critique of myth, *Gravity's Rainbow* refrains from presenting what Max Weber calls the "world-disenchantment" as a viable alternative. Radicalizing the general critique of representation so prominent at the time of the novel's production and publication, Pynchon frames this problem historically within a narrative of World War II, into which he then blends textual elements of a postmodern apocalypse. *Gravity's Rainbow* thus challenges and complicates any theoretical discussion of a posthistory in which the end of history, representation, and the subject are already treated as fact. Reading *Gravity's Rainbow* urges one to pose the question of history, representation, and the subject from the perspective of a postmodern simulation of history. As an apocalyptic metafiction, this simulation paradoxically endows the end of history with a real sense of an ending.

Eschatological Fears and Delusions of Transcendence: The Rocket as Collective Myth

> The white whale is reborn . . . as Pynchon's Rocket.
> —*Thomas H. Schaub*

The object that inspires the myth of the Rocket is Hitler's V-2, which functions for many of Pynchon's male characters as a symbolic object onto which they project their eschatological fears. At the same time, however, a denial of those fears is already built into the construction of the myth.[7] The effects of the V-2 are transposed into the sphere of the uncanny, where its reality gives way to its phantasmatic cathexis. Like Melville's myth of the white whale, Pynchon's myth of the Rocket fulfills a paradoxical function: it provides a framework that centers the characters' desire for transcendence and unboundedness and endows this desire with a sense of teleological orientation and closure. For example, Kurt Mondaugen, the electromystic, sees the combustion chamber of the Rocket as a cosmological egg in which fire and water, creation and destruction form a unity. The ancient notion of a mystic unity of the self beyond history is revitalized in metaphors of electricity: "Think of the ego, the self that suffers a personal history bound to time, as the grid. The deeper and true Self is the flow between cathode and plate. The constant pure flow . . . Only at moments of great serenity is it possible to find the pure, the informationless state of signal zero" (p. 404).

The narrator leaves no doubt about the perversion of this mythology for political purposes when he laconically states that Mondaugen is "ready to accept Hitler on the basis of Demianmetaphysics" (p. 403). In order to understand the status of scientific mythologies in Pynchon's text, one must stress how the narrator pointedly exposes their complicity with political ideologies and, in this case, with fascism. Fahringer, the aerodynamic and "bodhissattva" of the Rocket engineers, also mystifies the Rocket when he develops a vision of mystic fusion inspired by Zen Buddhism and its art of archery: "The Rocket for this Fahringer was a fat Japanese arrow. It was necessary in some way to become one with the Rocket, trajectory and target—not to *will* it, but to surrender, to step out of the role of firer. The act is undivided. You are both aggressor and victim, rocket and parabolic path" (p. 403).

The narrator shows how all these myths of transcendence, developed around the Rocket, form a powerful collective dream in which apocalyptic visions express a desire for primordial unity and mystic transcendence. The mysticism of death developed by Captain Blicero, who sees himself as a god of creation and destruction, forms the perverse culmination of these apocalyptic visions.

Inspired by Rilke's *Duino Elegies,* Blicero mystifies the Rocket as an object that opens the path to transcendence and to the state of pure being incorporated by Rilke's angels. After colonizing the African Hereroes, Blicero returns with a slave lover, a black youth whom he ironically names, after Rilke's elegies, "Enzian"—a white flower. Later this very Enzian will propagate an archaic counterculture free from the constraints of time and history and centered around the *schwarzgeraet* of the V-2 00000, which symbolizes the timeless and mystic state of absolute zero. A surreal search for the lost *schwarzgeraet* brings together numerous threads of disparate stories in a sacred act, in which Blicero ties Gottfried, Enzian's Germanic mirror image, to the *schwarzgeraet* in order to sacrifice him as a new Isaac.

They are mated to each other, schwarzgeraet and next higher assembly. His bare limbs in their metal bondage writhe among the fuel, oxidizer, live-stream lines, thrust frame, compressed air battery, exhaust elbow, decomposer, tanks, vents, valves . . . and one of the valves, one test-point, one pressure switch is the right one, the true clitoris, routed directly into the nervous system of the 00000. She should not be a mystery to you, Gottfried. Find the zone of love, lick and kiss . . . you have time—there are still a few minutes. (p. 751)

The perverse eroticism in this fantasy of transcendence is grounded in an androgynous myth of the Rocket. On the surface, the Rocket functions as a phallic symbol of masculine technology. But in his blasphemous ritual of sacrificing his juvenile son-lover Gottfried, Blicero envisions the Rocket as the archetypal Great Mother, whose metal body appears as a return of the feminine that had been repressed in the male fantasies. The androgynous myth of the Rocket thus shapes the repressed feminine within a decidedly male fantasy. The technological myth domesticates the threatening aspects of the feminine by containing it within the sphere of male power. Displaced onto the fetish object of an eroticized male war machine, the feminine is not only tamed but also perverted.[8] The androgynous quality of the myth of the Rocket thus turns out to be a mere surface phenomenon. Far from integrating masculine and feminine principles, the myth attempts to neutralize the feminine by absorbing it into the masculine. From this perspective, the Rocket functions as a kind of "bachelor's machine," to use Michel Carrouges's term for a male fantasy of self-generation. Blicero uses this fantasy to stylize the homoerotic ritual of Gottfried's sacrifice as a bachelor's birth. Following the mythology of a rebirth from death, Blicero has Gottfried killed in order to give birth to him—a symbolic rebirth into pure cosmic being. "A bachelor's machine is a fantastic image which transforms love into a mechanism of death," writes Michel Carrouges.[9] Following this perverse logic, Blicero creates a gigantic myth of the triumph of masculine technology over nature and the feminine.

It began when Weissmann brought him [Enzian] to Europe: a discovery that love, among these men, once past the simple feel and orgasming of it, had to do with masculine technology, with contracts, with winning and losing . . . Beyond simple steel erection, the Rocket was an entire system *won,* away from the feminine darkness, held against the entropies of lovable but scatterbrained Mother Nature: that was the first thing he was obliged by Weissmann to learn, his first step toward citizenship in the Zone. He was led to believe that by understanding the Rocket, he would come to understand truly his manhood. (p. 324)

This passage reveals the ambivalent overdetermination of the myth of the Rocket. While using the fantasy of a bachelor's machine in order to replace the feminine power of the archetypal Great Mother, the myth also incorporates the technological object as a male fetish. Gottfried serves as the sacrificial victim in this technological Eros, which is of course inspired by futurism.[10] Tied to the *schwarzgeraet*, Gottfried's body merges with the Rocket. Together they unite the complementary utopian visions of a machine body and a body machine. This equation is not merely metaphorical. The myth of the Rocket in fact visualizes and externalizes the concrete psychohistoric impact of technology on the formation of the egos, the bodies, and the unconscious of historical subjects. By simultaneously mechanizing the body and anthropomorphizing the machine, the myth of the Rocket reenacts the old fantasy of a fusion between man and machine. We must only shift perspectives in order to see that this myth of technomystical transcendence works on both a metaphorical and a psychocybernetic plane. Withdrawn from the human body, psychic energies and cathexis are displaced onto the inanimate Rocket, which is in turn anthropomorphized. This can be seen as a special form of a flight into the inanimate in which lived emotions are only tolerated in relation to inanimate objects.[11] In this process, the anthropomorphic objects are connected with the technological subjects who have bound all libidinal energies.

Pynchon's presentation of the myth of the Rocket entails a psychohistorical critique of fascism that is above all directed against the hypermaniacal images of masculinity propagated by fascism. Fantasies of the war machine as a sexualized machine reach a peak in fascist ideology. As Klaus Theweleit has shown in *Male Fantasies*, this libidinal cathexis of the war was acted out on the male bodies of soldiers and prisoners in sadomasochistic rituals or in practices of "iron steeling."[12] Rebuilt and mechanized, these new bodies produce a soldier's ego, which forcefully rejects all inner impulses in order to persecute these impulses outside, as woman, nature, body, the primitive, the black, the Jew, or the communist.

Blicero/Weissmann, the proto-fascist, displays a masculinity completely adapted to the war machinery. In his private life, he acts out the dark instincts of this masculinity in sadistic rituals. With Katje Borghesius he performs a perverse enactment of the fairy tale of Hansel and Gretel, full of sadistic violence and cannibalistic desires. The perverse games of master and slave he plays with Enzian, his Herero lover, culminate in fantasies of fusion with the colonized Other. The text exposes these fantasies of transgression and fusion as effects of a repressive cultural dynamic. The rigid authoritarian socialization of soldier males under fascism is compensated with fantasies and rituals in which the repressed returns in regressive and destructive desublimations.

Gravity's Rainbow exposes the uncanny complementarity of these perverted desublimations of the body with fascist body politics at large. The violent practices against the body of the Other, its mutilation in torture, the extermination of masses of Jews, gypsies, and communists, the mechanized extinction and cynical utilization of their dead body parts, and the disposal of "waste" are—in Pynchon's as well as in Theweleit's perspective—intrinsically linked to the rigid politics toward the body of the soldier male and its reconstruction as a machine of combat. While this restructuring of the body is supposed to control or eliminate the excesses of subjectivity, these very excesses return with a vengeance in archaic fantasies and rituals of male domination. The obsession with control has gone wild and is transformed into a hatred of all living processes and all that is Other. What Sartre once criticized as a cultural desire for the inanimate and for the petrification of all living processes stems from the same rigid formation of subjectivity and culture. Pynchon shows how the most archaic instincts of destruction are lived out in the most rigid and refined systems of political and technological control. The willful destruction of subjectivity in the soldier male follows the same cultural logic as the colonization, if not extermination, of other races. *Gravity's Rainbow* shows how fascism feeds on archaic fears of otherness and perverts desires for fusion or transcendence in order to establish its imperial will to power and control.

Pynchon's critique of culture is rooted in an ambivalent critique of myth. Mythologizing violence, destruction, and control functions as a precondition for its social and historical practice. Myths of transcendence, purification, and ascendency to a higher plane of existence or a superior race are perversely used to justify the participation in global and local destruction. Instead of simply denouncing or rejecting the social construction of myths in general, *Gravity's Rainbow* alerts one to the dangers of underrating the deeply rooted cultural need for mythologies as well as the perils of exploiting them for political purposes. The textual critique of proliferating myths of transcendence is at the core of Pynchon's critique of fascism. But the text retains an ambivalence toward the desire for transcendence as such. Rather than seeing this desire itself as destructive, Pynchon exposes its mythologizing as an effect of cultural repression. The rigid systems of order imposed under fascism engender an often unacknowledged desire for fluid boundaries and a susceptibility to myths of transcendence or archaic and violent regressions. Moreover, the hatred of cultural otherness propagated by fascist ideology allows for a release of these violent instincts under the guise of a highly rationalized and impersonal system of destruction. The depersonalization of the Other is accompanied by the depersonalization of experience. The repressed affects are then displaced onto and lived out in fantasies and myth. Pynchon's text is extremely sensitive to the unacknowledged linkage between the cold, fascist rationality and its Other—barbarism. He thus overcomes the critical impasse of an ongoing debate whose proponents try to analyze fascism either according to a model of hyperrationality and cold technology of destruction or a model of irrationality and barbarism. Pynchon's novel insists on an inseparable link between these two complementary aspects of fascism.

From this perspective, a political strategy that aims solely at reinforcing rationalism necessarily fails, since the myths are not responsible for cultural destructiveness but rather their enactment within a paranoid system. However, a purely antirationalist political strategy (such as that of the Counterforce) also fails, since it blinds itself to the traps of regressive desublimation. *Gravity's Rainbow* insists upon a fundamental ambiguity at the heart of every myth: the flexibility and plasticity that myths share with unconsious productions allows one to use them in the most diverse ways, including perverted political practices.

Since *Gravity's Rainbow* posits the need for mythologies as anthropologically invariant not only for the fascists, but also for all the other characters from the most diverse cultural backgrounds, a rationalist or purist world disenchantment does not appear as a viable alternative.[13]

Myths pervade the formation of subjectivity as well as the making of history. And they are as prolific in a rationalist and technological culture as they were at the time of the early Puritans. They helped shape the politics of Germany under fascism as well as of the United States during the Vietnam War. Far from embracing the notion of an objectivistic, scientistic, or rationalistic disenchantment of the world, *Gravity's Rainbow* locates powerful myths at the core of politics, science, and technology. They appear as secret fantasies of the most rational engineers or scientists and within the most developed technological control of history.[14]

The Bounds of Representation

Gravity's Rainbow shows how all cultural systems of meaning are potentially susceptible to being mythologized. Due to their powerful psychological cathexis, myths contribute to the production of systems of meaning and knowledge in general, including political ones. Pynchon develops his implicit critique of mythologies from a decidedly historical and psychohistorical perspective. His focus is on how a specific ideology uses myths for its own purpose. The characters in *Gravity's Rainbow* use myths mainly to deny the reality of fascism and war, while at the same time tacitly supporting fascist, capitalist, colonialist, and imperialist ideologies with the same myths. Numerous scientific ideologies form part of this mythological system by mystifying the results as well as the political uses of their highly sophisticated research.

Textual demystification in *Gravity's Rainbow* thus entails a critique of ideology. Pynchon distinguishes between three types of myth: those used to enact private pathologies (Blicero's myth of the Rocket); collective myths disseminated by film and the media (such as the collective dream in Van Goell's film *Alpdruecken*); and unconscious myths, which lie at the heart of social codes, systems of order, and the organization of knowledge. *Gravity's Rainbow* reveals how a secret symbiosis between private pathologies and male myths of technological power serves the purposes of fascist ideology. The latter is further supported by the collective dream (to use Benjamin's term) of the cinema which, in *Gravity's Rainbow*, takes part in an imaginary semiotization of the characters and their fictional world.

Pynchon's historical novel traces the tacit mythologies operative in the systems of thought and modes of representation and enforces this perspective theoretically with intertextual references to contemporary critiques of myth and representation in science, cybernetics, and critical theory. Allusions to Wittgenstein's critique of language, to poststructuralist refutations of the "True Text," to cybernetic theories, and to theories of relativity and quantum physics all point to mythologies in our systems of knowledge. Pynchon shares the contemporary sensitivity to the traps of representation and conceptualization. From this perspective, one could see *Gravity's Rainbow* as one of many demystifying aesthetic or theoretical practices that supplement and counterbalance the cultural activity of forming systems of knowledge and thought. The cultural relationship to otherness—to Jews, Hereros, communists, Vietnamese, the counterforce, or Dodoes—is at the core of this critique of rigid systems of order based on a paranoid rejection of whatever is Other to the system. The monstrous paranoia of fascism is only the most radical historical manifestation of a much more widespread cultural paranoia revealed in *Gravity's Rainbow*.

Yet myth and representation are central to the textual composition of *Gravity's Rainbow* itself. Pynchon builds most of its narratives around the myth of the Rocket. Therefore, his fictional presentation of World War II must develop strategies to undercut the remythologizing effects of its own system of textual representation. Pynchon uses a form of literary self-reflection well known since the advent of modernism in order to critically expose the myths that form the core of his narrative by establishing the metaperspective of an artificial mythological system. Focusing on the ominous symbiosis between myth and political ideology, *Gravity's Rainbow* develops a system of textual representation in which history appears as an effect of multiple other systems such as politics, technology, science, the media, and myth itself. For Pynchon, to understand history means to represent it as a complex systemic interconnection of cultural spheres. The narratives of fictional characters traverse these spheres and are shaped by them—without ever becoming reduced to them. Refined technologies of communication are used by the media in order to create collective mythologies and dreams. But even these systems of representation fail to exert the total control they simulate: there is always a counterforce that eats away at the fringes of established myths and systems of representation.

The Myth of the True Text and the Logocentric Semiotization of the World

Metaphor creates a new reality from which the original appears to be unreal.
                                              —*Wallace Stevens*

Gravity's Rainbow raises the problem of representation within a general, often carnivalesque critique of language full of ironic allusions to contemporary philosophies of language. Wittgenstein's "The world is everything that is the case," for example, is transmitted from space in *Gravity's Rainbow.* At times, the characters' dialogues seem to be a pastiche of contemporary theoretical debates about the truth value of language. At other times, they seem to speak the credos of modernism and postmodernism or their theoretical spin-offs. Cybernetics, systems theory, and the New Physics figure most prominently next to contemporary theories of language and representation. Historically, it is interesting to recall that most of these theories developed around or during World War II. But many of them were only broadly received in the United States around the time when Pynchon wrote his encyclopedic novel. Voiced by its characters, the core issues of contemporary theories of language have often already hardened into theoretical stereotypes and commonplaces about language and representation.

Certain characters mythologize the notion of language and representation. The myth of silence and the myth of the True Text bespeak a desire to purify language from the excesses, slippages, and wastes of representation. Both myths are rooted in the romantic idea of a primordial self in touch with its origin. During the alphabetizing campaign in Syberia, Galina, the "connoisseuse of silences" (p. 340) who the narrator says is "shut in by words, drifts and frost-patterns of white words" (p. 388), learns through silence the fear of this primordial self. She tries to obtain a magic protection against this fear by performing an archaic act of naming. In a similar way, Enzian, who harbors the dream of creating a Herero-community in the spirit of "Pre-Christian Oneness," evokes the magic force of naming: "There may be no gods, but there is a pattern: names by themselves may have no magic, but the *act* of naming, the physical utterance, obeys the pattern" (p. 322).

We are reminded that the archaic act of naming lies at the root of both myth and *logos.*[15] Language can be used as a protective screen against fear, but at the same time it also functions as a dividing screen that cuts the speaking subject out of a primordial unity with nature. In a symbolic "order of Analysis and Death" (p. 722), speech has become an ambivalent medium, capable of both repression and protection. The desire for primordial unity is betrayed by speech, which admits it only in the form of displacements and distortions. Some of the characters believe that the symbolic order, which was once established for the purpose of domesticating a threatening nature, has rigidified to a point where everything that recalls nature or a primordial oneness is perceived as a threat—regardless of whether it comes from outside or from within the self. Or, to use Lacan's formulation, within the symbolic order the subject is barred from its truth by the wall of language.

The characters are not only driven by their desire for primordial unity, they are also haunted by its other—the fragmented body. Pynchon has driven the phantasmatic anatomy of body images and body performances to a nightmarish excess. They even pervade the myths of transcendence, which are organized around images of self-preservation and primordial unity or, conversely, of aggressive fragmentation and mutilation of the body. By acting out such phantasms, the characters resymbolize in displaced form what has been repressed or excluded, or what functions as a taboo or perversion within the social code. In this context, the romantic myth of a primordial, presymbolic unity forms the inverse of the abundant sadomasochistic performances. The Herero's cabalistic dream of a primordial unity preserved in a lost "real Text" exposes this dynamic within the myth of the Rocket:

> Say we [the Zone Hereros] are supposed to be the Kabbalists out here, say that's our real Destiny, to be the scholar-magicians of the Zone, with somewhere in it a Text, to be picked to pieces, annotated, explicated, and masturbated till it's all squeezed limp of its last drop . . . well we assumed—natuerlich—that this holy text had to be the Rocket . . . Its symmetries, its latencies, the *cuteness* of it enchanted and seduced us while the real Text persisted, somewhere else, in the darkness, our darkness. (p. 520)

The Rocket as holy text is only one of many myths of a primordial unity of word and thing behind which we can trace the absolutism and the tacit verdict on metaphor practiced in Romanticism's insistence on literality.[16] The myth of an absolute text, which appears in figurations of a "real Text," "True Text," or "Holy Text," is of the same order as the verdict on metaphor. It operates through a confrontation of absolutisms. In this purist conception of language, some characters infuse the Puritan search for signs of grace or condemnation with a romantic desire for reading the world as inviolate nature.[17] This semiotization of the world is, however, radically different from the one that founded the "Chain of Being" and degenerated into a "Chain of Order and Command." *Gravity's Rainbow* reminds us that the readability of the world as text began long before the advent of modernity. Once the world and the signs were so tightly woven that distinguishing them was irrelevant. Most characters in *Gravity's Rainbow* preserve a nostalgia for such a time and experience the semiotization of the world as a loss of reality. It seems as if for them the reliability of the world has dissolved into the instability of signs. From this perspective, their mythologies—especially the myth of the Rocket as Holy Text—are compensatory social constructions aimed at semiologically stabilizing the inherent instability of signs.

Pynchon thus exposes a fundamental ambivalence in these myths of textuality. *Prima facie,* they appear to be developed to counter what he calls the symbolic order of analysis and death. But *Gravity's Rainbow* shows how transgressions of the code can also be instrumentalized. The rigid order of codes appears to be as problematic as their pure inversion in myths of transgression. In order to remain a flexible living system, language has to speak simultaneously within and beyond the bounds of the code. This ambiguity is, in fact, what most characterizes language. The transgression of rhetorical conventions and linguistic boundaries must challenge the code without mythologizing a True Text hidden beneath the code. Pynchon depicts literary characters who harbor various mythologies of language—such as the myth of the True Text or the myth of silence—and at the same time establishes a textual perspective that critically exposes these mythologies. Often this double coding verges on textual entropy; but even more often it celebrates the excesses of carnivalization.

Intertextuality: Fiction, Film, and Theory

Pynchon's strategy of using double coding and metaperspective is enforced by a dense network of intertextual references. The semiotization of the world in *Gravity's Rainbow* is embedded in a new development in the history of signs: the dramatic impact of film as the new medium of a collective dissemination of images. Film in Pynchon's novel frames and shapes the subjectivity of numerous characters and, at a different level, informs the literary devices of Pynchon's text. At one point or other in the novel, nearly all of the main characters become replicas of the celluloid patterns of subjectivity provided by the films of the time. Twenty-five films, nine directors, and about fifty actors appear in the text.[18] A whole canon of key texts and films from the time before and during World War II provides a network that connects characters and plots through transsubjective threads. Intersubjective, socioeconomic, and political connections are enforced by affinities and relations generated by the collective dreams of film. The whole final sequence of the novel, for example, including the mystic rebuilding of the Rocket for the purpose of the sacrifice of Gottfried, is staged after Fritz Lang's *Dr. Mabuse*. Fritz Lang himself serves as a model for the character of von Goell, the film director, whose film *Alpdruecken* creates another collective dream featuring the star Greta Ermann—also a central character in Pynchon's novel.

The rocket engineer Franz Poekler is one among many who, after watching *Alpdruecken*, engenders one of the "shadow-children fathered on Erdmann" (p. 397). Poekler illustrates a mental diffusion between the real and the imaginary. After experiencing a permanent trauma of war, Poekler begins to perceive his whole environment as a film. He becomes unable to decide whether the child sent to him each summer is his daughter Ilse or her double, a child actor. His desire to deny the fact that Ilse lives in a nearby concentration camp induces him to define the serial sequence of their meetings as reality even though he experiences them as a filmic illusion. Only years later will this psychic economy break down and force him to admit the devastating reality of his real daughter.

Poekler in fact incorporates a new type of imaginary personality. He uses film or other collective dreams in order to deny the reality of war. Different from the Sartrean "imaginary personality,"[19] Poekler no longer enacts an imaginary life in order to live real emotions in a displaced form, but, on the contrary, in order to repress them. The function of his flight into fantasy is inverted. Instead of creatively inventing an imaginary personality as a survival strategy for a subject whose reality is denied, Poekler rather passively dissolves his subjectivity into the foil of an imaginary film. In both cases we witness a certain adaptation to a socially expected or produced image. But while the Sartrean protagonist becomes the star of an individual self-performance, Poekler remains an anonymous extra in a performance directed by others—a mere reflection of characters from the collective dreams of film.

Exaggerated to the point of pastiche, if not parody, the device of casting literary characters as film stars turns them into flat characters. They become almost literalizations of Freud's astute definition of the ego as the "projection of a surface"—in this case a surface already copied from the two-dimensional surface of a filmstrip. Siegfried Kracauer observes that the prewar film classics (some of which figure as the core films in *Gravity's Rainbow*) portray the psychological disposition of Germany between 1918 and 1933.[20] Most important among those films in Pynchon's text are Robert Wiene's *The Cabinet of Dr. Caligari* and Fritz Lang's *Die Frau im Mond (Woman in the Moon)* and *Metropolis. Die Frau im Mond* is particularly interesting in relation to the myth of the Rocket. Key advisor for this technically dazzling film was the pioneer rocket enthusiast Willy Ley, who collaborated with Hermann Oberth (later a rocket designer for the Nazis) in designing a two-step rocket model for the film. In 1937 the film, as well as all models of its spaceship, were confiscated by the Gestapo.

The second book of *Gravity's Rainbow* is centered around Katje Borgesius, who mirrors Fay Wray, star of *King Kong*. She is introduced with the remark Merian C. Cooper made to Fay Wray: "You will have the tallest, darkest leading man in Hollywood" (p. 179). In addition to these classic films, which serve as foils for Pynchon's characters, are many allusions to other films, some from the 1960s, which figure as distinct elements of Pynchon's historical collage. Blending later films into the historical frame further disrupts the chronology of historical time and creates an achronological simultaneity of sceneries, spaces, and times. The formative status of film is also enforced in the narrative simulation of camera perspectives and filmic techniques.

This macrostructural frame turns *Gravity's Rainbow* into a simulated film narrative from the 1960s about World War II—a "film" whose serial images use space and time freely and whose narrative structures are guided by camera techniques.[21] The last passages of the novel, for example, are constructed after the model of the countdown, which was invented, as we are reminded in the text, in Fritz Lang's *Die Frau im Mond.*

Even film music becomes a theme and a structural element in
Gravity's Rainbow. Apart from numerous textual allusions to film
music, we find references to theories of serial and electronic music,
and the premises of those theories are used as a model for structuring
the novel. Music as a paradigm for "orders beyond the visible"
(p. 188), which escape or even oppose the cultural dominance of the
eye, is evoked in its sensual qualities as an interface between the visible
and the hidden orders of the text. Like the order of polyphonic music,
the order of *Gravity's Rainbow* is not immediately accessible to experience. Both rely on structures that disturb the hierarchy of gestalt
and background. Narrative sequences in Pynchon's novel form multiple and nonhierarchical connections among each other. What *Finnegans Wake* generates on the level of words and syntax, *Gravity's
Rainbow* simulates in its network of narratives. More strongly even
than in *Finnegans Wake,* however, the semantic density of language
counters this dehierarchizing tendency, since the reader will inevitably
follow the multiple narrative strands with the focused attention that
a plot commands. Language cannot disperse focused attention in the
same way as polyphonic music does. The affinities with polyphonic
music are thus only established after the fact—that is, in a retrospective
interpretation of structure or in a process of remembering textual
echoes. The less focused the memory, the easier it is to detect subtle
resonances between the different narratives, characters, themes, myths,
or styles.

The allusions to music are further enforced by Pynchon's use of the
musical as a structuring element. Throughout the novel, characters
suddenly break into musical songs that parody the narrated events.
Since the narratives themselves are often already staged as parodies of
other narratives or films, these musical sequences function as meta-
parodies of the whole novel.

Pynchon's literary assimilation of devices from film or musicals is
not a mere exercise in experimental intertextuality, but aesthetically
reflects the historical impact of the media on subjectivity and secular
history. Intertextual montages blend remote historical periods into an
integrated fictional simultaneity. The textual staging of a historical
period as a reflex of models from film, literature, music, opera, and
musical translates a new condition of historical experience into the
medium of literary representation. It unearths an imaginary reservoir
of collective dreams and mythologies that cannot be divided from

historical experience, since this reservoir forms the very historical perception of Pynchon's characters.

In addition to the dominant role of film as a structuring model, Pynchon uses Rilke's *Sonnets to Orpheus* and Wagner's *Tannhäuser* as models for both the subjectivity of characters and his literary devices. The Angel from Rilke's *Duino Elegies* figures as a crucial symbol of transcendence.[22] As a being who transcends the limitations and contradictions of human existence toward a unity of thought and action, actuality and ideality, will and force, time and eternity, Rilke's angel inspires such different myths as the myth of the Rocket, the Herero myth, or Blicero's myth of transcendence. It also motivates the numerous mandalas used throughout *Gravity's Rainbow.* Even textual transgressions of boundaries can be formally traced back to the *Duino Elegies.* Slothrop's erotic adventures during his quest for the *schwarzgeraet,* which is ironically cast as *tannhaeuserism* and as a quest for the holy grail, culminate in his gradual dissolution as a literary character. Pynchon announces this process with a pastiche of verses from *Tannhäuser* and structures it according to the phases of transformation and transcendence in Rilke's elegies (see pp. 533, 742). The holy fool quoted from Wagner's *Parsifal* also recalls Slothrop's tarot card, the tarot fool being of course yet another symbol of transgression. Breaking social rules and taboos, he creates chaos in order to initiate a new cycle of life.

Woven seamlessly into the exuberant narratives, Pynchon's dense intertextuality also forms the literary subjectivity of his characters. Most of the literary texts, films, operas, and theories quoted by Pynchon deal with transcendence or dissolutions of subjectivity. His intertextuality has a decidedly psychohistorical dimension. Far from being a mere aesthetic formalism, intertextuality appears as the literary equivalent of the general infiltration of historical subjects by alien texts and scripts. From this perspective, literary intertextuality formally reflects a specific vision of the world in which fictions are integral aspects of historical reality.

Gravity's Rainbow reorganizes its historical material into various and shifting ecological units that unsettle the institutionalized boundaries between politics, economy, technology, science, religion, art, and subculture. Pynchon's historical fiction highlights the ways in which all these sectors are part of and inseparable from the concrete lives and dispersed stories of historical subjects. Intertextual and intercultural references are used as systemic connections that refuse to replicate the segmentation of different social or cultural spheres or the exclusion of certain spheres from historical narratives.

Mendelson has analyzed this intertextual density of Pynchon's fictional perspective on history within the tradition of the encyclopedic novel. Underscoring its larger cultural implications, I would rather call Pynchon's intertextuality ecological, if not holistic. It does not aim—as, for example, do Nabokov's historical narratives—at a playful accumulation and exhibition of historical knowledge or at literary allusions for a group of initiated readers; rather, it attempts a fictional simulation of a holistic perspective upon domains whose internalized classification segments our historical experience. This notion of history recalls an ecology of mind more than an encyclopedia. Even though *Gravity's Rainbow* dismisses conventional patterns of historical novels, it reconstructs a fiction of history on a different level of abstraction.

For this purpose, Pynchon uses a strange blend of intertextuality and conventional narrative devices. Compared to, say, Joyce's or Beckett's disruptions of narrative in favor of artistic transgressions of boundaries in language, Pynchon's historical fiction rather celebrates the return of an exuberant storyteller. Built around documented historical events, Pynchon's fictional projection of history uses some of the neorealistic devices popular at the time he was writing and seamlessly weaves them into his intertextual network. References to film, historical novels, science fiction, spy novels, comics, erotic literature, opera, and musicals are so perfectly absorbed by the flow of narration that one can become quite oblivious of the artful construction of Pynchon's literary devices. Our deeply ingrained disposition to focus on narrative as soon as a text is again willing to tell stories at all testifies to the historical hunger for narrative after a time of high experimentalism. Since Pynchon packages his conceptual experiments into consumer-friendly stories, they are often as easily absorbed by the reader as other simulacra of postmodern culture.

In this respect, Pynchon's readers resemble those of his characters who forget the extent to which their world is semiotized. Pynchon grasps this semiotization of the world through the various media and through institutional and scientific apparatus not simply as a partial aspect of history, but as constitutive for history in general. He pursues a similar strategy with the status of theoretical models in his presentation of history. Even though in less directly visible ways, theories, much like media, form the history and subjectivity of an epoch. This is why in *Gravity's Rainbow* theories figure as cultural objects. Like everything that can be invested with emotions or affects, theories make their own contributions to the staging of history.

Intertextuality between Literature and Theory

The abundant theoretical references in *Gravity's Rainbow* refer to different dispositions of knowledge, which in turn predicate specific structures of understanding the world. Pynchon's hobbyhorse entropy forms the core of scientific allusions that pervade theoretical discussions of characters, scientific metaphors and images of the narrator, quotations of theoretical paradigms, and the use of scientific models as a structuring device for textual organization.[23] Entropy seems to be an ideal metaphor because it provides a foundation in physics and cybernetics for general systemic tendencies toward dedifferentiation. Entropy in *Gravity's Rainbow* is anthropomorphized and serves as a conceptual background for the apocalyptic myths of transcendence. Norbert Wiener's notion that the universe is running downhill, according to which there is no possibility for negentropic processes in closed systems, is evoked in *Gravity's Rainbow* along with Heisenberg's quantum theory. Both belong to the so-called physics of irreversible processes. The abundant number of scientists among Pynchon's characters show how theories of entropy or irreversibility become a fertile ground for popular myths of transcendence. Pynchon uses entropy as a metaphor and as a concept in order to show the tendency of historical subjects to adapt scientific discoveries to psychohistorical needs and interests. Myths of transcendence and debates about entropy were extremely popular both at the historical time portrayed in *Gravity's Rainbow* (the forties) and at the time of the novel's writing and publication (the sixties and early seventies). Pynchon thus links the scientific mythologies of entropy shared by the World War II scientists who figure in his novel to the revival of similar mythologies in the sixties. "Entropy has always had a somewhat magical and mystical aura about it" writes Anthony Wilden in "Cybernetics and Machina Mundi,"[24] and as early as 1919 P. W. Bridgman, in his article about Heisenberg's uncertainty principle, predicted a range of new mythologies aimed at overcoming the shock of Heisenberg's attack on the closed image of the physical world:

The immediate effect of the uncertainty principle will be to let loose a veritable intellectual spree of licentious and debauched thinking. This will come from the refusal to take at its true value the statement that it is meaningless to penetrate deeper than the electron, and will have the thesis that there *is really* a domain beyond, only that man with his present limitations is not fitted to enter this domain . . . The existence of such a domain will be made the basis of an orgy of rationalizing. It will be made the substance of the soul.[25]

Theories of entropy and uncertainty challenge traditional models of order. Yet Pynchon's characters turn these theories into popular myths and thus undermine the critical implications of these theories. This ambiguity is crucial for the status of entropy and uncertainty in Pynchon's text. *Gravity's Rainbow* mediates the model of entropy mainly through its adaptation by Norbert Wiener for cybernetics and by Henry Adams for social sciences.[26] Both Wiener and Adams emphasize uncertainty, indeterminacy, and contingency as factors of experience and knowledge. Pynchon transposes this emphasis onto the macrostructural organization of his text. Indeterminacy and contingency are formative for the structures and organization of *Gravity's Rainbow*. Moreover, a built-in tendency toward textual dissolution figures as a simulacrum of entropy. In its last chapters the text formally simulates its own dissolution. This integration of theoretical concepts into the text's formal structures and into its strategies of communication carries intertextuality much further than the mere allusions to other texts or theories do. Pynchon uses such allusions not only to make historical connections, but also to provide indispensable signals for his readers, to help them understand the textual composition and its larger cultural implications.

In his historical narratives Pynchon emphasizes how the immediate historical popularity of the concept of entropy followed from its suitability as an object for the projection of apocalyptic fears engendered by the disasters of World War II. The text even reflects (and the narrator playfully mocks) possible reactions of readers to its entropic structure and thus poses the problem of dissolution and chaos as a phenomenon of textual reception. The status of entropy in Pynchon's historical fiction, however, is quite different from the playful simulation of textual entropy. The simulated dissolution of characters and their narratives is in fact not supported but counterbalanced by the overall textual perspective. The law of entropy is restricted to closed systems. *Gravity's Rainbow*, however, does not constitute itself as a closed entropic textual system, but as an open text. Pynchon reflects closure on two different levels: as a problem in the ecology of social systems and as a problem in the ecology of the text. Entropy can also result from a culturally induced disturbance in the ecology of the subject as, for example, in the case of Slothrop, who experiences an implosion of his inner world as a result of his being cut off from his sociohistorical environment.

While the narrative perspective presents entropy as a dynamic resulting from the enforced closure of social systems, the text itself resists closure even throughout its simulation of entropy and apocalypse. Cultural resistance against the habit of thinking in closed systems is emphasized and practised as a negentropic force against the Cartesian-Newtonic heritage. The very communicative strategies of the text, which presuppose skills in handling complexity and indeterminacy, also refine one's ability to think in open systems. The narrative perspective in fact not only constitutes an open, flexible system, it also anticipates forms of consciousness that expand three-dimensional systems of order. What is perceived as a system depends on the boundaries that an observer (recipient) draws toward interacting systems—or toward the environment of a literary text. The more complex the network of relations between different heuristic systems becomes, the smaller the danger of creating an artificially closed entropic system of thought.

The many allusions to *The Education of Henry Adams* in *Gravity's Rainbow* suggest that, in addition to using entropy as a conceptual category, Pynchon also uses this metaphor to describe historical and social processes. In his reflections about social entropy, Henry Adams criticized the despotism of artifical order. *Gravity's Rainbow* highlights the ways in which this despotism affects the subjectivity of all those characters who become obsessed with a specific ideological, scientific, or religious system—be it Pavlovian behaviorism, rigidly practiced Puritanism, zealous imperialism, or a military myth of transcendence.

On a macrostructural level, Pynchon's text retains a certain balance between structure and its dissolution, between complexity and openness. During a linear process of reading we are exposed to the development and dissolution of multiple storylines that never seem to find any closure. If we try, however, to grasp their interconnectedness from a macroperspective, we can detect a whole network of linkages, resonances, and historical affinities. A linear increase of textual differentiation in the form of more and more information about characters and historical events would induce entropy into a closed textual system. Pynchon's simulated entropy, however, is embedded in a connective system of cross-references and thus introduces negentropy, opening the text up for new interpretations of history, subjectivity, and ecology.[27]

In this context it is interesting to recall that Jean Baudrillard criticizes the basic assumptions of cybernetics and information theory by claiming that information as such is not negentropic but entropic. Distinguishing between information and meaning, he convincingly argues that only meaning is able to resist entropy. The increasing complexity of a closed system of information absorbs its own object as a consequence of linear differentiation: "All subject matter (the message) is absorbed by the single dominant form of the medium."[28] Baudrillard consequently insists that it is not the increase of information, but rather the creation of open systems that will prevent social entropy. This perspective—which historically extends McLuhan's theory—explains why the myths of transcendence in *Gravity's Rainbow* fail to become negentropic carriers of meaning. Despite the fact that the characters create myths in order to ward off chaos and entropy, they remain powerless in the face of an entropy that stems from transpersonal social systems, since they oppose closed systems with other closed systems.

This tension between transpersonal institutional systems and individual systems is fundamental for the status of entropy and the conception of history in Pynchon's text. History is not made by either of the two systems but generated by a complex interaction between the two. This dynamic, however, is no longer clear to the characters, the subjects of history, who are governed by and live in systems of order that they cannot experience as such. Opacity is not only a consequence of controlled strategies of dissimulation deployed by transpersonal systems, but also an effect of emergent new orders. Pynchon's historical subjects must continually adapt to changing differentiations and levels of complexity in their symbolic and social orders. Certain opacities in a system can become transparent only through a change in the patterns of experience.

This is also true for the opacity of a literary system and internalized patterns of aesthetic experience. In *Gravity's Rainbow* the tension between quotidian experience and more differentiated forms of consciousness, which can be anticipated theoretically, becomes formative for the aesthetic experience of the text. Its literary devices are inspired by the idea of a multidimensional and transpersonal order that at this point in history can only be deduced from theoretical positions. Human subjects are forced to adjust their systems of order to that "sphere of middle dimensions" that is accessible to sense perception.[29] On the other hand, those same subjects can develop theories of orders that transcend the boundaries of the senses. By using such theories aesthetically, Pynchon grounds his literary devices and communicative textual strategies in this very tension.

Historically as well as aesthetically the possibilities and limitations of a communicative mediation of such orders determine their very experience.[30] In *Gravity's Rainbow*, Pynchon projects complex patterns of order that go beyond the familiar axes of orientation provided by space, time, and causality. But because not only the characters in the text but also its potential readers can be assumed to use these familiar axes, a constant mediation is required to convey the sense of a different order. As Thomas Schaub has convincingly argued, the narrator functions as a pilot figure in this process by playfully simulating a four-dimensional perspective, which situates the text at an interface between three- and four-dimensional visions of order.

Some critics have interpreted this narrative device as the return to an omniscient narrator. This view, however, overlooks the self-ironical position of relativity the narrator constantly stresses. He in fact places himself in an experimental narrative space outside the history of the characters from which he simulates a simultaneous fiction of various historical periods. The narrator uses the structure of simultaneous fiction in order to blend the contemporary historical background of the United States in the late sixties and early seventies into the historical fiction of World War II. Malcolm X, John F. Kennedy, and Richard Nixon emerge as symbolic markers in a historical collage. They become pilot figures for links between past and present, leaving it up to the reader to draw conclusions from the historical affinities. This use of prolepsis and analepsis in order to blend different times into a simultaneous historical fiction generates the effects of a four-dimensional perspective. In the reading process this perspective appears at times as a mere contingency of accumulated facts and memories. Despite the densely woven intertextual network, the narrated stories generate the effects of a secondary facticity. Readers may engage the text at the level of narrative without necessarily perceiving the intricacies of textual composition. They may lose themselves in the pseudofacticity of fictional history or follow the narrator's experiments with a multidimensional order.

Schaub has compared this ambivalent process of reception with a psychotic dissolution of internalized orders. "Meaning in Pynchon is always a medium, not an answer; his goal is to induce that medium, verging on psychosis, whereby the sterile and false world of 'official' forms is given the lie by a protective and inquisitive alertness, leaving an uncertain reality which both terrifies and releases."[31] Readers however will inevitably try to adapt Pynchon's seeming contingency and chaos to their own internalized order. The psychotic lacks such skills of receptive appropriation and would therefore be unable to project a new order along the lines of Pynchon's experiments. But Pynchon's implied reader does more than merely appropriate the text, and if we follow the traces of the implicit reader we end up mentally playing through the experimental new order of the text. Since many signals in *Gravity's Rainbow* suggest the idea of a four-dimensional order, we may perceive the interception of the familiar chronology of events occuring between 1944 and 1945 with past, future, and remote events as the simulation of a space-time continuum in a four-dimensional world that is governed by the structural principles of simultaneity, synchronicity, and seriality. Schaub argues that only the notion of such a simultaneous fiction can adequately describe Pynchon's concept of history:

> In his development toward simultaneous fiction, Pynchon exploits the curious relations of our familiar three-dimensional world to the four-dimensional world that encloses it. In his books, the time-bound world of the senses is suffused with the four-dimensional world of the space-time continuum. The four-dimensional world is used by Pynchon as the scientific expression of continuity unavailable to us on "this side," and is a figure for the continuities of timeless meaning and connection which exist at once with the historical time his characters and readers experience.[32]

While Schaub describes the experience of reading *Gravity's Rainbow* in terms of an artificial pseudopsychosis, I would rather stress the crucial difference from psychosis, dream, or primary processes. Unlike dreams, *Gravity's Rainbow* does not present simultaneity as undifferentiated and nonhierarchical, but as highly structured and hierarchical. In order to grasp this simultaneity, the reader must distinguish between macro- and microstructure. Initially, the process of reading follows the microstructure, whereas the macrostructure can only be discerned by reconstructing the intricacies of the narrative perspective.[33] But even if a reader takes the trouble to reconstruct the macro-perspective, this activity remains secondary compared to the reading process as such.

A crucial problem in aesthetically mediating the narrative perspective of *Gravity's Rainbow* is that language, as a medium linked to our three-dimensional system of order, can only suggest the idea of a four-dimensional order; it cannot operate from within this order. This gives Pynchon's simultaneous fiction a utopian and artificial effect. It plays with the discrepancy between the boundaries of experience imposed on historical subjects and theoretical models that transcend these boundaries. But whatever can be theorized or anticipated as order can also be aesthetically simulated. In this respect, *Gravity's Rainbow* is indeed a kind of science fiction, albeit of a different order.

This conceptual perspective complements the polarization between lived history and a history generated by transpersonal systems. Theoretical fictions partake in both the transpersonal systems and the systems of order and meaning that govern the social world. To separate those two spheres theoretically or experientially is a pragmatic reduction of complexity that might be unavoidable given the limitations of quotidian experience. Like the characters in *Gravity's Rainbow,* we must produce pragmatic fictions to order our daily lives and our historical experience. In Pynchon such fictions are confronted with the aesthetic simulation of an order with higher differentiation and complexity.

The narrative perspective of *Gravity's Rainbow* thus incorporates a utopian dimension by playfully simulating an expanded consciousness modeled on theoretical projections of a four-dimensional world. At the same time, however, the narrator undermines a position of omniscience, since such a position would simulate total control over the order of the text and hypostatize it as a closed system. Borrowing from a novelistic tradition of self-ironical or self-critical narrators, Pynchon self-ironically carnivalizes the narrative perspective. His narrator repeatedly teases the reader explicitly by refuting expectations of consistency and causality in his historical fiction. Ironically commenting on his own impact as a fictional observer on the observed historical period, he playfully exposes multiple manifestations of his own persona, which he transforms or dissolves as he pleases.[34] Like the unnamable, Pynchon's narrator is a figure without clear boundaries. But unlike Beckett's unnamable, Pynchon's unnamed narrator does not reflect upon the impasse between subject and discourse, but upon the artificiality of a narrative perspective that can do what neither the characters nor historical subjects in general can do—namely, to experience history as a space-time continuum and to play with different dimensions of its manifestation.

From this perspective, the simulation of a fourth dimension can be seen as an attempt to adapt narrative techniques to the explosive complexity of contemporary societies and to their theoretical knowledge.[35] Moreover, it reflects the limits within which we can experience complexity since, above a certain level, complexity is simply experienced as chaos. As Baudrillard has shown, increasing information cannot reduce complexity, because a linear increase in information turns entropic. In *Gravity's Rainbow* there is little of the type of historical information usually transmitted in more conventional historical novels. Rather, the text reveals how historical subjects must deal with an ever increasing quantity of abstraction. As Habermas has argued, in our century those abstractions surpass the tolerable amount of complexity of even a highly differentiated lifeworld organized according to our sense of space, time, and sociality.[36] In *Gravity's Rainbow* the abundance of mythologies is exposed as a misdirected cultural response to this overcomplexity.

Apart from the fear of war and the unacknowledged horror of fascism, the apocalyptic myth of the Rocket also reveals a more anonymous terror concerning a new category of literally invisible risks that can only be understood from a systemic perspective; risks that threaten the lifeworld while at the same time exceeding its dimensions.[37] In contrast to these myths, the narrative perspective calls for a renunciation of the treacherous protection of closed systems—not in order to propagate antiparanoia but in order to use the small space of creative paranoia, which still leaves a glimmer of hope.

Cyborgs

Subjectivity in *Gravity's Rainbow* is pervaded by the effects of transpersonal systems. Even though produced by humans, these systems develop a dynamic of their own, and their impact can no longer be understood or experienced concretely. Pynchon radicalizes this transpersonal formation of subjectivity. Many of his characters resemble cyborgs—cybernetic organisms that are controlled, if not rebuilt, by current technologies and modes of information.[38] Tyrone Slothrop, for example, had been used in his childhood in order to test the newly invented "krypotosam." Since by coincidence this same material was later used in the construction of the V-2, Slothrop developed a sensitivity to the Rocket, which appeared, to himself and to every outsider, to be completely paranormal. Grotesquely, the map of his amorous adventures anticipates exactly the map of the Rocket's future points of impact. The technological manipulation of Slothrop's body has transformed him into a cybernetic organism that reacts like an electronic machine to the stimulus of the Rocket.

We already take for granted some technological extensions of our body, such as the ear's extension by the telephone, the eye's by film, television, or telescope, and the brain's by computer. We have also become used to the increasing impact of cybernetics and computers on language. *Gravity's Rainbow* shows how transpersonal control systems generate a split within the subject that, like the split between consciousness and the unconscious, creates a dynamic tension between the separated domains. On their simplest level, the transpersonal systems exert their control on historical subjects from the outside through a concrete apparatus of power. In *Gravity's Rainbow,* the state, the media, and the sciences are the main vehicles of power. But the deepest effects on the changing cultural forms of subjectivity result from a tendency in the subjects to remain unaware of or even to repress the experience of transpersonal control. Such a structural repression establishes an illusory protective shield[39] against the overwhelming impact of outside controlling forces or stimuli. The transpersonal systems themselves have developed their own mechanisms to enforce such a structural repression and respective strategies of displacement.

In contemporary societies it is above all the mass media that help to internalize transpersonal control. This control becomes unconscious not in a dynamic Freudian sense, but in a more mediated sense by shaping unconscious fantasies and collective dreams. Some cultural critics argue that the mass media contribute to a cultural colonization of the unconscious. But such a colonization works only to the extent to which transpersonal systems of communication are able to produce a collusion with the unconscious of concrete historical subjects. In the fictional world of *Gravity's Rainbow* the power of the technological systems and their communicating organs, the media, increases in proportion to their ability to reach the unconscious. The proliferation of technological myths of transcendence is the most striking example. They become the symbolic carriers of an unconscious cathexis of technology and of an internalization of its power. Pynchon exposes the attempted colonization of the unconscious as part of a more general cybernetization of subjectivity and a new type of cultural semiotization anchored in the mass media.

This semiotization induces a process of cultural change that moves in two directions. One direction is the widespread cultural desensitization that Herbert Marcuse has analyzed in *One-Dimensional Man* and that seems to express itself in the flatness of most of Pynchon's characters. Frederic Jameson refers to the same phenomenon when he criticizes "the waning of affect" in "postmodern schizophrenia" which produces only "surfaces" and discards the validity of categories of depth. Baudrillard envisions this process in a more complicated way, reflecting possible ambiguities in cultural desensitization. In "The Implosion of Meaning in the Media and the Implosion of the Social in the Masses," he analyzes new forms of passive protest against the social control of the mass media, or an involuntary immunization against its effects.[40]

But postindustrialist media culture also further differentiates the means of communication. Theories already anticipate a possible transition from three-dimensional to four-dimensional systems of order, and computer techniques make nonlinear, simultaneous systems of ordering information feasible. As we have seen, Pynchon already mediates the cybernetization of the subject through the simulation of a four-dimensional narrative perspective. However, Pynchon's presentation of the cyborg, with its utopia of a cybernetically unbounded subjectivity, remains ambivalent. On the one hand, cyborgs appear as subjects under the spell of entropy and alien determination. Highly susceptible to regressive desublimation, they are prone to indulge in fascistic rituals of destruction. On the other hand, the text also emphasizes the utopia of a cyborg with a higher differentiation of subjectivity.

This ambivalence implicitly critiques the mystification of technology in late Romanticism as much as the wholesale demonization of technology. Concrete functions of technology in *Gravity's Rainbow* are always embedded in its historical uses. But regarding such historical uses, Pynchon's perspective is as grim as the historical period he fictionalizes. The dream of a pretechnological paradise offers no alternative either, since such a paradise is as lost as the dream of a preverbal or presymbolic unity, or—as it is formulated in *Gravity's Rainbow*—the Pre-Christian unity of the True Text.

Gravity's Rainbow in fact makes a strong historical connection between the cybernetization of the subject and the experimental expansion of language: the activation of primordial presymbolic forms of thought and speech offer a rudimentary model for simulations of a four-dimensional order. *Gravity's Rainbow* experiments with a literary representation that mediates the notion of a four-dimensional order within the three-dimensional order of poetic language. Pynchon makes such an order imaginable without using or representing it in the conventional sense of the word.

Because it remains bound to the temporality and relative linearity of language, Pynchon's project of a four-dimensional narrative perspective collides with the boundaries of language. We can already develop such conceptual notions as, for example, the undefinable character of the temporal order of coexisting phenomena, or the conception of movement as timeless or directed back into the past. But there is as yet no adequate expression in language of the *object* of such notions. Pynchon's simulation of a four-dimensional order may be seen as a postmodern version of the aesthetic paradox of representing the unrepresentable. Those of his characters who are themselves interested in transcending the boundaries of language fall back onto mythologies of a presymbolic unity. The members of the counterforce, for example, who "talk mandalas" (p. 706) in order to escape the prison-house of a disowned and entropic language, translate the experience of a loss of meaning into that of lost messages, and take refuge in mythologies of primordial unity. *Gravity's Rainbow* itself performs a stylistic anticipation of a four-dimensional experience after the age of writing.

Script and Postscript

Paradoxically, the vision within which such an anticipation appears moves toward what one could term a dystopia of the entropy of writing.[41] The affinities with Derrida's conception of *écriture* are embedded in numerous other affinities with poststructuralism and deconstruction such as, for example, with Lacan's notions of the real and of truth, or with Foucault's archeology of marginal histories. The whole narrative of the Hereros could, in fact, easily be modeled according to a Foucaultian archeology of history.

One could read *Gravity's Rainbow* as a literary version of the poststructuralist critique of Western history and philosophy and of a symbolic order based on logo- and phallocentrism. The first wave of a popularizing reception of poststructuralism in the United States coincides with the time in which Pynchon wrote *Gravity's Rainbow*, and we can already hear his characters voice utterances that sound like popularized versions of poststructuralist theorems. *Gravity's Rainbow* thus illustrates the danger of their mystification within an intellectual subculture (such as the New Age movement) or their hardening into closed systems of theoretical thought. While fully integrating poststructuralism's theoretical challenge to traditional philosophical and epistemological assumptions, Pynchon also exposes a mystifying historical appropriation, which leads to an erosion and closure of its major assets.

Poststructuralism is not the only theoretical movement prone to popularizing mystifications in *Gravity's Rainbow*. The New Physics and relativity theory share the same destiny. The characters easily absorb into their pop mysticism diverse theoretical assumptions, such as the entropy principle or relativity theory. They adapt the New Physics, cybernetics, and systems theory, and they play with the notion of an entropy of writing or of a violent symbolic order similar to those developed by poststructuralism and deconstruction. In this way, Pynchon's text dramatizes how avant-garde theories seep into the collective consciousness of popular culture. At the same time, he traces the roots of contemporary theoretical concerns with openness, relativity, fluidity, ambiguity, and ambivalence back to Romanticism, if not to older mystic philosophies.

In this context, Derrida's reflections on *écriture* are especially relevant. Numerous mythologies of a primordial unity evoked in *Gravity's Rainbow* are based on nostalgic dreams of the lost multiplicity of oral culture. In *Gravity's Rainbow* it is not language as such, but the linearity and teleology of onedimensional writing that institutes the order of analysis and death. Pynchon's poetic language tries to undermine such order with its multidimensional forms of expression. This recalls a vision of language in Jacques Derrida's *Of Grammatology*, where he takes the notion of four-dimensional thought from the French archeologist Leroi-Gourhan.[42] Leroi-Gourhan links the crisis of writing to a development of multidimensional, simultaneous forms of presentation:

> Curiously enough one may wonder if the audiovisual techniques really change the traditional behavior of anthropiens. One may also wonder about the fate of writing in a more or less distant future. Due to its one-dimensional linearity, writing has doubtlessly consti-tuted, during several million years and independent of its role as a repository for collective memory, the instrument of analysis for philo-sophical and scientific thought. Nowadays we are able to conceive of the conservation of thought differently . . . An immense "mag-netic library" with electronic selection will in the near future instantly deliver preselected and restored information. Reading will still main-tain its importance for centuries to come, despite a distinct regression for the vast majority, but writing [*écriture*] is likely to disappear rapidly and be replaced by automatic dictaphones . . . The long-term effects on the forms of reasoning and on a return to undifferentiated and multidimensional thought are at present unpredictable . . . It is certain that if there existed a procedure that would allow for a form of presenting books such that their different chapters were offered simultaneously and in all their contexts, the authors and their users would find a considerable advantage in this mode of presentation.[43]

Leroi-Gourhan's utopian speculation provides an ideal framework for interpreting the aesthetic devices in *Gravity's Rainbow* as a break with the linearity of writing and three-dimensional thought. Like Leroi-Gourhan, Pynchon does not propagate the end of writing but an expansion of its boundaries from within. The literary form Pynchon creates for this purpose—especially the four-dimensional narrative per-spective and the macrostructure of *Gravity's Rainbow*—is so complex that one may well describe its aesthetic experience as a practice of multidimensional reading within the transitional space of literature.

Stylistic Carnival and Infantile Regression

There is yet another form of transgressing the boundaries of language that is as prominent as Pynchon's conceptual experiments. This transgression was historically inspired by Dadaism and its forms of cultural resistance. In *Gravity's Rainbow*, the counterforce, an exotic group consisting of members of the schwarzkommando, former double agents, and other "preterites," is inspired by the vanguard movements of the Weimar republic and has its contemporary equivalent in the "Dada of the sixties." Pynchon dedicates *Gravity's Rainbow* to the memory of his friend Richard Fariña, an underground writer and cult figure of the sixties. The last section of the novel, "Counterforce," displays the most obvious similarities to the "roaring sixties." The dialogue of the counterforce characters mimics the resigned self-analysis of sixties groups facing their impotence vis-à-vis the establishment and the State.

And yet, even the narrator's satirical perspective of the counterforce does not diminish its being the only force of resistance against the order of analysis and death—a mobilization of irrational anarchy that articulates itself in an "isolated voice refusing to be routinized and consumed like a piece of coal."[44] The most positively drawn characters of the book form the counterforce and undoubtedly own the sympathy displayed in the textual perspective. On the other hand, they never gain the status of a utopia. Their powerless protest shows signs of infantile regression, and they indulge in aggressive anal provocations. At one level, counterforce members deliberately stage their unbounded regression to ward off their sense of impotence before the terrors of destruction. Their conscious renunciation of both a deadly reality principle and compensatory mythologies of transcendence shows that their unboundedness pursues a very different goal than metaphysical transcendence. Against the transcendence toward pure being, they oppose a transcendence downward into a world of farcical meaninglessness.[45] Feeling hopelessly excluded from all social spheres of political influence and exposed to the destructive irrationality of anonymous systems of power, the characters transform their inherited puritan paranoia into "creative paranoia." At an anarchistic "Gross Suckling Conference" (p. 706) they appear as childish rebels, as self-declared victims of a political system that, like a "Great Mother," nourishes and clothes them in order finally to devour them.[46]

Like its model, Dadaism, the counterforce acts against the spirit of gravity maintained even in the myths of transcendence. Their anarchism produces an art of militant irony.[47] But Dadaism was highly ambivalent toward the political currents of its own time, especially toward fascism; it wavered between aesthetic affirmation and relentless opposition. And like the dadaism of the Weimar republic and of the 1960s, the counterforce, anticipating its own defeat, eventually succumbs to ecstatic destruction. They hurl their nonsensical contaminations of meaning against the mythologizing semiotization of war. Using the old weapon of designification, they express their resistance in hopeless political acts of transgression—rejecting all available systems of meaning and power while knowing full well that they will fail.

The counterforce may also serve as a model for analyzing some of the aesthetic devices of *Gravity's Rainbow*. It is tempting to read certain of its communicative strategies as a grandiose ironic performance of an aesthetic counterforce. Like Roger Mexico in his last appearances, the aesthetic counterforce of this text does not shy away from any violation of taboos or any stylistic regression in opting for a trancendence downward into a world of farcical insignificance.

The baroque richness of Pynchon's grotesque, exotic, and obscene images and narratives and the mixture of high and low forms of expression turn Pynchon's novel into a prime example of a postmodern carnivalesque text.[48] Carnival mediates the historical material as well as the forms of discourse in this novel. Due to its simultaneous fiction, which blends past and future into the historical setting of World War II, the text creates more than a "restoration of an active, accumulated memory" in Bakhtin's sense.[49] It makes historical connections that have been repressed from or never admitted to the collective memory.

Forgotten marginal events or buried mythologies of World War II move to the center stage of *Gravity's Rainbow*, while the historical period threatens to move into the present with the reality of the Vietnam War. The carnivalesque parade of alien and bizarre figures through the World War II setting—from the Puritan settler William Slothrop to Richard Nixon, King Kong, and Plastic Man, including such oddities as the trained gigantic octopus Grigori and the immortal lightbulb Byron—evokes a postmodern carnival that plays with the effects of simulation produced by bizarre collages. The narrator's carnivalesque gaze uncovers subversive connections that violate historical taboos. *Gravity's Rainbow* becomes a zone of contact between history and the present as well as between official history and marginal histories. This carnivalesque gaze looks behind the recorded scenes of war and the defensive narratives of its participants. It installs itself as a fictional memory that retains and uncovers what is repressed by those immersed in the historical situation as well as what escapes the linearity of conventional historical narratives.

Pynchon's intertextuality reinforces this carnivalization. The contamination of high with low (or what some critics call "sub-literary") forms celebrates a postmodern anarchy of literary forms and genres. Pynchon's mixture of different forms and styles appears less constructed and artful than the familiar forms of intertextuality. His carefree style and his refusal to integrate the diverse intertexts into a homogenizing structure reminds one of an aesthetic transcendence downward. Or, as Bakhtin formulates it, we have "not the simple violation of a norm, but the negation of all abstract and rigid norms which claim absolute and eternal validity."[50]

Just as Pynchon contructs an artificial myth in order to counteract the myths of his characters, he also uses the carnivalesque simulation of styles—including decidely "bad" styles—against established literary and rhetorical conventions. Often he stages this as a carnivalesque laughter at death—as, for example, in the song "Carry on the Show," which appears in several variations:

> It never does seem to mat-ter if there's daaaanger,
> For Danger's a roof I fell from long ago—
> I'll be out-one-day and never come back,
> Forget the bitter you owe me, Jack,
> Just piss on m'grave and car-ry on the show! (p. 12)

"Carry on the show" signals a collective denial of fear, an adaptation to the performance of war that helps one to forget its reality. "It's all theatre" (p. 3) says one of the characters at the beginning of the novel. But instead of a Baudrillardian free play of simulation, we witness a special form of what Walter Benjamin called aesthetization of politics. Pynchon's characters stylize Rilke as the guru of a mystified death drive and turn Wagner and Humperdinck into soap operas of apocalypse and transcendence. From this perspective it is true that "it's all theatre"—but it is the theater of imaginary subjects who either act out illusionary realities or participate in the big Show without illusions. When, during the performance of Humperdinck's *Hänsel and Gretel,* a rocket crashes into the theater, Gretel appears on stage and sings:

> With a peppermint face in the sky-y,
> And a withered old dream in your heart

You'll get hit with a piece of the pie-e
With a pantomime ready to start!
. . .

And those voices you hear, Boy and Girl of the Year,
Are of children who are learning to die. (p. 175)

This core scene anticipates the structure of the novel's ending. "Descent," the last section of the "final Count-Down," starts in the Orpheus theater in San Francisco with a rhythmically clapping audience requesting: "Come on! *Start*—the—show!" But the Show turns out to be the silent fall of the apocalyptical Rocket on the imaginary *theatrum mundi*. The laconic exhortation "Now everybody" ends both film and novel.

The carnivalesque transgressions function as a counterbalance for the cultural pessimism of this apocalyptic metafiction. They introduce a pleasure of the text, not by indulging in apocalyptic fantasies but by celebrating a sensual, creative, and actively staged resistance. Grotesque scenes and images—as, for example, little Ludwig who, accompanied by Slothrop in the costume of the pig hero Plechazunga, searches for his female lemming Ursula—display a carnivalesque sensuality that opposes the deadly logic of war, if not a collective death drive.[51] The same can be said of Pynchon's kaleidoscopic plays with ever more unusual mirror effects and echos, in which incompatible elements—what has been parceled off into closed systems or different historical times—are brought together in a simultaneous fiction that opposes the particularizations, fragmentations, and segmentations of linear consciousness.

Pynchon's aesthetic carnival formally revives an old carnivalesque tradition of demystifying cultural or religious norms, collective mythologies, and conventions of poetic language. It works against thinking in closed systems and totalities and against the entropy of writing. And it functions as a counterforce against the cultural flight into the inanimate and the gravity of the psyche. Those in ancient Rome opposed the spirit of *gravitas* with the lightness of their humor and an Epicurean delight in flying and gliding. The poetic language of *Gravity's Rainbow* is located in a transitional space where the gravity of systems and psyches meets the color and weightlessness of the rainbow. It is written in the spirit of Nietzsche, who said, "Not by wrath does one kill, but by laughter. Come, let us kill the spirit of gravity."[52]

8

Basic Configurations of Transitional Texts

The previous readings of twentieth-century novels focus on the multiple forms in which experimental modern and postmodern texts have crossed what at their time functioned historically and culturally as boundaries of language and subjectivity. They have performed such crossings both within established systems and between systems, using astounding formal experiments that challenge and change poetic language, literary subjectivity, narrative, history, characters, textual composition, and notions of order in general. They have subverted not only literary and aesthetic conventions but also contemporary epistemological, ontological, and philosophical assumptions as well as conceptual categories. Adapting Winnicott's theory of the transitional space of play to a theory of the intermediacy of poetic language, I have called these texts "transitional texts," recalling the fact that they are the cultural descendants of so-called transitional objects.

To outline the basic configurations of transitional texts is to project a heuristic notion of order onto a complex and ongoing process. Transitional texts are highly self-reflexive and often immanently challenge their own modes of representation. They confront the reader with a radical otherness that cannot be appropriated through available categories of aesthetic order. The reader may well have to search for or invent new categories in order to account for a quite singular experience of reading.

Often transitional texts expose their readers to an excruciating experience of a loss of order. But such an initial shock is a necessary condition to awaken the reader's sensitivity to the otherness of those texts. As a rule, transitional texts deploy strategies that initiate the reader into new, often more complex configurations of differentiation. Most of the transitional texts under consideration challenge systems of linear order with a poetics of multidimensional spatial form. The following attempt to trace epistemological—if not anthropological—functions of transitional texts tries to theorize their new configurations of language and subjectivity. This orientation assumes a certain "family likeness," in Wittgenstein's sense, between literary texts and reading subjects or, more generally, between language and subjectivity.

Specific similarities in the communicative strategies of these transitional texts may indicate ways in which they aim at changing the very structure of aesthetic experience. We may assume that their implied reader is modeled according to their new notions of subjectivity and that their communicative strategies affect the subjectivity of recipients. Finally, the last chapter discusses transitional literary subjectivity in light of current theoretical concepts and debates that focus on indeterminacy, openness, and flexibility of boundaries.

Boundaries, Language, and Subjectivity

Despite the multiplicity of aesthetic devices and the multifaceted literary subjectivity displayed in transitional texts, they also share distinctive historical features. Their unbounded subjectivity is so intricately tied to their experimental language that one cannot be understood without the other. Each of the transitional texts under consideration develops its own aesthetic play of boundaries.

The transgression of boundaries in Virginia Woolf's *The Waves* is motivated mainly by the specific poetic mood of Woolf's "playpoem," which in turn resonates with the psychology of its literary characters. Inspired by the Bloomsbury group's keen interest in psychoanalysis, Woolf attempts to translate her emphasis of psychology and the unconscious into the poetics of her text. The characters' desire for primordial unity and fusion with others also entails a threat of disintegration and loss of self. On the surface their dialogues cast their fictional lives by tracing the rift between their rigid social identities and their unbounded desires. Aesthetically, however, these interior dialogues are used as transitional spaces for exploring an unbounded subjectivity able to access unconscious moods or emotions—their own or others'—which the characters are cut off from in their social world.

The formal qualities of the interior dialogues counterbalance the horizontal split between primary and secondary modes of experience that the characters expose in their narratives. This formal transgression of boundaries is based on the aesthetic paradox of a literary presentation of subjectivity that transcends the consciously experienced subjectivity of the speakers.

Emphasizing the absolute priority of language, *Finnegans Wake* creates a highly artificial symbolic order that ignores linguistic as well as aesthetic conventions. While *The Waves* works against a horizontal division of subjectivity, *Finnegans Wake* works against the linguistic foundation of such a division. The gradual suppression of primary processes in the genesis of the subject corresponds to a suppression of primary processes in the symbolic order at large, and the acquisition of language mediates the formation of social subjects oriented toward secondary processes. However, since language retains a capacity to use primary processes in order to voice the unconscious within speech, transgressions of the symbolic order are thus already built into the potential of language.

Finnegans Wake uses this potential by deliberately expanding its poetic language toward primary processes. With this aesthetic device, the text overcomes the polarization between the two modes of expression and experience. The integration of diverse languages and linguistic forms into the polylogue of the *Wake* dissolves what Paul Ricoeur terms the "structure of double meaning" that divides speech into distinguishable layers of manifest and latent meaning. The emphasis on primary processes in the *Wake*'s poetic language can be understood as a regression—less in the sense of a disintegration of language than in the sense of a recuperation of a form of expression that has historically been suppressed in the development of language and linguistic codes. By reactivating primary processes within poetic language, *Finnegans Wake* also revives the mode of the so-called prelinguistic or primordial experience. This transitional text thus reshapes both the material elements and the boundaries of language.

In the process of this reshaping, *Finnegans Wake* dissolves its literary characters into condensed literary forms. Instead of being anchored in characters, subjectivity in this text is anchored in language. This new form of language subjectivity mimics aesthetically the empirical and epistemological foundation of subjectivity in language. In exploring the possibilities of a subjectivity created through language alone,

Finnegans Wake pushes a contemporary figure of thought to its utter extreme—namely, the notion of a desubstantialized textual subjectivity that does not correspond directly to any experience of subjectivity in the social world. Poetic language thus becomes a privileged paradigm of transitional speech: by temporarily suspending the rules of the symbolic order, it creates a linguistic universe of its own in the transitional space between primary and secondary processes.

Just as *Finnegans Wake* crystallizes a transitional speech, *The Unnamable* portrays a transitional character. Beckett's first-person narrator voices his subjectivity by exploring the limits of representing subjectivity within speech. This literary subject attempts to practice a radical renunciation of fictions of the self within speech, knowing full well that this is a paradoxical project for any subject, let alone a fictional one. Given this epistemological and ontological dilemma, the unnamable invents himself as a paradoxical fiction hovering over the boundaries between I and Not-I, differentiation and dissolution. Without ontological substance, he linguistically materializes as a transitional character in perpetual flight from self-manifestation. Conventional notions of subjectivity—empirical, literary, or philosophical—are merely negative foils for him, implanted into his mind against his will by anonymous others. But the alternative of an autopoietic self-generation of a purely literary subjectivity does not work either, since the unnamable finds that even his own fictional voices are contaminated by alien voices.

The unnamable implodes language from within in order to subvert the differentiating systems of the symbolic order and hence the very possibility of self-constitution. Despite the fact that the techniques of his discourse are highly differentiated and self-reflexive, this process threatens the foundations of subjectivity and language. Like Joyce, Beckett experiments with the boundaries between primary and secondary processes. But while *Finnegans Wake* explores a purely linguistic subjectivity, *The Unnamable* demonstrates how language can erode the very ground for experiencing subjectivity. Playing with notions of a subject lost in language, *The Unnamable* evokes one of the central paradigms of contemporary theories of language and subjectivity. On one level, this discourse constitutes a critical aesthetic reflection of the poststructuralist absence of the subject in language. But on yet another level, *The Unnamable* challenges empirical and psychological notions of subjectivity, as well as conceptual schemata of subjectivity developed throughout the history of philosophy. While resisting its own reduction to a new concept, Beckett's text ultimately explores the paradox of voicing the subject.

Mediated through the frame of a historical novel, *Gravity's Rainbow* develops a new form of fictional presentation of history. Pynchon's novel exposes the effects of an increasingly transpersonal organization of the social world on historical subjects. Fragmentation, violence, paranoia, superstition, and mythology reveal the inherent irrationality of a hyperrationalized, technological, and hopelessly overcomplex social order. Multinational industrial networks and a state apparatus controlled by the logic of monopoly capitalism create a superstructure that becomes increasingly opaque to historical subjects, who internalize this transpersonal logic without ever consciously experiencing it. Because the communicative infrastructure becomes saturated with information, historical interpretation can no longer simply be rooted in the lived experience of historical subjects.[1] The characters' experience of social reality is reduced to special sectors and social subsystems and thus becomes partial and fragmented. They compensate for their unanswered need for global syntheses with myths of primordial unity and transcendence. The narrator, however, in turn demythologizes these myths as the unacknowledged imperatives of totalized subsystems.

The contrast between the fragmented perspectives of characters who hunger for totalizing myths and the demythologizing narrative perspective becomes the basis for a new conception of fictional history. Like *The Unnamable*, *Gravity's Rainbow* plays with diffusions between the real and the imaginary. Pynchon couples the imaginary semiotization of social reality with a technological invasion of the transitional space. Instead of a creative autopoiesis, *Gravity's Rainbow* stresses a subtle colonization of the unconscious through the controlled production of collective dreams and mythologies. Characters become anonymous extras in a show directed by transpersonal forces. And yet at times even the extras fall out of their roles and, resisting the attempted colonization, reshape the prefabricated images of a technological dream factory with their own excessive desires.

The wholesale change in social conditions, however, imbues the transgressions of boundaries in *Gravity's Rainbow* with a new ambivalence. This text exposes how transgressions become susceptible to manipulations and perversions. Under certain social conditions, transgression can degenerate into a purely regressive desublimation, supported by a media- or "culture industry" that incites controlled desublimations as a leisure compensation for the increasing social control over the subject in all other spheres, especially in the workplace.[2] We might see such an invasion of the transitional space as the cultural equivalent of an invasion of the inner core of the subject by an other—an intrusion Winnicott describes as a form of psychological rape. *Gravity's Rainbow* portrays the increasing impact of film and other media on the imagination of historical subjects as a cultural violation of the "protected" transitional space.

Poetic language in *Gravity's Rainbow* often appears as a pastiche of current theories of language. For the characters, language is an instrument of logocentric order as well as a carrier of personal identity. Like the characters in *The Waves*, Pynchon's characters are torn between two desires, "personal identity and impersonal salvation" (p. 406). The narrator, however, mocks such a mystifying polarization. The text's carnivalesque language subverts the codified order of language as well as the gravity of myths with a subjective anarchy, celebrating the excesses of speech over all rules, conventions, and norms.

Pynchon retains a fundamental ambivalence toward transgressions of boundaries. Under certain historical circumstances they form a resistance against a rigid "order of analysis and death," which cultural critics, from the Frankfurt School to Deleuze/Guattari and Theweleit, have linked to an authoritarian or fascistic socialization. But sadomasochistic rituals and organized violence under fascism also perform a transgression of boundaries—this time as a destructive return of the repressed. One is reminded of Deleuze and Guattari's warning that the free-floating energies and transgressions of the schizo are always haunted by a fascist double. In a different way, *The Unnamable* conveys the fallacies of unbounded transgressions. *Gravity's Rainbow* further reveals their underlying sociopolitical conditions, thus shifting the emphasis from the philosophical or epistemological realm to a social pathology. Pynchon shows how state apparatus and war machinery convert an archaic desire for transcendence and primordial unity into the destructive instincts needed to maintain their own paranoid structures. While the earlier transitional texts react against a horizontal division of subjectivity, *Gravity's Rainbow* reacts against a vertical split in the cultural formations of subjectivity brought about by an unintegrated contiguity of rigid social control, uncontrolled desublimation, asocial anarchy, and collective aggression on the one hand, and mysticism, superstition, and archaic rituals on the other.

The double exposure of this historical fiction—its insertion of characters and events from the sixties and early seventies—provides a historical retrospective of World War II inspired by the postmodern United States and the Vietnam War. Under these conditions, the historical ambiguity of the boundaries of subjectivity gains a new concreteness. Transgressions have acquired a high market value and are made consumer friendly by a media culture indulging in an inflationary politics of sex and crime. Pynchon links this politics with the sector of macropolitical domination. His most perverse and criminal characters have the highest power in the military, politics, war research, or technology. From Pynchon's perspective, we can no longer simply presuppose an authoritarian society in which rigid social structures are subverted by cultural transgressions. Or, from a different perspective, we can no longer simply assume that the mere enforcement of primary processes has an integrative cultural function. The status of primary-process experience varies according to the specific historical conditions. *Gravity's Rainbow* reveals how film and other media engage the unconscious for their production of new mythologies. All of Pynchon's characters indulge in fantasies of transgression or transcendence—the fascists and the authoritarians as much as the anarchists, revolutionaries, and individualists. Moreover, formal transgressions and simulations of textual entropy are among the most important aesthetic devices in Pynchon's text.

Gravity's Rainbow indicates that the most far-reaching change in contemporary subjectivity lies in the cultural formation of cyborgs, cybernetic organisms whose senses and whose unconscious are expanded but also determined technologically. Historical subjects are invaded by alien technological bodies or body parts. Pynchon probes the resistance of a counterforce against such an invasion. While some of Pynchon's characters, such as Slothrop, try out the art of Baudrillardian simulation and the possibilities of passive resistance or immunization against culturally transmitted information and messages, the members of the counterforce practice collective anarchy. Pynchon's text, however, with its simultaneous fictions and its playful transgression of our three-dimensional perspective, follows the earlier transitional texts in experimenting with formal transgressions that affect the modes of reading and thereby the cultural formation of subjectivity in general.

The Break with Cartesian Subjectivity

Sink deep or touch not the Cartesian spring!
—*Finnegans Wake* (301.24–25)

Transitional texts, like most current theories of the subject, refute the paradigm of Cartesian subjectivity. This trend has its roots in the nineteenth century where, for example, the narrator in Melville's *Moby-Dick* rejects the burden of a Cartesian ego. The raging desire for unboundedness that underlies the myth of the white whale can be understood as a rebellion against the constrictions of Cartesianism. Moreover, Ishmael problematizes his own negative fixation to the Cartesian heritage that marks his narrative perspective. The aesthetic of blankness implicitly developed in Melville's text turns the empty space, which Descartes proscribes absolutely, into a metaphor for transcendence and the sublime. Blankness becomes the paragon of desire and the utopia of a new aesthetic. The epistemological dilemma described by the narrator, however, forces this conception to remain largely programmatic in *Moby-Dick*. Fully aware of the limitations of Cartesian reflexivity, Ishmael still cannot transcend them. His intuitive aesthetic experience of a defaced painting anticipates what he himself cannot yet realize or live.

In *The Unnamable,* the Cartesian ties emerge from within a consciousness that has radicalized the systematic doubt ad absurdum. *Cogito ergo sum,* carnivalized in *Finnegans Wake* as "cog it out, here goes a sum" (304.31), appears in *The Unnamable* as the metaphor for an obsolete identification of the subject with his mind. Not even the *cogito* itself remains unchallenged, since the unnamable can no longer unquestionably presuppose an I linked to a thought. His insistence on being thought by others expresses at one level the narrator's self-reflexive awareness of his own fictionality. But it also voices a subjectivity whose status and place in the mind have become problematic. The unnamable extends the Cartesian refusal to trust the body with its senses to encompass even the mind and subjectivity in general. "Where I am there is no one but me who am not" springs from a reflection that no longer finds any ground in the self-affirming *cogito ergo sum*.[3] Carried to their extreme, Cartesian methods of self-exploration are undermined from within. The unnamable's unlimited doubt materializes in spirals of verbal negation that weaken the Cartesian tie between self-reference and binary schematization. Thus they withdraw one of the basic conditions of Cartesian thought: the self-referential organization as a closed system.[4] For the unnamable, the binary oppositions of Cartesian epistemology are imaginary oppositions, artificial constructs of a language failing to grasp the complexity of a mind that rejects each "either . . . or" as an entrapment in the systematic Cartesian spirit. The narrator prefers his endless series of "no . . . or . . . but. . . if" or an inclusive "be it that . . . or that"[5] in order to produce his irresolvable paradoxes and to remain faithful to his dictum "the thing to avoid is the spirit of system" (p. 4).

Regardless—or perhaps precisely because—of all these anti-Cartesian moves, *The Unnamable* can be seen as a late product of Cartesian self-consciousness. Yet the concrete fictionalization of Cartesian figures and theorems (stressed mainly in Anglo-American Beckett criticism) subverts the Cartesian heritage. The narrator's all too concrete radicalizations of Cartesian reflection release him from the boundaries of a Cartesian logic into the paradoxical discourse of a hopelessly self-reflexive subject without ontological substance, a subject who no longer finds consolation in the Cartesian optimism of a self-affirming identity between thought and subject.[6]

While *The Unnamable* mirrors the aporias of Cartesian self-consciousness through the conception of a literary character, *Gravity's Rainbow* develops an archeology of subjectivity that pursues the psychohistorical traces of Cartesian thought up to the present. This perspective reveals that Cartesianism is still ingrained in the very categories of most natural sciences. But the "old perfect Cartesian harmony" (p. 655) is irretrievably lost—even though some of the characters still try to escape from the reality of war into the security of Cartesian coordinates. The Cartesian dream has become one of their quotidian mythologies. Like the myths of transcendence, this dream is projected onto the symbolic object of the Rocket. Poekler, for example, mystifies the Rocket as an "immaculate Cartesian object." But the comforts of the Cartesian ego appear as an illusion that operates beyond history. *Gravity's Rainbow* couples Cartesian thought with the paranoid structuring of a subjectivity that, separated from its own ground, pursues the destruction of whatever is perceived as Other.

The Inclusion of Primary Processes

The transitional texts under consideration identify the formation of a Cartesian ego with a horizontal division within the subject and direct their anti-Cartesian discursive strategies against this split. Their fictional subversions of Cartesianism problematize the genesis of the philosophical subject, which still marks contemporary conceptions of subjectivity. The Cartesian ego appears as a privileged theoretical paradigm for the exclusion of primary processes from the symbolic order. In *Moby-Dick* the primordial domain figures as the lost core of the subject. The holistic myth of the white whale introduces a subject that internalizes the primordial as an integral part. From this perspective, the drama of Ahab and Ishmael is one of a subjectivity severed from its ground.

The transitional texts of the twentieth century are increasingly concerned with the imaginary aspects of subjectivity. Through diverse aesthetic techniques they try to integrate primary processes and the unconscious into language and communication. The interior dialogue in *The Waves*, the condensation of poetic language in *Finnegans Wake*, and the implosion of language in *The Unnamable* all testify to this process. *Gravity's Rainbow*, on the other hand, introduces an ambivalent historical turning point by exposing mythologies of transgression and dissolution without ever reverting to old notions of closed orders.

As opposed to the Cartesian notion of the subject, transitional texts create unbounded literary subjects who often display characteristics that would be considered pathological in the social world. But contemporary literary subjectivity does not simply depict the pathologies of schizophrenia. Such a theoretical assumption would fall back onto a framework of literary mimesis, if not social realism, that cannot explain the antimimetic or transmimetic devices of transitional texts. On the other hand, it is certainly no coincidence that the pathology of schizophrenia—namely, its rigid horizontal division between primary and secondary modes of experience—appear as the exact inverse of the horizontal division inherent in the Cartesian model of subjectivity. While the schizophrenic is totally inundated by primary processes, the ideal Cartesian subject would be completely purged of primary processes and thus under the total control of secondary processes. Literary subjectivity gains its relevance through its specific differences from both schizophrenia as well as Cartesian subjectivity. Transitional literary texts reveal both forms of horizontal division as cultural pathology. From their perspective, it is the rigid division between the two modes of experience, not the transgression of the boundaries between them, that creates the pathology.

Still, we must account for the fact that, from Melville to Pynchon, schizoid or schizophrenic characters are among the most prominent literary subjects. Two dispositions mark the formation of schizoid subjectivity in these texts: paranoia and incomplete psychological birth. According to Margaret Mahler, the latter results from disturbances in the ways in which a subject is mirrored. Philosophical and psychological or psychoanalytic theories share the assumption that modes of mirroring are decisive for the cultural formation of specific types of subjectivity. The *esse est percipi* still figures among the most powerful cultural notions of subjectivity. Metaphors and allegories of mirroring pervade the imagery of transitional texts. Many passages in *Moby-Dick* suggest that Ahab compensates for the absence of a mirroring mother by turning the whole world into a mirror of his grandiose self and by pursuing the white whale, whose most terrifying aspect, according to Ishmael, is that "he has no face" and thus incorporates the absence of a mirroring look. Rhoda in *The Waves* also does not "have a face" in the mirror, and for the unnamable, the *esse est percipi* has the connotations of a petrifying gaze.

At one level, such literary fantasies can be related to historical changes in the cultural formations of subjectivity, a process that Foucault sees accompanied by a "great anxiety"[7] and fear of losing shape and boundaries, once the model of a clearly bounded Cartesian subject is no longer viable. But such diverse critics as Theweleit, Jameson, Lasch, and Ziehe interpret these fantasies as indications that narcissistic disorders and schizophrenic disintegration characterize the current cultural formation of subjectivity in general. Narcissism, paranoia, schizophrenia, incomplete birth become allegories for a cultural (and sometimes, as in the case of Lasch, ultra-conservative) critique that aligns itself with literary theories that read contemporary literature as an expression of a larger cultural fragmentation and depravation. Other theorists, following Deleuze and Guattari, celebrate unbounded forms of subjectivity as an anarchic resistance to political domination. My own reading of transitional texts emphasizes their creative potential over their symptomatic value. Rather than merely reproducing a symptom, literary forms of unbounded subjectivity often explore alternate forms of subjectivity that counteract cultural symptoms.

This is also true of the ways the texts deal with cultural paranoia. The paranoid suffers less from a disorder in the modes of mirroring than from a diffusion of the boundaries between I and Not-I.[8] In both *The Unnamable* and *Gravity's Rainbow* anonymous others figure as phantasmatic instances of a paranoid division between inner and outer reality. The first person narrator in *The Unnamable* is obsessed with the thought that anonymous others impose their own images on him and force him, paradoxically, to both speak of himself while at the same time preventing him from ever doing so because they make him speak their words. His rhetorical gestures of withholding and his constant denials of all his utterances are discursive strategies to ward off the fear of being devoured or intruded by others. From this perspective, the unnamable appears as a schizoid subject in a paranoid world, spoken by alien voices who have disowned his speech.

Paranoia in *The Unnamable* is derived from and supported by the narrator's transference of philosophical conceptions of the subject onto a fictional world conceived under the conditions of empirical subjects. The unnamable as a self-reflexive literary subject thus occupies a transitional space between philosophy and an imagined everyday world. This allows him to lay bare a whole spectrum of paranoid constructions that underlie our Western philosophical tradition. By merging the two horizons of philosophy and paranoia, the discourse of the unnamable develops a powerful cultural critique that equates the epistemological premises of our cultural heritage with the symptomatology of paranoia.

While in *The Unnamable* the paranoid projection of anonymous others is linked to the narrator's epistemological doubts, in *Gravity's Rainbow* paranoia appears as a structural foundation of systems of interpretation in general. Apart from classical schizophrenic paranoia, Pynchon develops notions of an "operational paranoia" as well as a "creative paranoia." One can either become the passive victim of a paranoid delusion or use paranoia operationally or creatively in order to survive in a destructive world at war. Creative paranoia inverts the loss of creativity and control from which the clinical paranoid suffers.

In *Gravity's Rainbow* paranoia ceases to be a mere delusion; it becomes a mechanism that controls the formation of symbolic orders under specific historical conditions such as fascism, puritanism, and militarized societies in general. Paranoia thus no longer signals a failure to adapt to the symbolic order but, on the contrary, marks an overadaptation to that order. Just as the unnamable's hyperreflexivity implodes the rational system from which it developed, the overadaptation to a politics of exclusion of otherness produces cultural paranoia in *Gravity's Rainbow*. This form of cultural paranoia erodes the symbolic order from within. The repression of the Other provokes a return of the repressed, followed by a destructive impulse to completely exterminate the Other. Creative paranoia, instead, is directed against the paranoia of the whole system. Just as Pynchon's artificial mythological system counteracts primordial myths, his creative paranoia works in small doses, like a homeopathic drug, in order to counteract the general cultural paranoia.

The paranoid structuring of subjectivity in *Gravity's Rainbow* is only one manifestation of a more general cultural tendency in which systems pursue a rigid conservation or a successive differentiation of structures along the same lines. Ultimately, Pynchon's text exposes paranoia as the founding principle underlying the social semantics of its fictionalized historical worlds. At one level, paranoia seems to be a doomed attempt to ward off an unbearable reality. Behind the characters' flight into the inanimate lies a desperate effort to maintain minimal structure amid the destruction of war and the regressive desublimation that threatens them from within. Once the paranoid structure of the social semantics is internalized, it tends to create artificially closed social systems that maintain themselves either by becoming immune to their environment or by destroying it violently to protect their own boundaries.

In his essay on the regulation of systems, Dieter Wellershoff writes, "If one understands the conservation of structure as the primary function of a system, then systems of madness *(Wahnsysteme)* are the ideal systems . . . By refusing any insight into their founding principles, they conceal their own selectivity, they ignore that there is an environment to the system and thus resist their elimination."[9] Wellershoff describes precisely the petrification of a system that Bateson attributes to the internalization of epistemological errors. The latter form a political unconscious of sorts, the dynamic of which is comparable to the unconscious effects of paranoia in social contexts. Pushing Wellershoff's notion a step further, one can say that, by trying to prevent any change in their structure, those systems contribute to their own destruction from within.

Gravity's Rainbow suggests a very similar systemic conception of cultural paranoia and reveals its historical foundations. Pynchon's text traces the overadaptation to a politics of exclusion, which lies at the basis of cultural paranoia, back to the epistemological premises of Cartesianism. The text also reveals paranoia as the deep structure of such different historical formations as Calvinist puritanism and fascism. Paranoia thus figures in Pynchon's text as a cultural symptom produced by very different types of closed social systems that aim at a violent stasis or ossification of living processes and the destruction of otherness. From this perspective, paranoia is a pathological cultural formation of subjectivity that complements narcissism and schizophrenia. *Gravity's Rainbow* no longer presents these pathologies as deviations from the norm, but suggests that they have already become the norm. Paranoids, narcissists, and schizos alike react against a cultural praxis of rigid inclusion and exclusion: the paranoid exaggerates and totalizes the social structures of exclusion, the narcissist tries to refuse the social altogether, and the schizo invades it with a flood of unbounded drives and intensities.

While the subjectivity of characters in *Gravity's Rainbow* thus extends between the pathologies of cultural paranoia and the return of the repressed in regressive desublimation, the overall perspective and structure of the text introduces utopian aspects of a subjectivity able to break through these historical constraints. The narrator's playful simulation of a four-dimensional perspective creates a simultaneous fiction that engenders new modes of aesthetic experience. *Gravity's Rainbow* thus practices a textual transgression of boundaries as an act of resistance against the rigid closure of systems, the horizontal division of subjectivity, and reactive forms of regressive desublimation. Pynchon's transgression of boundaries is embedded in a dialectic of utopia and pathology. Against the dissolutions and fragmentations of its fictional world or its microstructure, *Gravity's Rainbow* asserts a macrostructure that introduces the transgression of boundaries as an expansion of narrative possibilities, mental structures, modes of representation, and aesthetic experience.

Mythologies of Transcendence

In one way or another, transitional texts all draw some connection between their transgressions of boundaries and historical visions of transcendence. Even though these visions are no longer presented as viable cultural options, they often function as symbolic evocations of the unrepresentable or the sublime. Their appeal lies in the structural tension between forces that shape and forces that resist confinement to a shape. A desire to transcend boundaries is aesthetically controlled by a delineated mythology. Even experimental texts that reject harmonizing mythologies and aesthetic closure still display a tension between gestalt formation and resistance against gestalt.

In *Moby-Dick,* the holistic myth of the white whale forms the core of the narrative. It symbolizes a metaphysical search for the transcendent ground of subjectivity. But this archaic challenge of decentered subjectivity is demythologized by the narrator. In *The Waves,* the mythological character Percival fulfills a similar function. Through his absence, Percival centers the subjectivity of the other characters, who project their desire for primordial unity and transcendence onto him. In his final monologue, however, Bernard demystifies this function of Percival by introducing trivial quotidian memories of his friend. *Finnegans Wake* plays with the holistic myth of the Great Letter, a miniature mirror of the textual universe, which, in turn, is supposed to mirror the human universe. At the same time, this holistic myth of the Great Letter functions as an ironic self-quotation. Supposedly containing the truth of all truth beyond space and time, it is nonetheless deposited in the mud and displayed as the prop of a grandiose textual carnival. *The Unnamable* desubstantializes the holistic myth by reenacting it as a myth of silence. What cannot be represented is no longer figured as a well-defined shape, but as emptiness. The unnamable willfully uses the myth of silence in order to undermine representation. His endless spirals are the paradoxical self-figuration of a subject who, despite his resistance to all speech as an imaginary representation, cannot remain silent. Finally, the characters in *Gravity's Rainbow* share a holistic myth of the Rocket. Like Moby Dick, Percival, and even the Great Letter, the Rocket, too, is an androgynous myth of transcendence. As Holy Text, the Rocket is supposed to contain the lost "Real." But the narrative perspective demonstrates how, through their myth, the characters aestheticize politics. The destructive potential of the Rocket becomes increasingly unreal—precisely the condition required to maintain the Rocket as a real object of destruction. The "lost original" stands here not only for the unrepresentable ground of subjectivity, but also for the unrepresentable ground of a reality that has become unavailable in the simulacrum of history.

From this perspective, the myths of transcendence—which, according to Eliade, are all holistic myths—take shape as the Other within the open forms of transitional texts. By quoting these myths as past historical forms, the texts retain their insistent desire for holism. This desire paradoxically pervades their broken and fragmented forms of language. From this perspective, the transgression and dissolution of boundaries in these texts might even be seen as an attempt to fulfill this desire by overcoming the horizontal division of subjectivity or by temporarily traversing the bar within the subject that marks the separation from the unconscious and the primary processes, the unrepresentable ground, the real, or the inner core. In their refusal to mythologize this desire, transitional texts view the holism of subjectivity no longer as an entity, but as a process.

The fragmentation or dedifferentiation of their surface structure would then offer a new attempt to present the unrepresentable. Instead of confining the unrepresentable to a symbolic shape and thus presenting it as an entity, transitional texts emphasize the processual structuring, destructuring, and restructuring of subjectivity. From this perspective, the desire for the transgression of boundaries appears perfectly compatible with the desire for a holistic subjectivity. Since, however, the aesthetic paradox of unrepresentability remains unresolved, holism may appear to be an impossible heuristic fiction—as, for example, in Beckett, Lacan, or Derrida.

In light of the postmodern infatuation with transgression, openness, flexibility, fluidity, and refusal of closure, it seems important to stress once again that, in transitional texts, structuration is as important as destructuration. Even the most open textual forms with their various dissolutions of boundaries are not immune to being mythologized during the course of history. The current theoretical discussion tends toward mystifying the transgression of boundaries by ignoring the complementary restructuring processes. Celebrating the fluid, volatile, open, oceanic, and lawless anarchy of unboundedness has already created new myths of openness and transgression. Those very metaphors already dominate a whole pop-theoretical appropriation of the new episteme, especially in the New Age movement. Mythologies of transcendence have pervaded pop culture since the sixties. The artificial myths of Pynchon's apocalyptic metafiction, however, indicate that new differentiations are necessary. We might perceive Pynchon as marking the transition toward a new paradigm, accompanied by a new phase of literary production.

Phenomenology of Transitional Techniques

The history of the novel suggests a correlation between the invention of new literary techniques and accompanying changes in the cultural formation of subjectivity. We can observe a cultural trend toward an increasing differentiation of the inner worlds of literary characters, especially in the wake of psychoanalysis, which has exerted a powerful impact on both thematic orientation and formal experimentation in twentieth-century literature. The challenge to find different modes for the literary presentation of the unconscious has inspired many experimental forms in modernism. A second trend is marked by increasingly complex explorations of the relationship between language and the unconscious. Instead of focusing on fictional constructions of the unconscious of literary characters, the focus begins to shift toward explorations of a structural unconscious as it speaks itself in the folds and fissures of language. To a certain extent, this trend is mirrored by the historical development of psychoanalytic theories and their increasing emphasis on language—especially in France through the strong impact of Lacan. But at the same time we can observe how the new experimental literary forms inspire new theoretical concepts of the relationship between language and the unconscious.

Inspired by romantic conceptions of the unconscious, *Moby-Dick* voices the unconscious in its myth of transcendence and primordial unity. For both the hero and the narrator, self-realization requires a transgression of the boundaries of subjectivity. But they both fail in their pursuit of transcendence. The bounded myth of the white whale is contrasted by an aesthetic of blankness, which suggests that the desire for transcendence requires aesthetic techniques of mediation able to convey the indeterminacy and opacity of the object. Such techniques engendered a whole new aesthetics in the twentieth-century novel.

Virginia Woolf's *The Waves* uses stylizations of poetry and drama to expand the scope of novelistic devices. This novel transgresses the boundaries between characters in order to fictionalize tacit knowledge and the unconscious. Challenging the cultural dominance of secondary over primary processes, *The Waves* inverts the usual hierarchy and emphatically expresses what usually remains barred from direct communication. The rhetorical device of the interior dialogue aesthetically simulates a communication about tacit knowledge, if not an unconscious communication between the characters. Suspending conventional boundaries between characters, these dialogical exchanges establish a deliberate aesthetic manifestation of the unconscious within poetic language. The speaking agency of this highly artificial interior dialogue is the core self of the characters. This aesthetic practice overturns a social boundary that keeps the core self separate from conscious interaction and direct communication. In contrast to the characters' bounded and conventional bourgeois lives, their interior dialogues voice and realize a burning desire for primordial unity and fusion. The literary form thus simulates the fulfillment of a desire they can never experience in their social lives. Speech as a form of conscious articulation is chosen to stylize what otherwise remains relegated to the status of tacit knowledge.

This experiment with the boundaries of language marks a new development in the language of the novel. Its most characteristic feature is the opening of poetic language toward the primary process. *Finnegans Wake* already carries this process to an extreme with its systematic polyvalence of signs, syntax, and semantics, its condensation and overdetermination of all textual elements, and its linguistic dissolution of characters and fictional world. As the fundamental aesthetic technique in *Finnegans Wake*, poetic condensation simulates the basic operation of primary processes. Interestingly, this condensation leads to a formal depsychologization of fictional characters: they dissolve into condensed textual subjectivities.

While *Finnegans Wake* pushes its experiments with poetic language toward the limits of readability, the experimental devices in *The Unnamable* are grounded in a paradoxical extension of the boundaries of reflexivity, which also affects the boundaries of language. Through the pastiche of a Cartesian reduction of subjectivity to consciousness, the unnamable inverts the very epistemological and linguistic foundations of an I. Literary subjectivity feeds off the aporias of philosophical and empirical subjectivity. Fictionalizing a subject without an ontological ground aesthetically counters the reduction of the subject to its linguistic manifestations. The discourse of the unnamable translates epistemological paradoxes or paradoxes of the order of language into narrative paradoxes. The most fundamental paradox resides in the "I" of a first person narrator who rejects any self-manifestation.

Gravity's Rainbow challenges the boundaries between the real and the imaginary in a different way. Pynchon uses three techniques to

break through the conventions of historical fiction and to sever its ties
to a tradition of narrative realism: a specific use of intertextuality and
carnivalization, the development of an artificial mythological system
and the simulation of a four-dimensional perspective. The artificial
mythological system demystifies the characters' myth of transcendence
through a critical narrative reenactment of the myth. The narrator's
self-ironic simulation of a four-dimensional perspective presents temporally and spatially separate events in a simultaneous fiction that
playfully anticipates future events within the literary presentation of
history. This perspective accounts for the complexity of a historical
reality, which the historical subjects can no longer experience with
immediacy but which they can theoretically conceive and aesthetically
present.

Stylistically, this device is supported by multiple voices quoted from
other literary texts and genres, as well as by the dense intertextuality
with theoretical texts. Instead of a quasi-realistic representation of
history, Pynchon's historical fiction is a conglomeration of styles and
forms borrowed from different genres and epochs, from the media,
from mythologies and even from theoretical conceptions. Rather than
being merely a new form of self-reflexive aesthetics, intertextuality in
Gravity's Rainbow constructs not only a theoretically inspired multidimensional vision of history, but also playfully includes "lower" forms
of popular expression from the margins of social semantics or the
official recordings of history.

Reading Transitional Texts

Despite their esoteric language games, their opacity and self-reflexivity,
their intertextual simulation and experimentalism, transitional texts
relate directly to the cultural experience and subjectivity of readers at
large. As Dieter Henrich has convincingly argued, the perceptual
structure of aesthetic experience can be described with the same ter-
minology as the structure of subjectivity.[10] Moreover, the structures
of literary subjectivity can be related to textual strategies that seek to
affect the subjectivity of the reader and cultural notions of subjectivity
in general.

It is no coincidence that the growing aesthetic interest in the unconscious has produced experimental stylizations and formalizations
of poetic language—a literary practice already prominent in the "bor-

rowed language" of *Moby-Dick*. In *The Waves*, the artificial literary stylization is supposed to prevent the reader from reading the characters' speeches as quasirealistic interior monologues. The literary creation of interior dialogue creates a new aesthetic experience of literary subjectivity. Even though the characters' language is not disrupted by primary processes, their speeches direct the reception toward tacit knowledge and the unconscious. But this shift is still more an effect of what the characters say than an affect of poetic language and literary form. The semantic crutches remain intact, and the reader can follow the development of a narrative even though the rhythm, musicality, and visuality of poetic language underscore the thematic appeal to the unconscious. Since Woolf's musicality and visuality retain basic values of aesthetic harmony, they support rather than disrupt the narrative structure. The conscious reception of a narrative may therefore unfold independently from and undisturbed by the unfocused attention to formal qualities. Textual presentation and reception thus open out toward the unconscious without structurally altering the experience of reading.

By contrast, *Finnegans Wake* establishes a radical break in our reading habits. By refusing to provide a stable semantic orientation, a transparent narrative, or an immediately accessible meaning, Joyce's text provokes a crisis of literary communication that radicalizes the disruptive communicative strategies of literary modernism. *Finnegans Wake* challenges the internalized structures of aesthetic perception and constitution of meaning so thoroughly that the text has been called unreadable. As Sybille Kisro-Völker argues, the *Wake* creates its own unreadability as a topic.[11] Because its textual subjectivity can no longer be equated with any other existing form of subjectivity, and because its language resists all receptive habits, *Finnegans Wake* becomes paradigmatic for a fundamentally new interaction with readers. It offers a provocative challenge to the cultural boundaries of subjectivity. In addition to an endless semiosis, the *Wake*'s polylogicity and polyphonicity incite new forms of reading with unfocused attention. For readers who insist on conventional meaning, the text can become a lifelong obsession—a lifetime is not enough to exhaust its current potential of meaning, let alone that of new meanings opened up in the future. But a "normal" reading time is enough for an exemplary reading. As soon as the reader shifts from focused to unfocused attention, he or she becomes receptive to the simultaneous perception of multidimensional structures beyond the conscious capacity for reception, thus adding to the further differentiation of subjectivity.

The aesthetic experience of the *Wake*'s textual subjectivity combines otherwise separated modes of experience. Being neither totally primary nor secondary process, the *Wake* initiates an intermediate experience of their complementarity. In addition to an unfocused reception of language, it stimulates a mimetic production that playfully integrates the two modes of aesthetic creativity. Reflexive skills of deciphering, mnemonic retention, and association are activated in conjunction with the capacity for unconscious scanning. The enjoyment of language games and the pleasurable cathexis of order are complemented and counterbalanced by the rewards of unconscious association or scanning of rhythm and patterns. Conscious and unconscious responses interact with each other as a result of the *Wake*'s doubling of communicative strategies. The limits of a conventional reading the reader experiences in facing the complex multidimensional order of the text can only be compensated for by a shift to a different mode of reception.

The explosive complexity as well as the limitations of reflexivity become major themes in *The Unnamable*, affecting narrator and reader alike. Here, transgressions between primary and secondary processes once again mark the aesthetic experience. The discourse of the unnamable engenders a pointed apprehension of transitional subjectivity. Theoretical paradoxes undermine systems of order in which primary and secondary processes, or I and Not-I, are incompatible opposites. Forced to abandon the basic security of linguistic rules and binary oppositions, the reader must adapt to the materiality of the unnamable's discourse. But while the forms of poetic language in *The Unnamable* channel the reader's unfocused attention, the text also requires a doubled reflexivity. The reader must not only follow the high reflexivity of the narrator, but also establish a reflexive distance on a narrative perspective that negates every one of its own manifestations. The crisis of communication that results from this strategy of negation can only be solved from a metaperspective. Numerous signals in the text itself invite the reader to construct such a perspective. In contrast to the reflexivity that follows the spirals of the unnamable's discourse, this secondary reflexivity does not remain entangled in the implosive complexity and the paradoxes of the text. As soon as one reflects upon the aesthetic devices and intermediary processes from an outside perspective, the aesthetic paradoxes can be seen in their philosophical and cultural functions and thus become integrated at a different level of reception.

Finnegans Wake and *The Unnamable* generate tension between familiar categories of order and textual complexity mainly as a problem of aesthetic experience. In *Gravity's Rainbow* this tension becomes a central theme and a structural element. At the same time, however, the text retains much more narrative coherence in its historical representation than the previous texts. Its exotic stories about hundreds of narrative characters are told in an unbroken poetic language, free from eruptions of primary processes. But at one level this seems to be an illusion, a trap. The text displays just as many breaks in the conventions of aesthetic representation as Joyce's or Beckett's texts, but they seem to happen outside the numerous stories about characters and do not interfere with them in any direct way. Rather, the breaks manifest themselves as functions of a narrative perspective that has at its disposal systemic perspectives reaching beyond the experiences possible in the text's spatiotemporal and sense-oriented fictional worlds.

This double coding generates an intermediate receptive position in which the reader is simultaneously inside and outside the historical narrative. The simulation of a four-dimensional narrative perspective induces an outside view of the fictional worlds of the characters, which emphasizes both the impact of transpersonal systems on the fictional historical world and the artificiality of a fictional presentation of history. Moreover, since Pynchon uses this four-dimensional narrative perspective only sporadically, the reader becomes as intricately involved in the stories of characters as they themselves are in their historical world. Only when the narrative perspective is emphasized in a textual self-reflection are the transpersonal and the textual systems brought into an explicit tension and interaction with the stories and fictional worlds of Pynchon's historical fiction. At this level of reception, the fragmentation of stories and events stimulates the synthesizing functions of a historical gaze and induces the reader to oscillate between different historical perspectives.

At the level of the characters' fictional world, the utopia of a four-dimensional perspective has its correlate in the literary conception of cyborgs, cybernetic organisms whose perceptions of self and world are rooted in a technological imagination. Transpersonal semiotic systems and apparatus of power infiltrate their minds and even their bodies. The interplay between narrative perspective and the perspectives of the characters suggests a new form of reading that accounts for the new formations of subjectivity under postindustrial and postmodern conditions. Under such conditions a linear reading that focuses exclusively on the stories of characters and historical events seems reductive, since it maintains the illusion of cognitive control over narrative histories—an illusion equivalent to the illusion some characters still believe, that they can understand or even control the cause and effect of historical events.

The implosive complexity of Pynchon's social semantics seems to call for multidimensional forms of thought and experience, and Pynchon's "implicit reader" is constructed on this premise. At the same time, however, the self-irony with which the narrator simulates a four-dimensional perspective indicates that the realization of such a perspective under present historical conditions remains an illusion. Like some of his characters, Pynchon's postmodern readers are left with the choice of either compensating for the complexity, contingency, and opacity of this text through mythological readings, or cultivating a creative paranoia and counterbalancing the transpersonal semiosis with individual patterns. Or finally they may, like some of the other characters, renounce their linear or totalizing conceptions of history in order to listen to the alien voices dispersed through Pynchon's fictions of World War II and the United States during the Vietnam War.

The Horizontal Division of Subjectivity

With their dynamic integration of primary and secondary processes into poetic language, transitional texts work against a horizontal division of subjectivity. Their formal qualities require an aesthetic experience that presupposes an increased flexibility between the two modes. Even though the literary transgressions dedifferentiate secondary-process orders, they aim at a higher differentiation of subjectivity. As we have seen, it is not the transgression of boundaries between primary and secondary processes that leads to a dissolution of subjectivity, but the rigid division between the two. In extreme isolation from each other they tend either toward entropic degeneration or sterile petrification. Cut off from primary processes, the structures of subjectivity rigidify, while a flooding by pure primary processes disintegrates the boundaries of the subject. Temporary dedifferentiations of secondary processes are necessary stages in an ongoing process of reorganization and higher differentiation. Order and differentiation, as well as dissolutions of order and dedifferentiation, are different stages in the continual reorganization of decentered subjectivity. Cultural pathology does not result from the dissolution of secondary processes, but from an attempt to repress primary processes within the symbolic order. The subject can only cope with its fundamental decenteredness if the boundaries between primary and secondary modes of experience are kept flexible in order to allow for transgressions between them, which, in turn, lead to new differentiations. The fact that contemporary transitional texts practice such transgressions excessively indicates that the cultural formation to which they react is threatened by a horizontal division of subjectivity.

The analysis of reader response to these texts has shown that they do not activate unfocused attention at the cost of reflexivity but that on the contrary they increase the intensity of both forms of reception. This indicates that literary subjectivity gains a new complexity through the inclusion of primary processes in poetic language. In this process of mutual integration, the self-reflexive structure of literary texts plays a specific role. The modes of reception are shifted from the so-called middle dimension—such as identification, empathy, or the cognitive constitution of the meaning of narratives—toward the extremes of possible responses, such as unconscious scanning and heightened reflexivity. Often the texts force such extreme responses by refusing to allow for any immediate meaning or emotional involvement. They thus attempt to enforce experience at the limits of our receptive dispositions.

In addition to activating those extreme receptive dispositions separately, transitional texts generate an interaction between them. The reader's heightened reflexivity, for example, is also steered toward an awareness of the effects of simultaneous unfocused attention. To this purpose, transitional texts develop communicative metasystems that aim at illuminating the function of the new modes of reception for a change in subjectivity. According to Bateson, each metacommunicative system defines a psychological frame.[12] From a psychological perspective, the self-reflexivity of transitional texts also intensifies awareness of and sensitivity to the reader's own receptive attitudes and habits. Specific forms of intertextuality heighten this awareness. Aesthetic illusion reveals itself as such and endows imaginary transactions with a new status. This process often incites the intellectual pleasures of constructing ever more abstract and complex levels of fictionalization, which release the imaginary from the status of a mere illusion but which nonetheless create an imaginary world in the transitional space between I and Not-I, or the real and the imaginary. Even when we engage in a literary metafiction, we are, after all, not beyond fiction but within the aesthetic paradox of being simultaneously within and without. The effects of such a transitional position become part of our subjectivity. Literature thus appears as a privileged medium for the formation of new orders of the subject with new forms and levels of differentiation.

9

Toward a Holonomy of
Texts and Subjects

The Ecology of the Text

The following speculations trace the striking affinities between transitional texts and a variety of contemporary theories. Transitional texts fulfill different functions in relation to a larger postmodern episteme. Both postmodern theories and transitional texts challenge the antagonistic cultural polarization of primary and secondary processes and related linear and binary models of thought. The intriguing combination of formal dissolutions with a highly differentiated literary self-reflexivity is one of the most characteristic features of transitional texts. Critics have tended to discuss these phenomena in isolation from each other, emphasizing one of these features at the expense of the other or discussing them as separate. A completely different picture appears once we view the dynamic interaction between literary self-reflexivity and formal dissolution as the basis of a new type of aesthetic experience. The perceptual matrix of transitional texts often resists our perceptual and cognitive habit of shaping what we experience into an organized gestalt.[1] Wolfgang Iser has shown how our tendency automatically to divide our perceptions into figure and ground also works during the reading process.[2] But aesthetic experience is formed by a dynamic interplay between conscious and unconscious processes. As long as the focused attention is absorbed by an orienting gestalt, unconscious reception may unfold undisturbed by and separate from conscious reception. Only when a text lacks or deliberately undermines this focusing quality does the polyvalent structure of a literary text become dominant in the reading process, favoring a free-floating attention that does not automatically differentiate salient features.

Ehrenzweig has argued that the fragmented forms of modern art and literature provoke a remarkable shift toward a new mode of synchretistic reception that cannot be explained by the theoretical tools of gestalt psychology.[3] The deliberate activation of primary processes and the temporary dissolution of cognitive orders in transitional texts deeply affect the reader's subjectivity. Ehrenzweig describes how recipients with rigid or badly integrated self-boundaries react with anxiety and defensiveness to ambivalent forms—the so-called "counterchanges"—and even more to the "chaotic forms" of polyvalent texts.[4] According to Ehrenzweig, such strong reactions reveal a dissociation between the undifferentiated basic structures of subject organization and the highly differentiated surface structures.[5] We may assume that a culture that promotes such a dissociation too vigorously produces a pathological horizontal division in its various formations of subjectivity. Schizophrenia and paranoia have been identified as two related pathological subject formations based on an overly rigid separation of the primary from the secondary processes. Schizophrenia is characterized by a complete breakdown of secondary processes and a subsequent flooding of the subject by primary processes. In the case of paranoia, a rigid separation of conscious perception from the unconscious causes a loss of judgment and creativity. The paranoid builds fortresslike walls in a futile attempt to enclose the enemy from within or to eject him or her from the self.[6]

It is significant that both schizophrenia and paranoia are marked by a violation or petrification of the boundaries of subjectivity. If we recall that schizophrenia and paranoia have been identified as the cultural pathologies of the twentieth century, it becomes evident why aesthetic games with the boundaries of language and subjectivity play such a crucial role in twentieth-century literature. Because their poetic language uses primary processes as well as abstraction and self-reflexivity, transitional texts continually traverse or blur the boundaries between primary and secondary processes, thus rendering them more flexible and undermining the cultural polarization or horizontal division of subjectivity. As we have seen, from Melville's *Moby-Dick* to Pynchon's *Gravity's Rainbow* this process develops in pointed response to Cartesian subjectivity. We have become accustomed historically to link the cultural tendency toward horizontal division of subjectivity with the Cartesian model. Even more radically, because of its theoretical devaluation of primary processes, Cartesianism is understood as the philosophical version of this division. From a psychohistorical perspective one could argue that, by undermining this division, transitional texts reactivate a mode of subjectivity that has been culturally underrepresented and devalued at least since Descartes. Given the fact that Cartesianism does not have a very good press in our current critical climate, this anti-Cartesian trend might not strike us as a particularly remarkable cultural event. However, in light of the critical reception of the fragmented literary forms of modernism and postmodernism, this trend gains a new significance in that it inverts the very premises of the most common evaluations. Due to formal and structural affinities between the fragmentation and dissolution of boundaries in schizophrenic and schizoid disorders and transitional literary texts, critics have tended to interpret these literary forms as a mere aesthetic expression or reproduction of these disorders. By contrast, the previous reflections lead to a different conclusion: by enforcing the coexistence of and interaction between primary and secondary processes, these texts work in the opposite direction; instead of enforcing a split or horizontal division of subjectivity, they create an increased activity between the two modes, thus increasing their flexibility within the subject. In other words, these texts do not aesthetically reproduce but, on the contrary, work against the cultural pathologies of schizoid disintegration, paranoia, regressive desublimation, cultural narcissism, and fascistic destruction.

The hypothesis of a cultural horizontal division of subjectivity helps us understand why many contemporary theories hypostasize schizophrenia as the pathology of our century (if not as its excluded Other), in contrast to hysteria, which figured as the pathology of the nineteenth century. Furthermore, to speak of a postmodern schizophrenia indicates that the horizontal division of subjectivity has reached a stage where the relationship between what constitutes the cultural norm and what is a deviation from it threatens to be reversed. Archaic forms of primary-process experience, which the Cartesian tradition seemed to have brought under control, celebrate a return of the repressed in manifold cultural manifestations of regressive desublimation. But it would be a mistake to conclude that one could simply reverse this trend by either reinforcing or, on the contrary, by further repressing primary processes in cultural experiences at the expense or in favor of secondary processes. This would only reverse the hierarchical order between the two modes, while leaving their horizontal division intact.

The perspective developed in the previous readings of transitional texts, rather, suggests that these texts work against the horizontal division as such.

As we have seen, the transgressions of established cultural boundaries of subjectivity in modern and postmodern literature are deeply ambivalent and reach from a utopian expansion of subjectivity to regressive desublimation. While modernism (with the exception, perhaps, of dadaism and surrealism) has mainly explored the former, postmodernism increasingly explores the latter—a trend that can be directly related to the implosion of primary-process experience in our current media culture.

In this study—which is, at its core, a rereading of modernism—I have deliberately chosen transitional texts that explore and practice the expansion of the boundaries of subjectivity through language. I thus highlight a dimension of experimental modernism and postmodernism that I see as undervalued, if not ignored, in most critical and theoretical debates about these periods. I have read the intermediacy of these texts as actively contributing to the cultural production of subjectivity in ways that counteract its threatening horizontal division. With what Ehrenzweig called "a savage attack on our surface sensibilities,"[7] the transitional texts in question indirectly reinforce the mental faculties of unfocused attention and unconscious scanning, which have for a long period been culturally marginalized—especially as forms of knowledge or aesthetic judgment. Transitional texts thus not only influence the reader's subjectivity through their forms of imaginary world-making, but they also change the very perceptive structure of aesthetic experience. In many respects, this impact is more forceful and reaches deeper than the mere representation of an imaginary world. Depending on their readers' mental flexibility or their willingness and ability to be truly affected—which means *changed*—transitional texts provoke extreme reactions, from a deeply rooted attraction to the most defensive rejection.

If they manage to break through the barrier of possible defenses, transitional texts become a zone of contact between the polarized modes of decentered subjectivity. Most important for determining the cultural function of transitional texts are the ways in which they affect the unconscious perception of form—an effect that may well reach much deeper than the cultural dissemination of unconscious fantasies through literature. Ehrenzweig assumes that we are capable of an

unconscious perception of form that precludes the conscious formation of a visible image—a process Ehrenzweig calls "structural repression": "It is possible to speak of a purely formal 'structural' repression
which gives an unconscious quality to split-second tachistoscopic ex-
posures and to the totally invisible subliminal images."[8] Thus, I have
argued that unconscious perception and structural repression also
operate in our reception of poetic language. In addition to consciously
received information, we unconsciously perceive formal qualities of
language and thus react to what Kristeva calls the semiotic. With their
resistance to the surface qualities of our readings and concomitant
insistence on formal qualities and unconscious scanning, transitional
texts may temporarily break through our structural repression and
incite us retrospectively to translate our syncretistic unconscious scanning into conscious abstraction.

Once more, what is at stake is not a privileging of primary processes
or a simple inversion of cultural priorities, but a change in the relationship between the two qualitatively different modes of experience.
This is confirmed by the crucial role played by reflexivity and self-referentiality in transitional texts. Reflexivity does not form an antagonistic opposition but occupies a complementary position to the
primary processes. Abstract thought does not (as presupposed in the
Cartesian model) exclude primary processes. Instead of using abstraction as a pure carrier of Cartesian rationality, transitional texts celebrate
abstraction as another form of excess. This complementarity may account for such seeming paradoxes as the abstract *jouissance* of the
unnamable or the convergence of mysticism and abstraction in *Gravity's Rainbow*. As Ehrenzweig has insisted, "abstract thought can be
seen as a success of the Eros."[9] We ultimately witness no more and
no less than a change in the symbolic order brought about by new
forms of interaction between primary and secondary processes in the
cultural field.

From a historical perspective, this change of subjectivity in the
transitional space of literature can be related to a more general historical change along the lines of a paradigm shift or the emergence
of a new episteme. Transitional texts themselves indicate as much
when they develop intertextual links with theories that propagate such
a shift. The move beyond Cartesian epistemology is one indication of
this process. In their formal transgressions and their resistance to
closure, transitional texts undermine the basic Cartesian categories of

the stable, the clear-cut, the constant, and the bounded. Sartre argues that these very categories reveal a culture-specific desire for the constancy and stability of petrification. Transitional texts oppose this Cartesian epistemology with their celebration of open and fluid boundaries.

Literary theories have responded to this epistemological shift with various models of the open text. Kristeva, for example, points to the affinities between her model of the subject-in-process and quantum physics by comparing the nonobservable objects of quantum theory with the ineffability of aesthetic experience: "We encounter an *inobservable* object (in the sense in which one speaks of inobservable objects in quantum mechanics), that is to say: poetic signification."[10] Accordingly, she conceives aesthetic experience not only as a conscious process, but also as a holistic experience within a dynamic field of movement. The constitution of semantic meaning is supplemented by a holistic response to the material body of the semiotic text. While the constitution of meaning apprehends the text as a product, the semiotic reading constitutes a holistic experience of the text-in-process, which is qualitatively different from the final product. (Kristeva describes it with the terms *saut, quantum leap, coupure,* and *blanc.*) According to Kristeva, only the mediation between process and product, between meaning-oriented and semiotic reading, unfolds the full potential of aesthetic experience.[11]

This transition from thinking in terms of entities and closed systems to thinking in terms of processes and open systems is replicated at the most diverse cultural and theoretical levels. In his essay "Pathologies of Epistemology," Bateson, for example, criticizes the tendency to transform open systems of the phenomenal world into closed systems of thought—a tendency he sees particularly enforced in Cartesian-Newtonian models of thought and in Puritanism. Bateson considers the formation of closed mental systems as one of the most consequential epistemological errors that dominate the history of Western culture. Since closed systems of thought tend to become epistemologically independent, they ossify into stable, self-referential systems based on imaginary oppositions. Bateson works with the basic notion of an ecology between a system and its environment, which is over and over again confirmed throughout history: a system that destroys its environment will inevitably become self-destructive in the long run. Such an ecology of mind might also release an ecology of texts and readings. From its systemic perspective, abstractions such as consciousness, subjectivity, intersubjectivity, texts, and readings appear as integral parts of larger cultural ecosystems. The horizontal division of subjectivity, for example, could be interpreted as a consequence of a cultural transformation of primary and secondary processes into antagonistically opposed closed systems. This transformation creates an imaginary opposition supported by the mind's tendency to internalize pragmatic binary schematizations. Such "epistemological fantasies," as Anthony Wilden calls them, create their own reality—as, for example, the disturbance in the ecology of the subject that we have termed horizontal division of subjectivity.

Bateson's ecology of mind reconceptualizes the notion of an organized system in a way that may be used to develop new perspectives on the aesthetic organization of a literary text, and, more specifically, on the status of transitional texts. Influenced by similar reconceptualizations in cybernetics and systems theory, Pynchon's *Gravity's Rainbow,* for example, adapts such notions to its textual organization. In this context, entropy has become the most popular metaphor to describe the new forms of textual production. The notion of textual entropy is, of course, directly relevant to a discussion of transitional texts. As Rudolf Arnheim has shown, the popularized notion of entropy is, ironically, based on a misreading of the second law of thermodynamics. This law holds that closed systems tend toward stabilizing at the lowest level of differentiation possible within their system, but the popularized notion of entropy has mystified this process, concluding that the world moves from a stage of relative order toward a stage of absolute chaos. Subsequently, the metaphor of entropy has been anthropomorphized with apocalyptic connotations and used to symbolize the discontents of civilization as well as the general dissolution of boundaries in contemporary culture.

The popularized use of the second law of thermodynamics in the humanities, literature, and the media differs significantly from the history of reception of this law in the sciences. The changing notions of the term *entropy* reflect changing cultural conceptions of order. Arnheim has pointed out that, over the hundred years of its history, the notion of entropy has changed from having negative to positive connotations. Immediately after the discovery of the second law of thermodynamics, entropy resonated with an increasingly apocalyptic zeitgeist: "When it began to enter the public consciousness a century or so ago, it suggested an apocalyptic vision of the course of events on earth. The Second Law stated that the entropy of the world strives towards a maximum, which amounted to saying that the energy in the universe, although constant in amount, was subject to more and more dissipation and degradation. These terms had a distinctly negative ring. They were congenial to the pessimistic moods of the times."[12] Interestingly enough, Arnheim refers to the reception of minimalist art as an example of the shift toward positive connotations of entropy. In order to evaluate this new development of minimalist forms in the arts, critics inverted the popular use of the notion of entropy during the nineteenth century and used the metaphor as "a positive rationale for 'minimal' art and the pleasures of chaos."[13] However, in Arnheim's own aesthetic evaluation of art, entropy remains negatively associated with dissolution of form and loss of aesthetic differentiation.

Like Ehrenzweig, Arnheim develops theoretical perspectives and concepts that reach beyond his more conservative aesthetic judgment. His cultural evaluation of entropy reveals the same tendencies as the literary critics' evaluation of modernism's fragmented or unbounded forms. In each case, critics presuppose their own conception of an organized system in order to understand changes in the organization of contemporary cultural systems. From this perspective, the dissolution of boundaries and closed systems in contemporary literature, culture, and theory appears to be nothing but a loss of their former organization, and is indicative of cultural entropy. Even Arnheim perceives entropy in art as a sign of degeneration—despite the fact that, in principle, he is inclined to accept a positive cultural revaluation of entropy. Astonishingly, Ehrenzweig equally deplores fragmented forms in modern art, ignoring that his own theoretical revision of the cultural status of primary processes has prepared the ground for a positive evaluation of formal dedifferentiations. Grounding his position in Freud's death drive, he writes, "Death is undifferentiatedness," thus invoking a cultural norm that identifies life with differentiation and death with undifferentiation—despite the fact that throughout his book he makes a strong case for the creative use of primary processes and dedifferentation in artistic production and reception. In a similar move, the German philosopher Hans Blumenberg ends his book *Die Lesbarkeit der Welt (The Readability of the World)* with a discussion of entropy and links Freud's death drive explicitly with the second law of thermodynamics: "When Freud invented the death drive in 1920, this was, after nearly a century, the psychological metaphor for the second law of thermodynamics: Life is not the fulfillment of an inner tendency of all matter, because it has itself the innermost tendency to return to its origin in the pseudopodium—if not in inorganic matter—in order to prove itself as the great, over-burdened exception which ultimately becomes insupportable to it-self."[14]

Freud maintains the duality of the two cosmic tendencies of differentiation and undifferentiation as a principle underlying his theory of drives, equating Thanatos with entropy and Eros with a negentropic principle of life. This duality also shapes Freud's theory of subjectivity, based on a cultural hierarchy between primary and secondary processes. But it is important to understand that for Freud this duality is never organized by way of a binary opposition. The tendency to understand differentiation and dedifferentiation as binary oppositions and then identify them respectively with life or death has only developed in some later versions of psychoanalysis. Freud, by contrast, understands life as a dynamic interplay between both principles, and consequently also attributes life-preserving functions to temporary or partial dedifferentiations.

We are confronted here with basic differences in how to conceive the order of living systems. If one understands entropy and dedifferentiation in pure opposition to order, this results in all likelihood in a purely negative evaluation of the two notions—unless one inverts the cultural norm and celebrates entropy as the advent of anarchy and chaos. Both perspectives, however, fail to perceive the dynamic that structures the involved systems. Arnheim criticizes the inadequacy of any notion of order that neglects to determine the level of order established by its specific structures. As we recall, he defines entropy not as a trend toward disorder, but toward a stage of relatively tension-free balance, a stasis that a system reaches once it has found its most simple structure. If one understands order in this way, as the result of a dynamic interplay between differentiating and dedifferentiating forces, then a perspective that polarizes the two becomes obsolete. Only this interplay can determine the status of dedifferentiation in each case. Dedifferentiating processes as such remain ambiguous; they can either destroy an order or pertain to a temporary process of reorganization.

Within the transitional space of literature, more static orders appear next to more flexible ones, or vanishing orders next to orders that are able to survive. The very boundaries of what we perceive as an aesthetic order are continually adapted to changing cultural norms. What each critic defines as an order will decide the status attributed to literary transgressions, dissolutions, and fragmentations and to the cultural function of transitional texts.

With respect to aesthetic orders, Arnheim distinguishes between two different forms of increasing entropy: the cosmic tendency toward simplicity, symmetry, and regularity immanent in natural systems; and the catabolic effect, which consists in a destruction of form caused by an intervention into a system from without. The catabolic effect finds its counterpart in the anabolic effect—that is, the introduction of a structural theme that creates and maintains tension.[15] This assumption of an interplay between the two effects shows that Arnheim, too, presupposes that aesthetic order depends upon a dynamic relation between differentiating and dedifferentiating forces. Most challenging in Arnheim's perspective is his assumption that the fundamental categories of a classical aesthetics of harmony—namely, symmetry and regularity—can result from either differentiation or dedifferentiation. This assertion only further underscores the malleability of categories such as order and dedifferentiation—that is, their basic sensitivity to context. Historically, the aesthetic order of a literary text must therefore be analyzed in relation to the various notions of order operative in the cultural system in which the text emerges. At the same time, however, literary texts form highly mobile cultural subsystems since they can be transferred to or brought in contact with other systems in which their own order assumes new dimensions.

Bateson's notion of culture contact helps to analyze this mobility of literary texts in its larger cultural implications. The transitional space of literature can be understood as a cultural subsystem whose functions unfold throughout history and across different cultures in contact with a whole variety of other subsystems—a process that results in mutual change. In "Culture Contact and Schismogenesis," Bateson argues that cultural systems brought into contact with each other gain a new balance through reciprocal differentiations. If the changes brought about by culture contact lack reciprocity, the systems involved tend to develop self-destructively toward what Bateson calls "schismogenesis"—that is, a tendency toward symmetrical or complementary linear differentiation at the expense of the cultural environment.

According to Bateson, any linear differentiation a system achieves at the expense of another system leads to the destruction of both systems, regardless of whether symmetrical or complementary forms of behavior are developed further. If one understands differentiation and dedifferentiation as complementary processes of systemic regeneration and reorganization, dedifferentiations appear not only as changes within a specific system but also as an effect of cultural contact between systems. Instead of conceiving entropy and negentropy as binary oppositions, Bateson understands them as complementary activities in processes of systemic development. Entropy may thus also appear as a reservoir of renewal or even of new differentiations. The strength of a system is not determined by its progressive linear differentiation, but by its flexible oscillation between differentiation and dedifferentiation. Or, to use the metaphor of entropy again, negentropy (system, organization, and differentiation) and entropy (dedifferentiation) are two sides of a double movement that belongs to each living process.[16]

This systemic perspective also informs Bateson's theory of subjectivity. If we understand the interaction between primary and secondary processes as a form of culture contact in Bateson's sense, we could say that the official symbolic order of the secondary processes constantly requires new negotiations with the alternate order of the primary processes. From the perspective of an ecology of the subject, the isolated development of secondary processes hypostasizes them to a closed psychic system that domesticates or excludes the primary processes instead of interacting with them.

The genesis of imaginary functions suggests that, among other functions, the transitional space of literature and cultural objects establishes a cultural balance between secondary and primary processes. If we now use this general systemic perspective in order to assess the cultural status of contemporary transitional texts, we must take into account that they activate the extreme poles of our receptive capacities. By refusing to communicate through familiar, narratively mediated middle dimensions, they elicit both unconscious scanning and complex operations of abstraction.

The fact that transitional texts activate metacommunication and self-reflexivity in conjunction with unconscious scanning also bears on their implied models of subjectivity. Bateson sees the formation of metasystems as the only way to escape the destructive patterns of schizoid communication, with its characteristic double binds. On a more general level, metasystems form a self-preserving operation of a system threatened by schismogenesis. Anthony Wilden describes this process as follows: "Opposing messages and codes within the ecosystem may be related symmetrically or complementarily (or both); when the intensification of their deviations ("contradictions") can no longer be controlled by negative feedback, the system will remain viable—be maintained and transformed (aufheben)—only if the ensuing exponential schismogenesis leads to the emergence of a metasystem."[17]

Bateson's ideas about the integrative function of metasystems opens up a new perspective on transitional texts. Dedifferentiation and self-reflexivity, or unconscious scanning and abstraction, are the two extremes of literary presentation and reception that characterize both modern and postmodern experimental texts. In the previous chapters I have criticized the notion of a contemporary cultural schizophrenia. Within a larger cultural framework, the narrative of postmodern schizophrenia fails to account for the productive interaction between literary dedifferentiations and tendencies toward higher formalization, abstraction, and self-reflexivity. Bateson points out that, tacit or explicit, the communicative message "this is play" already presupposes a capacity to think in terms of a metasystem. Accordingly, the transitional space formed during the genesis of the subject can be seen as a rudimentary metasystem whose function is to establish differentiations within the organization of subjectivity.

This function is preserved later when the psychogenetic transitional space merges with the transitional space of cultural objects at large. From this perspective, one of the most crucial functions of the intermediacy of cultural objects lies in creating ecologically balanced cultural formations of subjectivity. If we accept this, the idea that transitional texts are an expression of cultural schizophrenia can indeed be inverted. According to Bateson, schizophrenia is a disorder in the ecology of mind manifested when primary processes dominate the mental functions in isolation from the secondary processes. As a result, the schizophrenic becomes incapable of distinguishing between system/communication and metasystem/metacommunication—an incapacity that eventually leads to his or her complete disintegration.

As in the case of a destructive schismogenesis of interacting systems, Bateson sees the introduction of a metasystem as a possibility for redifferentiating the dissolved boundaries of the schizophrenic. As we have seen, transitional texts display a high degree of self-reflexivity and metacommunication. One of the basic assumptions of my readings, that transitional texts work against manifestations of cultural schizophrenia, can now also be supported by Bateson's theoretical perspective, which emphasizes metacommunication as an integrative counterbalance against schizoid dissolutions. The self-reflexivity of transitional texts allows the reader to integrate their formal dissolutions and thus to attain a more complex aesthetic experience. Crucial for this further differentiation is that this integration is not achieved by excluding or repressing primary processes, but through an increased flexibility between the two modes of subjectivity. The interplay between dedifferentiation and self-reflexivity thus creates a form of intermediacy that works against binary schematization and uncontrolled linear differentiation.

The Holonomic Paradigm

In addition to dissolving established orders, transitional texts develop their own alternative notions of order. The lowest common denominator for their dialectic of differentiation and dedifferentiation may be the shift from linear to multidimensional and overdetermined forms of order. A similar shift can be observed within literary subjectivity. To mark this shift, the texts recall—often ironically—historical models of multidimensional thought from the mystic tradition. Even a postmodern text such as *Gravity's Rainbow* still invokes this tradition by tracing connections between mysticism and contemporary scientific models such as the New Physics, relativity theory, or cybernetics. Many critics and scientists have commented on the affinities between the so-called postmodern sciences and mystic traditions.[18] Given the deeply ingrained scholarly prejudice against mysticism, and especially against the popmysticism of the New Age movement, the statement of such affinities has engendered many polemical debates. But *Gravity's Rainbow* shows that regardless of their scholarly validity, such affinities have already become part of our popular culture. How can we then determine the status of such affinities without mystifying them? As we have seen, the transitional texts themselves maintain an ironic distance from the quoted mystic traditions or symbols, at the same time retaining their notions of holism and multidimensional thought. Moreover, other critics who have no stake in mysticism—

such as, for example, Leroi-Gourhan—have claimed a cultural trend toward the reactivation of multidimensional thought whose only available models are the dream, the languages of early childhood, and the semiotics of mystic systems. Leroi-Gourhan points out that the technological development of our modes of production and communication requires a transition to multidimensional forms of thinking, and so far the archaic forms of primary-process experience provide the only available model.

The proliferation of nonlinear and multidimensional forms or modes of presentation in literature and theory calls for new theoretical models that may account for the function and emergence of these forms at different levels and in different spheres of culture. We have seen that historically the concept of entropy was used for such a purpose. But like the concept of cultural schizophrenia, entropy seems to focus exclusively on processes of dissolution and thus fails to grasp the importance of alternate notions of order implicit in transitional texts. Unless it is used as a dynamic category in Bateson's sense, entropy suggests the dissolution of complex structures to a point where they find equilibrium in minimal differentiation. In this sense, entropy remains tied to the notion of linear process. By contrast, transitional texts call for a model for nonlinear, multidimensional forms of writing.

One new paradigm seems ideally to meet this requirement: the holographic paradigm. A hologram is a three-dimensional pictorial representation made possible without the use of a photo objective— that is, without a focusing lens. The hologram is based on the patterns of interference produced by light and the principle of superimposition. In contrast to mechanical optics which are unable to use the waves produced by light and are restricted to the light reflected by objects, the hologram uses waves of light in order to produce a three-dimensional representation. Several characteristics make the hologram attractive for contemporary theories of mind or theories of representation. For example, Karl Pribram, inspired by the model of the hologram, has developed a holonomic theory of mind. In *Languages of the Brain,* Pribram argues that the human brain constructs "concrete" realities by interpreting frequencies of a space- and timeless order and then translating them into a spatial and temporal order. According to Pribram, the brain functions like a hologram that translates a holographic universe. Like a hologram, the brain not only possesses an enormous capacity for storing information, it also discloses the implicit structure of perceived objects. Due to the steering of frequences, several objects can either occupy the same space in a hologram or appear distinct and separate from each other. Holographic images can thus be perceived in isolation from each other, but they result from an "undifferentiated generative matrix."[19]

Here we can easily see why the model of the hologram attracts contemporary theories of mind. In his article "The Holographic Paradigm and the Structure of Experience,"[20] John Welwood argues that the order of the unconscious may generally be described according to the model provided by the holographic paradigm. This paradigm may serve to supplement psychoanalysis with a holistic theory of mental functions confirming, from a neurophysiological perspective, dynamic conceptions of creativity such as the one developed by Ehrenzweig. This double perspective also allows one to formulate some heuristic premises for a postmodern theory of transitional texts. Pribram's "holonomy of mind" has been developed under the impact of the English physicist David Bohm. Bohm argues that, while physical phenomena manifest themselves in a spatiotemporal order as separate and distinct, they also pertain to an "enfolded" order that encompasses the totality of phenomena. The explicate order of distinct and differentiated phenomena is, for Bohm, grounded in an undifferentiated whole, which nonetheless has its own enfolded order. Since, according to Bohm, the enfolded order is simultaneously and atemporally present in each distinct part of the explicate order, the physical universe can be compared to a gigantic hologram.

Pribram applies Bohm's concept to the structure of the brain and of consciousness: the manifest order of space and time, which organizes our mental functions and according to which objects appear as separate and discrete, is based on an enfolded order according to which the same objects pertain to an undifferentiated whole, which ignores the categories of time and space. The manifest order is a product of our conscious ordering, which functions like a focusing lens. This lens produces a differentiated order of space and time that is an abstraction of the implicit, fluid, and undifferentiated order—a perceptual construct we need in order to act in a spatial and temporal world. According to Pribram, the brain partakes in both orders, engaging different functions that are commonly considered exclusive: the analytic and digital function of the mind generates the secondary processes, and the syncretistic and analogic function generates the primary processes.[21]

One could ask to what extent this distinction becomes relevant once we deal with language, which is bound to a spatiotemporal order. We have seen that transitional texts release poetic language from its confines to a linear temporality. Moreover, their integration of primary processes already implies a transgression of the spatiotemporal order of consciousness. The affinities between Pribram's and Bohm's theories of mind and Ehrenzweig's theory of creativity are striking. Like Ehrenzweig, Bohm is interested in a continuous universal dynamic of simultaneous differentiation, undifferentiation, and redifferentiation that exceeds the boundaries of three-dimensional thought and experience. Both conceive the relationship between explicit and implicit order in terms of complementarity and polarization. A holonomic model of aesthetic production and reception may account for the equivalent dynamic in transitional texts. As outlined in Chapter 2, Ehrenzweig assumes that the discrete elements of an aesthetic order pertain to an undifferentiated matrix—which is, as we can now see, comparable to the matrix presumed by a holonomic theory of mind. Regarding aesthetic experience, Ehrenzweig's notion of an unconscious holistic memory is, in turn, comparable to the distributed memory of the hologram. With unfocused attention, this memory is able to grasp the generative matrix of a text, a painting, or a piece of music. The distributed memory of the hologram, with its capacity to store information about the whole in each of its parts, could thus also be taken as a model for one of the most basic activities in aesthetic production and reception: unconscious scanning.

As we have seen, transitional texts engage both conscious and unconscious modes of reception in extreme ways. Ideally, they would elicit a holistic reception in addition to the familiar reception, which focuses on narrative and the constitution of meaning. Ehrenzweig describes a syncretistic or holistic reception of the paintings of Jackson Pollock:

> Extreme examples of action painting such as the unending loops of Jackson Pollock could not but cause discomfort in people of the more rational visual type. To avoid discomfort we have to give up our focusing tendency and our conscious need for integrating the color patches into coherent patterns. We must allow our eye to drift without sense of time or direction, living always in the present mo-

ment without trying to connect the colour patch just now moving into our field of vision with others we have already seen or are going to see. If we succeed in evoking in ourselves such a purposeless daydream-like state, not only do we lose our sense of unease but the picture may suddenly transform itself and lose its appearance of haphazard construction and incoherence. Each new encounter now comes as a logical development and after a while we feel that we have grasped some hidden allover structure which is contained in each nucleus of color . . . Conscious surface coherence has to be disrupted in order to bring unconscious form discipline into its own.[22]

From the perspective of a holonomic model, such a process of reception may also be understood in terms of a transition from a mode of reception based on digital connections to one that makes more use of the analogic capacities for a simultaneous processing of information that functions according to holonomic principles. The nexus of theoretical affinities becomes even more dense if one recalls Bateson's assertion that the transition from thinking in digital connections to thinking in analogic and simultaneous processes requires a dramatic shift in epistemological premises. A holonomic theory of mind would thus also work toward an ecology of mind in Bateson's sense. By activating such extreme poles of mind and subjectivity as unconscious scanning on the one hand and self-reflexivity on the other, transitional texts engender an aesthetic experience that reaches beyond the middle domain of receptive capacities. We have shown earlier that, from the perspective of Bakhtin's dialogical model of aesthetic communication, this aesthetic experience creates a zone of contact between the two polarized modes of subjectivity. This process of cultural contact extends the accumulated or distributed memory of these texts in precisely the direction that both Bateson and Leroi-Gourhan call for: toward multidimensional and syncretistic models of mind and representation as well as toward abstraction and self-reflexivity. Such processes lead to a higher differentiation of our receptive dispositions and, as a result, of subjectivity in general. Modern and postmodern transitional texts thus establish a new aesthetic order whose otherness overturns the most familiar cultural and epistemological premises— and may already have developed new ones, which we theorists in time will discover.

Notes

1. The Insistence of the Subject

1. Jacques Lacan, "Of Structure as an Inmixing of an Otherness Prerequisite to Any Subject Whatever," in Richard Macksey and Eugenio Donato, eds., *The Structuralist Controversy: The Languages of Criticism and the Sciences of Man* (Baltimore: The Johns Hopkins University Press, 1970), p. 189.

2. Lacan, "Of Structure as an Inmixing," p. 194.

3. What contributes to this trend is also the fact that the two theoretical currents most critical of those parameters—feminism (with the exception of French feminism) and, more recently, ethnic criticism—hardly ever become positively engaged with the projects of modernism or postmodernism.

4. Michel Foucault, *The Order of Things: An Archeology of the Human Sciences* (New York: Vintage Books, 1973), pp. 299–300.

5. Foucault, *The Order of Things,* p. 300.

6. Foucault, *The Order of Things,* p. 374.

7. Wylie Sypher, *Loss of the Self in Modern Literature and Art* (New York: Random House, 1964).

8. Derek Attridge and Daniel Ferrer, eds., *Poststructuralist Joyce: Essays from the French* (Cambridge: Cambridge University Press, 1984), p. 10. A recent critique of the notion of the death of the subject can be found in Andreas Huyssen, "Mapping the Postmodern," in *New German Critique* 33 (1984), pp. 5–52. Huyssen argues that by proclaiming the death of the subject, poststructuralism renounces alternative notions of subjectivity. Critical voices come also from within feminist criticism: see Theresa de Lauretis, *Alice Doesn't: Feminism, Semiotics, Cinema* (Bloomington: Indiana University Press, 1984), pp. 158–186; Alice Jardine, *Gynesis: Configurations of Women and Modernity* (Ithaca: Cornell University Press,

1985), pp. 13–38. See also the remarks on Lacan's conception of the subject in Jane Gallop, *The Daughter's Seduction: Feminism and Psychoanalysis* (Ithaca: Cornell University Press, 1982); and Shoshana Felman, ed., *Literature and Psychoanalysis: The Question of Reading: Otherwise* (Baltimore: The Johns Hopkins University Press, 1982). Felman discusses poststructuralist notions of the subject from a perspective of aesthetic experience.

9. Cf. Jean Baudrillard, *Simulations* (New York: Semiotext[e], 1983); Guy Debord, *Society of the Spectacle* (Detroit: Black and Red, 1970); Gilles Deleuze and Felix Guattari, *Anti-Oedipus: Capitalism and Schizophrenia,* trans. Robert Hurley, Mark Seem, and Helen R. Lane (Minneapolis: University of Minnesota Press, 1983). Christopher Lasch, *The Culture of Narcissism: American Life in an Age of Diminishing Expectations* (New York: W. W. Norton & Co., 1979).

10. Julia Kristeva, "The System and the Speaking Subject," in Toril Moi, ed., *The Kristeva Reader* (New York: Columbia University Press, 1986), p. 29. See also "Le sujet en procès: Le langage poétique," in Claude Lévi-Strauss, ed., *L'Identité* (Paris: Grasset, 1977), p. 40.

11. Jacques Lacan, *The Seminar of Jacques Lacan,* Book 2, ed. Jacques-Alain Miller, trans. Sylvana Tomaselli (New York: W. W. Norton & Co., 1988), pp. 191–205.

12. See Kristeva, "The System and the Speaking Subject," p. 32.

13. Kristeva, "The System and the Speaking Subject," pp. 28–31. See also "Le sujet en procès," p. 238.

14. See Fredric Jameson, "Postmodernism, or the Cultural Logic of Late Capitalism," *New Left Review* 146 (1984), p. 53: "The last few years have been marked by an inverted millennialism, in which premonitions of the future, catastrophic or redemptive, have been replaced by senses of the end of this or that (the end of ideology, art, or social class; the 'crisis' of Leninism, social democracy, or the welfare state, etc., etc.): taken together, all of these perhaps constitute what is increasingly called postmodernism."

15. Jameson, "Postmodernism, or the Cultural Logic of Late Capitalism," p. 92.

16. Jameson, "Postmodernism, or the Cultural Logic of Late Capitalism," p. 80.

17. See Ihab Hassan, "Postface 1982: Toward a Concept of Postmodernism," in *The Dismemberment of Orpheus: Toward a Postmodern Literature* (Madison: University of Wisconsin Press, 1982), pp. 259–271; Ihab Hassan, *Paracriticisms: Seven Speculations of the Times* (Urbana: University of Illinois Press, 1975); Ihab Hassan, *The Right Promethean Fire: Imagination, Science and Cultural Change* (Urbana: University of Illinois Press, 1980).

18. In *Playing and Reality,* Winnicott uses the term "intermediate area." In

some of his articles, as well as in the literature about Winnicott, this term is often used interchangeably with "transitional space." I will use "transitional space," which resonates with "transitional objects" and with the key term I have coined for this investigation, "transitional texts."

19. I consider the notion of autopoiesis not only from the perspective of traditional aesthetic concepts, but also from a more general systems theoretical perspective as developed, for example, in Humberto R. Maturana and Francisco J. Varela, *Autopoiesis and Cognition: The Realization of the Living* (Boston: D. Reidel Publishing Company, 1980). This systems theoretical perspective becomes especially important in relation to the emphasis on self-referentiality in experimental modernist texts.

20. See Jean-François Lyotard, "Answering the Question: What is Postmodernism?" in Ihab Hassan and Sally Hassan, eds., *Innovation/Renovation: New Perspectives on the Humanities* (Madison: University of Wisconsin Press, 1983), pp. 329–341.

21. Jean-François Lyotard, "Beyond Representation," in *The Human Context* 3 (1975), pp. 495–502.

22. Lyotard, "Beyond Representation," pp. 499–502.

23. Floyd Merrell, *Deconstruction Reframed* (Bloomington: Indiana University Press, 1985).

24. Merrell, *Deconstruction Reframed*, p. 88.

25. See "The Enfolding-Unfolding Universe: A Conversation with David Bohm," conducted by Renée Weber, in Ken Wilber, ed., *The Holographic Paradigm and Other Paradoxes: Exploring the Leading Edge of Science* (Boulder: Shambhala, 1982), pp. 44–104.

26. I use the term in the sense of Gregory Bateson's notion of an ecology of mind.

27. The aesthetic, cultural, psychological, social, and political spheres are perceived in constant interaction with each other and with fluid, provisional boundaries between them. And, most important, they are considered intrinsic, not extrinsic, to textual concerns.

28. Cf. an earlier version of this chapter, "Genesis of the Subject, Imaginary Functions, and Poetic Language," *New Literary History* 3 (1984), pp. 453–474.

29. The term I use in my German version is *Entgrenzungstexte. Entgrenzung* is, in fact, a key term used in the title and throughout the German book. This term seems to be nearly untranslatable; it posed the greatest difficulty for my translation. *Entgrenzung* in German refers to activities that have to do with the crossing, lifting, and redrawing of boundaries as well as with their transgression, expansion, or change. The term thus designates a structural activity or a process of structuration and restructuration and is highly flexible in its implications. Rather than using one English term, such as "transgression" (with its connotations of violation), I have chosen

to shift between different English terms in order to gain the most precise connotation in each context. Even though this removes some of the abstractness of the German term, it renders a more precise sense of the implications in the specific contexts in which the texts play with the boundaries of language and subjectivity.

2. The Transitional Space of Literature

An earlier version of the first part of this chapter appeared as "Genesis of the Subject, Imaginary Functions, and Poetic Language," *New Literary History* 3 (1984), pp. 453–474. The original German version, "Die Subjektgenese, das Imaginäre und die poetische Sprache," appeared in Renate Lachmann, ed., *Dialogizität: Kommunikation in ästhetischen Prozessen* (Munich: W. Fink, 1982), pp. 63–84; a French translation (with Spanish and English translations) appeared in *Diogène* 115 (1981).

1. Mikhail Bakhtin, "Typen des Prosaworts," in *Literatur und Karneval: Zur Romantheorie und Lachkultur* (Munich: Hanser Verlag, 1969), pp. 129–131 (my translation). Cf. a similar passage in Mikhail Bakhtin, *The Dialogic Imagination*, ed. Michael Holquist (Austin: University of Texas Press, 1981), p. 293.

2. Bakhtin, *Literatur und Karneval*, p. 293 (my translation).

3. Jacques Lacan, *The Seminar of Jacques Lacan*, Book 1, ed. Jacques-Alain Miller, trans. Sylvana Tomaselli (New York: W. W. Norton & Co., 1988), pp. 52–61.

4. Helmuth Plessner, "Die anthropologische Dimension der Geschichtlichkeit," in Hans Peter Dreitzel, ed., *Sozialer Wandel: Zivilisation und Fortschritt als Kategorien der soziologischen Theorie* (Berlin: Neuwied 1972), p. 160.

5. This is the epigraph in Ernst Bloch, *Spuren*, Complete Works, vol. 1 (Frankfurt am Main: Suhrkamp, 1969). See also Ernst Bloch, *The Principle of Hope*, trans. Neville Plaice, Stephen Plaice, and Paul Knight, vol. 1 (Oxford: Basil Blackwell, 1986). (Because the English translation does not include the epigraph, its translation is mine.)

6. The mother's place can, of course, be taken by any primary caretaker with whom the infant forms symbiotic bonds. I follow Winnicott in using the term "mother" because we still live in a culture where primary care is largely a maternal function. The notion of the maternal is also crucial in Kristeva's concept of the semiotic. Regarding this early "mirror phase" between the infant and its mother, I find Winnicott's astute critique of Lacan's theory of the mirror stage in *Playing and Reality* entirely convincing, particularly his argument that the discovery of the infant's own

mirror image unfolds its effects on the matrix of the mother's earlier modes of mirroring through look and touch.

7. Freud has emphasized the fact that, during this early phase of development, the ego is still a bodily function, a *"Körperich."* See "The Ego and the Id" in *The Standard Edition of the Complete Psychological Works of Sigmund Freud,* trans. James Strachey (London: Hogarth Press, 1950), vol. 19, p. 33. See also Margaret Mahler, Fred Pine, and Anni Bergmann, *The Psychological Birth of the Human Infant* (New York: Basic Books, 1975), Part 2, Chapter 4, and Part 6, Chapter 15.

8. Jacques Lacan, "The Mirror Stage," in *Écrits,* trans. Alan Sheridan (New York: W. W. Norton & Co., 1977) p. 1.

9. See Sigmund Freud, "Beyond the Pleasure Principle," *Standard Edition,* vol. 18, pp. 10–11.

10. Donald W. Winnicott, *Playing and Reality* (London: Tavistock, 1971), p. 2.

11. See, for example, Jacques Lacan, *Seminar II: The Ego in Freud's Theory and in the Technique of Psychoanalysis, 1954–55,* trans. Sylvana Tomascelli (New York: W. W. Norton & Co., 1988), p. 137.

12. See Paul Ricoeur, *Freud and Philosophy: An Essay on Interpretation,* trans. Denis Savage (New Haven: Yale University Press, 1970). and Paul Ricoeur, *De L'Interpretation* (Paris: Seuil, 1965), vol 1.1 and vol. 3.4. See also Tzvetan Todorov, *Theories of the Symbol,* trans. Catherine Porter (Ithaca: Cornell University Press, 1982).

13. An interesting implication of the theories discussed above is that they provide a psychogenetic foundation for theories that argue for a qualitative difference between poetic and ordinary speech. Most of these theories ground their arguments either in the materiality of poetic language or in the process of reception. A paradigmatic instance of this critical debate can be found in the controversy between Murray Krieger and Stanley Fish. See Murray Krieger, *Poetic Presence and Illusion: Essays in Critical History and Theory* (Baltimore: The Johns Hopkins University Press 1979), pp. 169–187; and Stanley Fish, "How Ordinary Is Ordinary Language?" *New Literary History* 5 (1973), and "Normal Circumstances: Literary Language, Direct Speech Acts, the Ordinary, the Everyday, the Obvious, What Goes Without Saying, and Other Special Cases," in *Critical Inquiry* 4 (1978).

14. Anton Ehrenzweig, *The Hidden Order of Art* (Berkeley: University of California Press, 1967), p. 64.

15. Ehrenzweig, *The Hidden Order of Art,* p. 5.

16. Ehrenzweig explicitly refers to Jean Piaget's analysis of "syncretistic vision." See *The Hidden Order of Art,* p. 6.

17. Ehrenzweig analyzes this phenomenon in his chapter "The Fragmenta-

tion of Modern Art" in *The Hidden Order of Art* (see especially pp. 70–71). He reminds us that even Mozart's music was criticized by his contemporaries for its disharmonies. Mozart's polyphonic structures undermined the expectation of a linear melody. Schoenberg on the other hand hoped that his nonmelodic and ruptured work would produce the effect of a clear melody in the future.

18. See Hans Robert Jauss, "Literary History as a Challenge to Literary Theory," in *Toward an Aesthetic of Reception,* trans. Timothy Bahti (Minneapolis: University of Minnesota Press, 1982), pp. 3–45.

19. See Donald D. Winnicott, *The Maturational Processes* (New York: International Universities, 1965), p. 179.

20. Winnicott, *The Maturational Processes,* p. 186.

21. Ludwig Binswanger, *Erinnerungen an Sigmund Freud* (Bern: Francke, 1956), p. 58 (my translation).

22. See Michael Polanyi, *The Tacit Dimension* (New York: Doubleday, 1966). It is interesting to see that de Saussure assumes a similar tacit dimension in systems of rules in social behavior and language. Cf. Ferdinand de Saussure, *Course in General Linguistics,* ed. Charles Bally and Albert Sechehaye, trans. Wade Baskin (New York: Philosophical Library, 1959).

23. See Michel Leiris, *La Possession et ses Aspects théâtreaux chez les Éthiopians de Gondar* (Paris: Le Sycomore, 1980).

3. Aesthetics of Blankness in *Moby-Dick*

1. Herman Melville, *Moby-Dick; or, The Whale,* ed. Harold Beaver (Harmondsworth: Penguin Books, 1972), p. 295. This edition hereinafter cited in the text.

2. See Ernst Bloch's analysis of the connection between the discontents of civilization and the desire to explore foreign spaces *("Ferntrieb")* in Ernst Bloch, *The Principle of Hope,* trans. Neville Plaice, Stephen Plaice and Paul Knight (Oxford: Basil Blackwell, 1986), vol. 3.

3. Harold Beaver, "Introduction," in Melville, *Moby-Dick,* p. 22.

4. Beaver, "Introduction," p. 38.

5. The metallization of the human body plays a crucial role in literature, and deals with male fantasies of invulnerability. Walter Benjamin has analyzed its role in futurism and fascism. See Walter Benjamin, "The Work of Art in Its Time of Mechanical Reproduction," in *Illuminations,* ed. Hannah Arendt (New York: Schocken Books, 1969), p. 241.

6. Beaver, "Introduction," p. 38.

7. Cf. Heinz Kohut's analysis of the narcissist's grandiose self in *The Analysis of the Self: A Systematic Approach to the Psychoanalytic Treatment of Nar-*

cissistic Personality Disorders (New York: International Universities Press, 1971).

8. See the title of chapter 132.

9. Beaver, "Introduction," p. 10.

10. Regarding the aesthetic device of doubling in *Moby-Dick,* see also John T. Irwin, *American Hieroglyphics: The Symbol of the Egyptian Hieroglyphics in the American Renaissance* (New Haven: Yale University Press, 1980), Chap. 16. Irwin also discusses Queequeg's function as a "hieroglyphic doubling" of Ishmael.

11. "Les mythes se pensent dans les hommes, et à leur insu," Claude Lévi-Strauss, *Mythologies I: Le cru et le cuit* (Paris: Librairie Plan, 1964), p. 20. Cf. *The Raw and the Cooked,* trans. John and Doreen Weightman (New York: Octagon Books, 1979).

12. With regard to Melville's use of whale mythologies I follow the extensive research on this topic in H. Bruce Franklin, *The Wake of the Gods: Melville's Mythology* (Stanford: Stanford University Press, 1966). Unlike Franklin, however, I focus on the implications of Melville's use of mythologies for his literary presentation of subjectivity.

13. On the relationship between Ishmael as protagonist and as narrator see also Franz Stanzel, *Narrative Situations in the Novel,* trans. James P. Pusack (Bloomington: Indiana University Press, 1971); and Manfred Smuda, *Der Gegenstand in der bildenden Kunst und Literatur* (Munich: Fink Verlag, 1979), pp. 68, 105.

14. These texts are reprinted in an appendix to Harold Beaver's critical edition.

15. See Charles Olson's excellent study on the profound influence of Shakespeare in *Moby-Dick* in Charles Olson, *Call Me Ishmael* (New York: Grove Press, 1974), Part 2, "Source: Shakespeare," pp. 35–73.

16. See also the numerous allusions to Shakespeare mentioned in the commentary of Harold Beaver's edition.

17. These are only some of the most important intertexts of *Moby-Dick.* For further references to numerous other literary influences see the commentary in Harold Beaver's edition of the text.

18. John T. Irwin has convincingly emphasized the self-destructive element in Ishmael's experience of transcendence. I would, however, insist on the basic ambivalence with which this experience is described in the text. See Irwin, *American Hieroglyphs,* Chapter 16, pp. 286–287.

19. With regard to Melville's relationship toward metaphysics and anthropology, see Rowland A. Sherrill, *The Prophetic Melville: Experience, Transcendence and Tragedy* (Athens: University of Georgia Press, 1979), p. 99.

20. Sherrill, *The Prophetic Melville,* p. 100.

21. Edgar A. Dryden, *Melville's Thematics of Form: The Great Art of Telling the Truth* (Baltimore: The Johns Hopkins University Press, 1968), pp. 89, 98.

22. For an analysis of indeterminacy as a basic aesthetic category see also Wolfgang Iser, *The Act of Reading: A Theory of Aesthetic Response* (Baltimore: Johns Hopkins University Press, 1978), Chapter 4, pp. 163–231.

4. Eyeless Silence: Interior Dialogue in *The Waves*

An early version of this chapter was published in German in *Freiburger litera-turpsychologische Gespräche 1,* ed. Johannes Cremerius et al. (Frankfurt am Main: Peter Lang, 1981), pp. 149–165.

1. Nathalie Sarraute, "Conversation and Subconversation," in *The Age of Suspicion,* trans. Maria Jolas (New York: George Braziller, 1963), p. 79.

2. Virginia Woolf, *A Writer's Diary,* ed. Leonard Woolf (Frogmore, St. Albans: Triad Panther Books, 1978), p. 136.

3. Virginia Woolf, *The Waves* (Harmondsworth: Penguin, 1964). This edition hereinafter cited in the text.

4. Interestingly, for this device Virginia Woolf is indebted to Ivy Compton-Burnett, a writer to whom Woolf displays considerable ambivalence.

5. See Norman N. Holland, "Unity Identity Text Self," in Jane P. Tompkins, ed., *Reader-Response Criticism from Formalism to Post-Structuralism* (Baltimore: The Johns Hopkins University Press, 1980), p. 124.

6. Regarding the psychological implications of fantasies of fusing with plants, see Stanislav Grof, *The Realm of the Human Unconscious* (New York: Dutton, 1976).

7. Cf. Sigmund Freud, "On Negation," *The Standard Edition of the Complete Psychological Works of Sigmund Freud,* trans. James Strachey (London: Hogarth Press, 1950), vol. 14; and René Spitz, *The First Year of Life: A Psychoanalytic Study of Normal and Deviant Development of Object Relations* (New York: International Universities Press, 1965).

8. Regarding the symptom of autistic rocking, see Spitz, *The First Year of Life.*

9. Interpreting Rhoda's collisions with the outside world as intrusions of the real in the Lacanian sense adds an interesting twist to the characters' notion of a true self. Even though I do not want to overburden this specific psychoanalytic perspective, it is interesting to see how Woolf's implied conception of the self gains additional complexity if viewed from the background of the Lacanian categories of the real and the truth of the subject.

10. Stanislav Grof, *The Realm of the Human Unconscious* (New York: Dutton, 1976), Chapter 3.

11. The most comprehensive analysis of this dimension of Woolf's text is to be found in Harvena Richter, *Virginia Woolf: The Inward Voyage* (Princeton: Princeton University Press, 1970). Regarding interior speech in *The Waves* see also James Naremore, *The World Without a Self: Virginia Woolf and the Novel* (New Haven: Yale University Press, 1973). Naremore works with the categories of interior monologue, stream of consciousness, and dialogue, but at the same time he emphasizes that the real communication takes place below the surface of what is said. (See especially Naremore, p. 167.)

12. I think that Woolf's images are indeed "self-similar" in the sense of recursive patterns as described in chaos theory.

13. This is exactly what Virginia Woolf in her diaries called the "tunneling process." See also Paul Ricoeur, *Time and Narrative*, vol. 2, trans. Kathleen McLaughlin and David Pellauer (Chicago: University of Chicago Press, 1985), p. 187.

14. These mythologies in fact resemble those analyzed in Roland Barthes, *Mythologies*, trans. Annette Lavers (New York: Hill and Wang, 1972).

15. See also Michel Serres's reflections on the third interlocutor in a dialogue in *Hermes: Literature, Science, Philosophy* (Baltimore: The Johns Hopkins University Press, 1982), p. xxvi.

16. See also the notion of cliché in Alfred Lorenzer, *Sprachzerstörung und Rekonstruktion: Vorarbeiten zu einer Metatheorie der Psychoanalyse* (Frankfurt am Main: Suhrkamp, 1970), Chapter 3, pp. 72–92.

17. The textual irony against Louis's mechanical production of signatures gains new interest in light of Derrida's later theorizing on the impossibilities of signatures.

18. Woolf, *A Writer's Diary*, p. 136.

19. My reading offers an alternative perspective to the one presented by those critics who see the final chapter as an apotheosis of the artist. Cf. especially Howard Harper, *Between Language and Silence: The Novels of Virginia Woolf* (Baton Rouge: Louisiana State University Press, 1982), p. 249; and Madeline Moore, *The Short Season between Two Silences: The Mystical and the Political in the Novels of Virginia Woolf* (Boston: G. Allen and Unwin, 1984), p. 142.

5. "I, a Self the Sign": Language and Subjectivity in *Finnegans Wake*

1. See Edmund Husserl's notion of "lebendiger Oberflächensinn" in *Logische Untersuchungen*, Part 1, "Ausdruck und Bedeutung" (Tübingen: F. Meiner, 1968), nos. 9 and 18; and Edmund Husserl, *Logical Investiga-*

tions, vol. 1 (London: Routledge & K. Paul; New York: Humanities Press, 1970).

2. The metaphor of the dance also evokes the historical relationship between dance and linguistic nonsense enforced by the multiple allusions in *Finnegans Wake* to Lewis Carroll. Regarding the relationship between dance and nonsense, see also Edith Sewell, *The Field of Nonsense* (London: Chatto and Windus, 1952), p. 194.

3. James Joyce, *Finnegans Wake* (London: Faber and Faber, 1939), p. 3.1–3. This edition hereinafter cited in the text.

4. *Vicus* is the Latin form of the Italian *vico.* The allusions to Vico and their significance for *Finnegans Wake* have been widely commented upon. For more specific connotations of the first sentence, see also Joseph Campbell and Henry M. Robinson, eds., *A Skeleton Key to "Finnegans Wake"* (London: Faber and Faber, 1959), pp. 29–30.

5. See Adaline Glasheen, *A Census of "Finnegans Wake"* (London: Faber and Faber, 1957), pp. 38–39.

6. James Atherton has pointed out that Arthur Symons's *The Symbolist Movement in Literature* had formed the cultural sensibility and aesthetic norms at the time when Joyce began his university studies. See James Atherton, *The Books at the Wake: A Study of Literary Illusions in James Joyce's "Finnegans Wake"* (London: Faber and Faber, 1959), p. 28.

7. Apart from the fact that this critical endeavor inverted the Joycean process of production, it also worked against all those features that French feminists—especially Hélenè Cixous and Julia Kristeva—have identified as *écriture féminine* in Joyce.

8. Clive Hart, *Structure and Motif in "Finnegans Wake"* (London: Faber and Faber, 1962).

9. Among the numerous allusions to famous dreams is also the famous Wakean version of the Freudian dream.

10. Apart from its allusion to Freud, the term *family romance* here also invokes Christine van Boheemen, *Novel as Family-Romance: Language, Gender, and Authority from Fielding to Joyce* (Ithaca: Cornell University Press, 1987).

11. See Wolfgang Iser, "Patterns of Communication in Joyce's *Ulysses,*" in *The Implied Reader: Patterns of Communication in Prose Fiction from Bunyan to Beckett* (Baltimore: The Johns Hopkins University Press, 1974), pp. 196–233.

12. Glasheen, *A Census of "Finnegans Wake,"* p. xvi.

13. See also Margot Norris, The Decentered Universe of *"Finnegans Wake,"* (Baltimore: The Johns Hopkins University Press, 1976).

14. See also Sibylle Kisro-Völker, *Die unverantwortete Sprache: Esoterische Literatur und atheoretische Philosophie als Grenzfälle medialer Selbstreflex-*

ion: Eine Konfrontation von James Joyces "Finnegans Wake" und Ludwig Wittgensteins "Philosophischen Untersuchungen" (Munich: Fink Verlag, 1981), pp. 282–283.

15. Ihab Hassan, *Paracriticisms* (Urbana: University of Illinois Press, 1975), p. 90.

16. Apart from the above-mentioned collection of essays edited by Attridge and Ferrer, see also Hélène Cixous, *L'Exil de James Joyce* (Paris: Grasset 1968); Margot Norris, *The Decentered Universe of "Finnegans Wake"* (Baltimore: The Johns Hopkins University Press, 1976); Colin MacCabe, *James Joyce and the Revolution of the Word* (London: Macmillan, 1978); and John Paul Riquelme, *Teller and Tale in Joyce's Fiction: Oscillating Perspectives* (Baltimore: The Johns Hopkins University Press, 1983)—to mention just a few of the most influential books concerning the debates around Joyce and poststructuralism. See also the *James Joyce Quarterly: Structuralist / Reader Response Issue* of 1978–79.

17. Jacques Derrida, "Two Words for Joyce," in Derek Attridge and Daniel Ferrer, eds., *Post-structuralist Joyce* (Cambridge: Cambridge University Press, 1984), p. 147.

18. Attridge and Ferrer, eds., *Post-structuralist Joyce*, p. 10.

19. Hélène Cixous, "Joyce: The (R)use of Writing" in Attridge and Ferrer, eds., *Post-structuralist Joyce*, p. 27.

20. See Ferdinand de Saussure, *Cours de Linguistique Générale* (Lausanne, 1916), Chapter 4. See also Ferdinand de Saussure, *Course in General Linguistics,* ed. Charles Bally and Albert Sechehaye, trans. Wade Baskin (New York: Philosophical Library, 1959).

21. Sigmund Freud, "The Antithetical Meaning of Primal Words" in *The Standard Edition of the Complete Psychological Works of Sigmund Freud,* trans. James Strachey (London: Hogarth Press, 1950), vol. 11, pp. 155–161. With regard to the transformation of hermetic philosophy in *Finnegans Wake* see also Barbara di Bernard, "Technique in *Finnegans Wake,*" in Zack Bowen and James F. Carens, eds., *A Companion to Joyce Studies* (Westport, Conn.: Greenwood Press, 1984), pp. 652–57.

22. Clive Hart, *Structure and Motif in "Finnegans Wake"* (London: Faber and Faber, 1962). Even though Hart's work has been criticized by Joyceans who dispute the existence of the macrostructural orders he identified, *Structure and Motif in "Finnegans Wake,"* with its systematic perspective, remains a landmark in the history of the *Wake*'s reception and a crucial breakthrough in the study of the problem of its possible layers of order.

23. See *Upanishads, Breath of the Eternal: The Principal Texts,* trans. Swami Prabhavananda and Fredrick Manchester (New York: New American Library, 1957).

24. In addition to the cosmogonic models mentioned earlier, Clive Hart has also identified a "geometry" of the text, which resembles the archetypal symbols of circle and cross. Both of these symbols figure as mandalas used to induce meditative transcendence. Such a projection of macro-structures is, of course, a problem: they are hardly accessible during the reading experience. Hart's projection has also been challenged on the grounds of its validity as a reconstruction. If we leave such criticisms aside for a moment, however, Hart's ideas are very interesting from a systematic point of view, because they all evoke systems of order that depend on a dynamic of continual formation, dissolution, and reformation.

25. My translation.

26. I use the notion of culture contact in the general sense defined by Gregory Bateson in "Culture Contact and Schismogenesis," in his *Steps to an Ecology of Mind* (New York: Ballantine Books, 1972), pp. 61–72. I have elsewhere elaborated my own notion of reading as a form of culture contact. See Gabriele Schwab, "Reader Response and the Aesthetic Experience of Otherness," in *Stanford Literary Review* 3 (1) (Spring 1986): 107–136.

27. See Fredric Jameson, *The Political Unconscious: Narrative as a Socially Symbolic Act* (Ithaca: Cornell University Press, 1981). *Finnegans Wake* inspires a notion of the political unconscious that, rooted in the very form of language, reaches further than the one developed by Jameson and would allow one to expand Jameson's reflections on the ideology of form.

28. I use this term in the sense defined by Julia Kristeva in *Polylogue* (Paris: Gallimard, 1977). See also "The Novel as Polylogue," in *Desire and Language*, ed. Leon S. Roudiez, trans. Thomas Gora, Alice Jardine, and Leon S. Roudiez (New York: Columbia University Press, 1980).

29. Mikhail Bakhtin names all these devices as crucial for carnivalistic literature. See Mikhail Bakhtin, *The Dialogic Imagination,* ed. Michael Holquist (Austin: University of Texas Press, 1981).

30. Jean Michel Rabaté, "Lapsus ex machina," in Attridge and Ferrer, eds., *Post-structuralist Joyce,* p. 58.

31. My translation.

32. See Hassan, *Paracriticisms,* pp. 82–90.

33. Derrida, "Two Words for Joyce," p. 147.

34. Fritz Senn, "A Reading Exercise in *Finnegans Wake,*" in John Paul Riquelme, ed., *Joyce's Dislocutions: Essays on Reading and Translation* (Baltimore: The Johns Hopkins University Press, 1984), p. 89.

35. Stephen Heath, "Ambiviolences," in Attridge and Ferrer, eds., *Post-structuralist Joyce,* p. 58.

36. See Hélène Cixous, "The Laugh of the Medusa," in Elaine Marks and

Isabelle de Courtivron, eds., *New French Feminisms* (New York: Schocken Books, 1981), pp. 245–264.

37. See Jacques Derrida, *Speech and Phenomena*, trans. David B. Allison (Evanston: Northwestern University Press, 1973), Chapter 6, "The Voice That Keeps Silence."

38. Derrida, "Two Words for Joyce," p. 156.

39. The remarks that follow refer mainly to Edmund Husserl, *Logical Investigations*, Part 1, nos. 9 and 18.

40. See Jacques Derrida, *Of Grammatology*, trans. Gayatri Chakravorty Spivak (Baltimore: The Johns Hopkins University Press, 1976), p. 235.

41. Derrida, "Two Words for Joyce," p. 156.

42. Karl Pribram, *Languages of the Brain: Experimental Paradoxes and Principles in Neuropsychology* (Englewood Cliffs: Prentice Hall, 1971), p. 370.

43. Quoted in Richard Ellmann, *James Joyce* (New York: Viking Press, 1959), p. 559.

44. Rabaté, "Lapsus ex machina," pp. 79–101.

45. See Fritz Senn, "Weaving, unweaving," in Edmund L. Epstein, ed., *A Starchamber Quiry: A James Joyce Centennial Volume 1882–1982* (New York: Metheun, 1982).

46. See Jacques Derrida, "La différance," in *Marges de la Philosophie* (Paris: Minuit, 1972), pp. 4–5, 13–14. See also *Margins of Philosophy*, trans. Alan Bass (Chicago: University of Chicago Press, 1982).

47. Derrida, "Two Words for Joyce," p. 156.

48. Derrida, "Two Words for Joyce," p. 156.

49. Sean Golden, *Bygmythster Finnegan: Etymology as Poetics in the Works of James Joyce* (unpublished manuscript, Indiana University, 1981), p. 122.

50. See Golden, *Bygmythster Finnegan*, "Introduction."

51. 1 Corinthians 2:9–10.

52. Senn, "A Reading Exercise," p. 89.

53. Derrida, "Two Words for Joyce," p. 158.

54. Derrida, "Two Words for Joyce," p. 159.

55. Riquelme, *Teller and Tale in Joyce's Fiction*, p. 3.

56. James S. Atherton, *The Books at the Wake* (London: Faber and Faber, 1959), p. 34.

57. Klaus Reichert, "Von den Rändern her oder Sortes Wakeianae," (unpublished manuscript, Frankfurt University, 1981) p. 4.

58. Matters are further complicated by the fact that ideally the utopian reading would respond to the double coding of the text for eye and ear and perform the two types of reading simultaneously.

59. Anton Ehrenzweig, *The Hidden Order of Art* (Berkeley: University of California Press, 1967), p. 384.

60. See David Bohm, *Wholeness and the Implicate Order* (London: Routledge & Kegan Paul, 1981).

61. In their book *The Medium Is the Massage: An Inventory of Effects* (Harmondsworth: Penguin, 1967, pp. 120–121), Marshal McLuhan and Quentin Fiore have captured this audiovocal reading of *Finnegans Wake* in a photo collage by Peter Moore of a face in which one of the eyes has been replaced by an ear.

6. Not-I Fiction of a First Person Narrator: *The Unnamable*

A shortened and revised version of the original German chapter appeared as "'Where I am there is no one but me who am not'—Die Nicht-Ich Fiktion eines Icherzählers," in Manfred Frank and Anselm Haverkamp, eds., *Individualität*, Poetik und Hermeneutik 13 (Munich: Fink Verlag, 1988).

1. Samuel Beckett, *The Unnamable* (New York: Grove Press, 1958). This edition hereinafter cited in the text.

2. Israel Shenker, "An Interview with Beckett," in Lawrence Graver and Raymond Federman, eds., *Samuel Beckett. The Critical Heritage* (London: Routledge and Kegan Paul, 1979), p. 148.

3. Beckett is especially interested in philosophies that work with the notion of a transcendental subject precisely because this allows him to endow his literary characters with features that differ radically from those of empirical subjects.

4. Regarding ontological insecurity see Ronald D. Laing, *The Divided Self* (Harmondsworth: Penguin, 1970), especially pp. 39–45.

5. The allusions in *The Unnamable* are to such diverse philosophies as those of Plato, Plotinus, Descartes, Berkeley, Leibniz, Spinoza, Kant, Schopenhauer, Kierkegaard, Heidegger, Merleau-Ponty, Sartre, Wittgenstein, Lacan, and Derrida, as well as Western and Eastern mysticism.

6. Allen Thiher, *Words in Reflection: Modern Language Theory and Postmodern Fiction* (Chicago: University of Chicago Press, 1984), p. 131.

7. Thiher, *Words in Reflection*, p. 133.

8. See Plato, *The Republic*, trans. H. D. P. Lee (Baltimore: Penguin Books, 1961), Part 7, The Philosopher Ruler, no. 7: "The Simile of the Cave," pp. 278–286.

9. See Peter Erhard, *Anatomie de Samuel Beckett* (Stuttgart: Birkhauser, 1976).

10. On the notion of the organless body, see Gilles Deleuze's and Felix Guattari's *Anti-Oedipus*, trans. Robert Hurley, Mark Seem, and Helen R. Lane (New York: Viking Press, 1977).

11. See Deleuze and Guattari, *Anti-Oedipus*, especially Chapter 1.

12. I deliberately use the masculine gender here, since I have the impression

that Deleuze's and Guattari's schizosphere is a decidedly masculine sphere—despite its ambition to transcend the boundaries of gender. I would even read their economy of production in light of Michel Carrouges's concept of the bachelor's birth in his work *Les machines célibataires* (Paris: Arcanes, 1954). See also Alice Jardine's reading of Deleuze and Guattari in *Gynesis* (Ithaca: Cornell University Press, 1985).

13. See Leo Navratil, *Schizophrenie und Kunst* (Munich: Deutscher Taschenbuch Verlag, 1965), pp. 69–80.

14. See Sigmund Freud, "The Ego and the Id," *The Standard Edition of the Complete Psychological Works of Sigmund Freud,* trans. James Strachey (London: Hogarth Press, 1950), vol. 19. See also Gilles Deleuze, *Logique du Sens* (Paris: Minuit, 1969), pp. 11–20.

15. Ruby Cohn, *Back to Beckett* (Princeton: Princeton University Press, 1973), p. 101.

16. See Dieter Henrich, "Identität," in Odo Marquard and Karlheinz Stierle, eds., *Identität,* Poetik und Hermeneutik 8 (Munich: W. Fink, 1979), pp. 177–178. See also Ernst Tugendhat, *Self-Consciousness and Self-Determination,* trans. Paul Stern (Cambridge: MIT Press, 1986), p. 59.

17. Ernst Tugendhat, *Selbstbewusstsein und Selbstbestimmung* (Frankfurt: Suhrkamp Verlag, 1979), p. 75. See also *Self-Consciousness and Self-Determination,* p. 62.

18. Tugendhat, *Self-Consciousness and Self-Determination,* p. 66.

19. Of course, at one level, the presupposition that a literary text has to be meaningful at all is challenged in *The Unnamable.* By repeatedly calling for a willful suspension of belief, the unnamable inverts one of the most basic literary conventions. Nevertheless the presupposition remains valid, since that very inversion establishes a metalevel of discourse. The problem of meaning is accordingly shifted to a different level of abstraction. In addition, Beckett's strategy of withholding meaning on an immediate level engages the reader in a very different process of meaning constitution. For a detailed analysis of this dynamic, see Gabriele Schwab, *Samuel Becketts Endspiel mit der Subjektivität: Zur Psychoästhetik des Modernen Theaters* (Stuttgart: Metzler Verlag, 1981). Regarding the same problem from the perspective of a theory of language, see Michel Foucault, *Archéologie du Savoir* (Paris: Gallimard, 1969), pp. 116–117. See also Michel Foucault, *The Archaeology of Knowledge,* trans. A. M. Sheridan Smith (New York: Pantheon Books, 1972).

20. This paradox also necessarily affects the critic, since it is impossible to immediately situate oneself outside the textual perspective on a metalevel.

21. Tugendhat, *Self-Consciousness and Self-Determination,* p. 273.

22. Regarding Beckett's metalanguage and textual self-reflexivity see Manfred Smuda, *Becketts Prosa als Metasprache* (Munich: Fink Verlag, 1970).

23. Regarding a critical reading of Derrida from the perspective of Beckett's texts, see Floyd Merrell, *Deconstruction Reframed* (West Lafayette: Purdue University Press, 1985), Chapter 7, "Beckett's Dilemma: or, Pecking Away at the Ineffable," pp. 165–195.

24. See Manfred Frank, "Das Individuum in der Rolle des Idioten: Die hermeneutische Konzeption des Flaubert," in Traugott König, ed., *Sartres Flaubert lesen: Essays zu Der Idiot in der Familie* (Reinbek bei Hamburg: Rowohlt Verlag, 1980), p. 90.

25. Ulrich Pothast, *Die eigentlich metaphysische Tätigkeit: Über Schopenhauers Ästhetik und ihre Anwendung durch Samuel Beckett* (Frankfurt am Main: Suhrkamp, 1982), p. 355 (my translation).

26. Søren Kierkegaard, *Fear and Trembling* and *The Sickness unto Death*, trans. Walter Lowrie (Garden City: Doubleday Anchor Books, 1954), p. 146.

27. Kierkegaard, *Fear and Trembling*, pp. 163–164.

28. Kierkegaard, *Fear and Trembling*, p. 166.

29. Kierkegaard, *Fear and Trembling*, p. 165.

30. Regarding Beckett's affiliations with mysticism, see Waltraud Gölter, *Entfremdung als Konstituens bürgerlicher Literatur, dargestellt am Beispiel Samuel Becketts: Versuch einer Vermittlung von Soziologie und Psychoanalyse als Interpretationsmodell* (Heidelberg: Carl Winter Verlag, 1976), pp. 209–226.

31. See Bruce Kavin, "On Not Having the Last Word: Beckett, Wittgenstein, and the Limits of Language," in Peter S. Hawkins and Anne H. Schotter, eds., *Ineffability: Naming the Unnamable from Dante to Beckett* (New York: AMS Press, 1984), p. 195.

32. See Sigmund Freud, "On Negation," *Standard Edition*, vol. 19; and René Spitz, *No and Yes: On the Genesis of Human Communication* (New York: International Universities Press, 1957).

33. Manfred Smuda has pointed out that with increasing complexity in Beckett's texts, the possibilites of writing have proportionally decreased. In this development, *The Unnamable* marks a turning point in Beckett's development toward the later, minimalist texts. See Manfred Smuda, "Kunst im Kopf—Becketts spätere Prosa und das Imaginäre," in Hartmut Engelhardt, ed., *Samuel Beckett* (Frankfurt: Suhrkamp, 1984), p. 212.

34. Merrell, *Deconstruction Reframed*, p. 191.

35. J. E. Dearlove, *Accommodating the Chaos: Samuel Beckett's Nonrelational Art* (Durham: Duke University Press, 1982), p. 61.

36. See Sigmund Freud, "Formulations on the Two Principles of Mental Functioning," in *Standard Edition*, vol. 12.

37. See Sigmund Freud, "Jokes and Their Relation to the Unconscious," in *Standard Edition*, vol. 8.

38. Kavin, "On Not Having the Last Word," p. 201.
39. For a detailed discussion of this effect of Beckett's texts, see Gabriele Schwab, *Samuel Becketts Endspiel mit der Subjektivität* (Stuttgart: Metzer, 1981), especially Chapter 4.
40. Merrell, *Deconstruction Reframed,* pp. 193–194. Herbert Blau, whose own work is deeply influenced by Beckett, describes a similar paradox of subjectivity in his staging of *The Donner Party.* His description precisely fits the unnamable's self-performances: "There is, then, an exploration of the dissolution of ego and the release of consciousness into structure, becoming an image of the ultimate subtraction, the death of self, which— as it materializes—is refused. In that respect, the works are emblematic arousals of residual will fighting off the loss of the self in the striations of thought." Herbert Blau, *Take Up the Bodies: Theater at the Vanishing Point* (Urbana: University of Illinois Press, 1982), p. 163.
41. See Pierre Maranda, "The Dialectic of Metaphor: An Anthropological Essay on Hermeneutics," in Susan R. Suleiman and Inge Crosman, eds., *The Reader in the Text* (Princeton: Princeton University Press, 1980), pp. 183–204. See also Gabriele Schwab, "Reader Response and the Aesthetic Experience of Otherness," *Stanford Literary Review,* 3, no. 1 (1986).
42. See also the following readings of Beckett, which use Winnicott's theory of the intermediate area: Kathleen Woodward, "Transitional Objects and the Isolate: Samuel Beckett's *Malone Dies,*" in *Contemporary Literature* 26, no. 2 (1985); and Gabriele Schwab, "The Intermediate Area between Life and Death: On Samuel Beckett's *The Unnamable,*" in Kathleen Woodward and Murray Schwartz, eds., *Memory and Desire: Aging—Literature—Psychoanalysis* (Bloomington: Indiana University Press, 1986).
43. Dieter Henrich, "Kunst und Kunstphilosophie der Gegenwart—Überlegungen mit Rücksicht auf Hegel," in Wolfgang Iser, ed., *Immanente Ästhetik—Ästhetische Reflexion,* Poetik und Hermeneutik 2 (Munich: Fink Verlag 1966), pp. 27–28.
44. Henrich, "Kunst und Kunstphilosophie," p. 30.
45. I think here not only of the unnamable's multiple phantasmatic bodies, but also of Jameson's imperative that postmodern culture help us grow new organs.

7. Carnivalesque Apocalypse of the Holy Text: *Gravity's Rainbow*

Parts of an earlier version of this chapter are included in Gabriele Schwab, "Creative Paranoia and Frost Patterns of White Words," in Harold Bloom, ed., *Thomas Pynchon's "Gravity's Rainbow": Modern Critical Interpretations*

(New York: Chelsea House, 1986), and are reprinted in Gerhard Hoffmann, ed., *Making Sense: The Role of the Reader in Contemporary American Fiction* (Munich: Fink Verlag, 1989).

1. Thomas Pynchon, *Gravity's Rainbow* (London: Pan Books, Picador edition, 1975). This edition hereinafter cited in the text.
2. See Marcus Smith and Khachig Toeloelyan, "The New Jeremiad: *Gravity's Rainbow*," in Richard Pearce, ed., *Critical Essays on Thomas Pynchon* (Boston: G. K. Hall, 1981), pp. 169–186.
3. Frank Kermode, *The Sense of an Ending* (New York: Oxford University Press, 1967), p. 12.
4. Kermode, *The Sense of an Ending*, p. 96.
5. Readers who ignore Pynchon's strategy of double coding remain entangled in the stories and myths of the characters and reduce the implicit textual critique of these myths. The critical reception of *Gravity's Rainbow* is marked by readings that suffer from the categorical error of confounding the perspective of the characters with the perspective of the narrative. I see David Leverenz's devastating critique of *Gravity's Rainbow* as an example: "Against the twentieth century complexities of bureaucracy, colonialism, markets, technology, interest groups, nations, Pynchon offers only the nineteenth-century fantasies . . . of anarchic individualism, momentary utopian communities and the Cult of Nature . . . They are peasant fantasies of a suburban alien. There's not much difference between Pynchon's call for a flight from manhood into Nature and any one of the late 1960s 'Youth Culture' books." David Leverenz, "On reading *Gravity's Rainbow*," in George Levine and David Leverenz, eds., *Mindful Pleasures: Essays on Thomas Pynchon* (Boston: Little, Brown, 1976), p. 243.
6. Roland Barthes, *Mythologies*, trans. Annette Lavers (New York: Hill and Wang, 1972), p. 135.
7. Douglas Mackey calls the Rocket "Pynchon's all-purpose symbol" and criticizes the ambiguity created by Pynchon's use of symbols. My own reading instead locates this ambiguity in Pynchon's characters, assuming that through them the narrative perspective exposes a historical ambiguity. See Douglas A. Mackey, *The Rainbow Quest of Thomas Pynchon* (San Bernardino: Borgo Press, 1980), p. 57.
8. See Klaus Theweleit, *Male Fantasies*, vol. 2, trans. Erica Carter and Chris Turner in collaboration with Stephen Conway (Minneapolis: University of Minnesota Press, 1987–1989), pp. 143–251.
9. Michel Carrouges, "Bachelor Machines," in Marc Le Bot et al., eds., *Le Machine Celebi—The Bachelor Machines* (New York: Rizzoli, 1975), pp. 22–23.

10. See René Girard, *Deceit, Desire and the Novel: Self and Other in Literary Structure*, trans. Yvonne Freccero (Baltimore: The Johns Hopkins University Press, 1965).

11. See Charles Russell, "Pynchon's Language: Signs, Systems and Subversion," in Charles Clerc, ed., *Approaches to "Gravity's Rainbow"* (Columbus: Ohio State University Press, 1983), pp. 251–272.

12. Theweleit, *Male Fantasies*, vol.2, pp. 143–270.

13. See Joseph W. Slade, "Religion, Psychology, Sex and Love in *Gravity's Rainbow*," in Clerc, ed., *Approaches to "Gravity's Rainbow,"* pp. 153–198. Slade uses Max Weber in order to analyze Pynchon's critique of the Calvinist disenchantment of the world.

14. See Khachig Toeloeyan, "War as Background in *Gravity's Rainbow*," in Clerc, ed., *Approaches to "Gravity's Rainbow,"* pp. 31–67. Toeloeyan analyzes the concrete historical function of the V-2 in connection with its function as a symbol of modern technology.

15. See Hans Blumenberg, *Work on Myth*, trans. Robert M. Wallace (Cambridge, Mass.: MIT Press, 1985). See also *Die Arbeit am Mythos* (Frankfurt am Main: Suhrkamp, 1979), p. 12; and Claude Lévi-Strauss, *Tristes Tropiques*, trans. John Russell (New York: Criterion Books, 1961).

16. Regarding the verdict on metaphor in Romanticism, see Hans Blumenberg, *Die Lesbarkeit der Welt* (Frankfurt am Main: Suhrkamp, 1981), p. 243.

17. See Blumenberg, *Die Lesbarkeit der Welt*, p. 276.

18. See David G. Cowart, *Thomas Pynchon: The Art of Allusion* (Carbondale: Southern Illinois University Press, 1980), p. 46. Regarding the function of film in *Gravity's Rainbow*, see Charles Clerc, "Film in *Gravity's Rainbow*," in *Approaches to "Gravity's Rainbow,"* pp. 103–152.

19. Jean-Paul Sartre, *The Family Idiot: Gustave Flaubert, 1821–1857,* trans. Carol Cosman (Chicago: University of Chicago Press, 1981).

20. See Siegfried Kracauer, *From Caligari to Hitler: A Psychological History of German Film* (Princeton: Princeton University Press, 1947).

21. See Cowart, *Thomas Pynchon: The Art of Allusion,* p. 47.

22. See Mark R. Siegel, *Pynchon: Creative Paranoia in "Gravity's Rainbow"* (Port Washington, N.Y.: Kennikat Press, 1978), p. 90.

23. Regarding entropy and other scientific metaphors and models in *Gravity's Rainbow*, see especially Alan J. Friedman and Manfred Pütz, "Science as Metaphor: Thomas Pynchon and *Gravity's Rainbow*," in Pearce, ed., *Critical Essays on Thomas Pynchon*, pp. 69–81. See also Alan Friedman, "Science and Technology," in Clerc, ed., *Approaches to "Gravity's Rainbow,"* pp. 69–102.

24. Anthony Wilden, "Cybernetics and Machina Mundi," in Kathleen Wood-ward, ed., *The Myths of Information: Technology and Postindustrial Culture* (Madison: Coda Press, 1980), p. 225.

25. Quoted from Thomas H. Schaub, *Pynchon: The Voice of Ambiguity* (Urbana: University of Illinois Press, 1981) p. 117.

26. See Norbert Wiener, *The Human Use of Human Beings: Cybernetics and Society* (Boston: Houghton Mifflin, 1950); and Henry Adams, *The Education of Henry Adams* (New York: The Modern Library, 1931).

27. See Bateson's analysis of destructive schismogenesis in *Steps to an Ecology of Mind* (New York: Ballantine Books, 1972) pp. 494–505.

28. Jean Baudrillard, "The Implosion of Meaning in the Media and the Implosion of the Social in the Masses," in Woodward, ed., *The Myths of Information*, p. 141.

29. Stanislav Grof, "The Holonomic Theory," in Hans Peter Duerr, ed., *Der Wissenschaftler und das Irrationale* (Frankfurt am Main: Syndikat, 1981) p. 603.

30. See Molly Hite, *Ideas of Order in the Novels of Thomas Pynchon* (Columbus: Ohio State University Press, 1983).

31. Thomas H. Schaub, *Pynchon: The Voice of Ambiguity* (Urbana: University of Illinois Press, 1981), p. 103.

32. Schaub, *Pynchon: The Voice of Ambiguity*, p. 4.

33. Peter L. Cooper has analyzed the dynamic opposition between macro- and microstructure in *Gravity's Rainbow* as an epistemological problem. See Peter L. Cooper, *Signs and Symptoms: Thomas Pynchon and the Contemporary World* (Berkeley: University of California Press, 1983), pp. 131–152.

34. Regarding Pynchon's multiple narrative perspective, see Cooper, *Signs and Symptoms*, pp. 196–222.

35. Cf. Tony Tanner's argument that reading *Gravity's Rainbow* is a practice in a new reading of the modern world. Tony Tanner, *Thomas Pynchon* (London: Methuen, 1982), p. 77.

36. See Jürgen Habermas, *Theorie des kommunikativen Handelns*, vol. 2 (Frankfurt am Main: Suhrkamp, 1981), p. 580; and *The Theory of Communicative Action*, trans. Thomas McCarthy, vol. 2 (Boston: Beacon Press, 1987), p. 395.

37. See Habermas, *The Theory of Communicative Action*, p. 395.

38. Regarding cyborgs, see Stanislaw Lem, "Die Cyborgisierung," in *Summa Technologiae* (Frankfurt am Main: Insel Verlag, 1976), pp. 583–602; Kathleen Woodward, "Cybernetic Modeling in Recent American Writing: A Critique," in *North Dakota Quarterly* 51, no. 1 (1983), pp. 57–73; Donna Haraway, "A Manifesto of Cyborgs: Science, Technology, and Socialist Feminism in the 1980's," in *Socialist Review* 80 (1984), pp. 65–

107; and David Porush, *The Soft Machine: Cybernetic Fiction* (New York: Methuen, 1985).

39. In the sense of Freud's stimulus-shield that provides a protection against overstimulation.

40. Fredric Jameson, *The Political Unconscious: Narrative as Socially Symbolic Act* (Ithaca: Cornell University Press, 1981). See also "Postmodernism, or the Cultural Logic of Late Capitalism," in *New Left Review,* no. 146 (1984). Jean Baudrillard, "The Implosion of Meaning in the Media and the Implosion of the Social in the Masses," in Woodward, ed., *The Myths of Information,* pp. 137–148.

41. Regarding the entropy of writing, see Manfred Frank, "Die Entropie der Sprache: Überlegungen zur Debatte Searle-Derrida," in *Das Sagbare und das Unsagbare: Studien zur neuesten französischen Hermeneutik und Texttheorie* (Frankfurt am Main: Suhrkamp, 1980), pp. 141–211.

42. Jacques Derrida, *De la Grammatologie* (Paris: Editions de Minuit, 1967), pp. 128–131.

43. André Leroi-Gourhan, *Le Geste et la Parole* (Paris: A. Michel 1964), pp. 261–262 (my translation).

44. William M. Plater, *The Grim Phoenix: Reconstructing Thomas Pynchon* (Bloomington: Indiana University Press, 1978), p. 212.

45. Regarding the phenomenon of countertranscendence in anarchistic groups, see Dieter Wellershoff, "Infantilismus als Revolte," in Wolfgang Preisendanz and Rainer Warning, eds., *Das Komische* (Munich: Fink Verlag, 1976), p. 351.

46. Wellershoff, "Infantilismus als Revolte," p. 351.

47. The social function of this form of irony is astutely described in Peter Sloterdijk, *Critique of Cynical Reason,* trans. Michael Eldred (Minneapolis: University of Minnesota Press, 1987).

48. See Tony Tanner, "Games American Writers Play," in *Salmagundi* 34 (1976), pp. 115–117.

49. Michail M. Bakhtin, "Rabelais und Gogol," in Rainer Grübel, ed., *Die Ästhetik des Wortes,* trans. Rainer Grübel and Sabine Reese (Frankfurt: Suhrkamp Verlag, 1979), p. 345 (my translation).

50. Mikhail Bakhtin, "Rabelais und Gogol," p. 347.

51. Regarding a collective death drive, see Lawrence C. Wolfley, "Repression's Rainbow: The Presence of Norman O. Brown in Pynchon's Big Novel," *PMLA* 92 (1977), pp. 873–889. See also Russell, "Pynchon's Language: Signs, Systems, and Subversion," in Clerc, ed., *Approaches to "Gravity's Rainbow."*

52. Friedrich Nietzsche, *Thus Spoke Zarathustra,* in *The Portable Nietzsche,* ed. and trans. Walter Kaufmann (Harmondsworth: Penguin, 1976), p. 427.

8. Basic Configurations of Transitional Tests

1. See Jürgen Habermas, *The Theory of Communicative Action*, trans. Thomas McCarthy, vol. 2 (Boston: Beacon Press, 1987), p. 395.
2. See Adorno's and Horkheimer's analysis of the historical development of a culture industry in *The Dialectic of Enlightenment*, trans. John Cumming (London: Verso, 1979).
3. See Niklas Luhmann, *Gesellschaftsstruktur und Semantik*, vol. 1 (Frankfurt am Main: Suhrkamp, 1980), p. 304.
4. Ibid.
5. See also Gilles Deleuze and Felix Guattari, *Anti-Oedipus: Capitalism and Schizophrenia*, trans. Robert Hurley, Mark Seem and Helen R. Lane (New York: Viking Press, 1977); and Gilles Deleuze and Felix Guattari, *L'Anti-Oedipe: Capitalisme et Schizophrenie* (Paris: Minuit, 1972), p. 18.
6. See René Descartes, *Meditations on First Philosophy*, trans. John Cottingham (Cambridge: Cambridge University Press, 1986), p. 18: "Thinking? At last I have discovered it—thought; this alone is inseparable from me."
7. See Michel Foucault, *Madness and Civilization*, trans. Richard Howard (New York: Pantheon Books, 1965). See also Michel Foucault, *L'histoire de la folie* (Paris: Plon, 1961), pp. 25–27.
8. I am, of course, aware of the fact that the categorical distinction of paranoia and schizophrenia is heuristic and pragmatic. Their concrete manifestations are more fluid and their appearance in literary texts is, most of the time, mixed.
9. Dieter Wellershoff, "Systemregulierung and Wahnsystem" in Harald Weinrich, ed., *Positionen der Negativität*, Poetik und Hermeneutik 6 (Munich: Fink Verlag, 1975), p. 551.
10. Dieter Henrich, "Ästhetische Perzeption und Personalität," in Weinrich, ed., *Positionen der Negativität*, p. 543.
11. Sybille Kisro-Völker, *Die unverantwortete Sprache* (Munich: Fink Verlag, 1981).
12. Gregory Bateson, "A Theory of Play and Fantasy," in *Steps to an Ecology of Mind* (New York: Ballantine Books, 1972), p. 188.

9. Toward a Holonomy of Texts and Subjects

1. See Rudolf Arnheim, *Art and Visual Perception* (Berkeley: University of California Press, 1966); and Ernst Gombrich, *Art and Illusion* (London: Phaidon Press, 1962).
2. See Wolfgang Iser, *The Act of Reading* (Baltimore: The Johns Hopkins University Press, 1978).

3. See Anton Ehrenzweig, *The Hidden Order of Art* (Berkeley: University of California Press, 1967), p. 67.

4. Ehrenzweig, *The Hidden Order of Art*, pp. 34–35.

5. Ehrenzweig, *The Hidden Order of Art*, pp. 292–295.

6. See also Lacan's metaphors for the "I."

7. Ehrenzweig, *The Hidden Order of Art*, p. 65.

8. Ehrenzweig, *The Hidden Order of Art*, pp. 32–33.

9. Ehrenzweig, *The Hidden Order of Art*, p. 284.

10. Julia Kristeva, *Semeiotike* (Paris: Seuil, 1969), pp. 257–258 (my translation). See also "Semiotics: A Critical Science and/or a Critique of Science," in Toril Moi, ed., *The Kristeva Reader* (New York: Columbia University Press, 1986), pp. 84–85.

11. As to its cultural implications, Kristeva's notion of the semiotic owes a great deal to Bakhtin's carnivalesque as well as to Foucault's ideas about modern literature as a space for the articulation of the excluded. Like many of the modernist texts that have inspired these critics, these theories all show how what is culturally excluded, repressed, or marginalized becomes the source for a transgressive aesthetic state or experience.

12. Rudolf Arnheim, *Entropy and Art* (Berkeley: University of California Press, 1971), p. 9.

13. Arnheim, *Entropy and Art*, pp. 11–12.

14. Hans Blumenberg, *Die Lesbarkeit der Welt* (Frankfurt am Main: Suhrkamp, 1981), p. 403 (my translation).

15. See Arnheim, *Entropy and Art*, p. 52.

16. See also Manfred Frank, *Das Sagbare und das Unsagbare* (Frankfurt am Main: Suhrkamp, 1980), p. 142.

17. Anthony Wilden, *System and Structure* (London: Tavistock Publications, 1972), p. 226.

18. See, for example, Fritjof Capra, *The Tao of Physics* (London: Wildwood House, 1975); Jeremy Rifkin, *Entropy* (New York: Bantam Books, 1981); David Bohm, *Wholeness and the Implicate Order* (London: Ark Paperbacks, 1983); Ken Wilber, ed., *The Holographic Paradigm and Other Paradoxes: Exploring the Leading Edge of Science* (Boulder: Shambhala, 1982); Ilya Prigogine and Isabelle Stengers, *Order out of Chaos: Man's New Dialogue with Nature* (New York: Bantam Books, 1984).

19. Karl Pribram, *Languages of the Brain: Experimental Paradoxes and Principles in Neuropsychology* (Englewood Cliffs: Prentice Hall, 1971).

20. John Welwood, "The Holographic Paradigm and the Structure of Experience," in Wilber, ed., *The Holographic Paradigm and Other Paradoxes*.

21. See also Anthony Wilden's extensive treatment of analogous and digital functions of systems in *System and Structure*.

22. Ehrenzweig, *The Hidden Order of Art*, pp. 74–75.

Index

275

Harvard Studies in Comparative Literature